CRIMINAL JUSTICE AND DRUGS

Kennikat Press
National University Publications
Multi-disciplinary Studies in the Law

Advisory Editor
Honorable Rudolph J. Gerber

CRIMINAL JUSTICE AND DRUGS
The Unresolved Connection

Edited by
JAMES C. WEISSMAN
and
ROBERT L. DuPONT

National University Publications
KENNIKAT PRESS // 1982
Port Washington, N.Y. // London

Manufactured in the United States of America

Published by
Kennikat Press Corp.
Port Washington, N.Y. / London

Library of Congress Cataloging in Publication Data
Main entry under title:

Criminal justice and drugs.

    (Multi-disciplinary studies in the law) (National
university publications)
    Bibliography: p.
    Includes index.
    Contents: "Nonaddictive opiate use" / Norman E.
Zinberg—"The 'maturing out' of drug use (and
deviance)" / Leonard D. Savitz—"The legislation
of drug law" / Patricia A. Morgan—[etc.]
    1. Drug abuse—United States—Addresses, essays,
lectures. 2. Drug abuse—Treatment—United States—
Addresses, essays, lectures. 3. Drug abuse and
crime—United States—Addresses, essays, lectures.
4. Narcotic addicts—Rehabilitation—United States—
Addresses, essays, lectures. 5. Criminal justice,
Administration of—United States—Addresses, essays,
lectures. 6. Drugs—Law and legislation—United
States—Evaluation—Addresses, essays, lectures.
I. Weissman, James C., 1947- . II. DuPont,
Robert L., 1936- . III. Series.
HV5825.C74   363.4'5   81-3701
ISBN 0-8046-9291-2   AACR2

During the preparation of this volume, drug research lost one of its pioneers and ablest practitioners, William H. McGlothlin of the UCLA Department of Psychology. Bill was a gentleman and fine scholar, and his presence will be sorely missed. We dedicate this volume to Bill's memory and to our children, Charlie Weissman, Caroline DuPont, and Elizabeth DuPont.

ACKNOWLEDGMENTS

The editors are grateful for permission to reprint the following materials (most of which have been condensed for inclusion in the present volume):

"The Legislation of Drug Law: Economic Crisis and Social Control," by Patricia A. Morgan; reprinted by permission from *Journal of Drug Issues* 8, no. 1 (winter, 1978): 53–62.

"Understanding the Drugs and Crime Connection," by James C. Weissman; reprinted by permission from *Journal of Psychedelic Drugs* 10, no. 3 (July–September, 1978): 171–92.

"Arrest Probabilities for Marijuana Users as Indicators of Selective Law Enforcement," by Weldon T. Johnson, Robert E. Petersen, and L. Edward Wells; reprinted by permission from *The American Journal of Sociology* 83, no. 3 (November, 1977): 681–99; copyright 1977 by The University of Chicago Press.

"Heroin Addiction, Criminal Culpability, and the Penal Sanction," by Ronald Bayer; reprinted by permission from *Crime and Delinquency* 24, no. 2 (April, 1978): 221–32.

"Drug Control Principles: Instrumentalism and Symbolism," by James C. Weissman; reprinted by permission from *Journal of Psychedelic Drugs* 11, no. 1 (January–March, 1979): 203–10.

"Marijuana and the Use of Other Drugs," by William H. McGlothlin, Kay Jamison, and Steven Rosenblatt; reprinted by permission from *Nature* 228 (December 19, 1970): 1227–29; copyright 1970 by Macmillan Journals Limited.

"Illicit Use of Central Nervous System Stimulants in Sweden," by Gilbert Geis; reprinted by permission from *Journal of Drug Issues* 8, no. 2 (spring, 1978): 189-97.

"Considerations in Sentencing the Drug Offender," by James C. Weissman; reprinted by permission from *Journal of Psychedelic Drugs* 9, no. 4 (October-December, 1977): 301-9.

"The Argument against Long-Term Addiction Treatment in Prison," by Robert G. Newman; reprinted by permission from *Drug Forum* 5, no. 4 (1976-77): 369-73.

"Drug Offender Diversion: Philosophy and Practices," by James C. Weissman; reprinted by permission from *Drug Abuse and Alcoholism Review* 2, no. 1 (spring, 1979): 1-8.

"We'll Make Them an Offer They Can't Refuse," by Robert G. Newman; reprinted by permission from *Proceedings of the Fifth National Conference on Methadone Treatment* (National Association of Prevention of Addiction to Narcotics, 1973), pp. 94-100.

"A Guide to the Treatment of Drug Addict Criminality," by James C. Weissman and George Nash; reprinted by permission from *Journal of Drug Issues* 8, no. 1 (winter, 1978): 113-22.

"The Concept of Prevention and Its Limitations," by Richard Brotman and Frederic Suffet; reprinted by permission from *Annals of the American Academy of Political and Social Science* 417 (January, 1975): 53-65; copyright 1975 by The American Academy of Political and Social Science.

Certain materials appearing in this volume are reprinted from government documents. The editors wish to note the original source of such materials:

"Nonaddictive Opiate Use," by Norman E. Zinberg, in DuPont, Robert L., Goldstein, Avram, and O'Donnell, John. *Handbook on Drug Abuse.* Washington, D.C.: Government Printing Office, 1979, pp. 325-36.

"The 'Maturing Out' of Drug Use (and Deviance)" by Leonard D. Savitz, in National Institute on Drug Abuse. *Drug Use and Crime: Report of the Panel on Drug Use and Criminal Behavior.* Springfield, Virginia: National Technical Information Service, 1976, pp. 205-11.

"The Future of Drug Abuse Prevention," by Robert L. DuPont, in DuPont, Robert L., Goldstein, Avram, and O'Donnell, John. *Handbook on Drug Abuse.* Washington, D.C.: Government Printing Office, 1979, pp. 447-52.

CONTENTS

PREFACE

The impact of drugs upon the criminal justice system has served as a popular topic of criminological and social policy concern. Embracing a variety of empirical and theoretical research strategies, social scientists subject the phenomenon to continuous assessment. Investigators examine and analyze the complex set of relationships that characterize interactions between drug control activities and the operation of the criminal justice system.

Two principal factors explain this elevated level of inquiry. First, it is commonly hypothesized that drug use is a major contributor to serious crime, particularly income-generating predatory crime. Consequently, the phenomenon merits rigorous scrutiny in terms of etiological analysis and assessment of preventive efforts. The vast majority of government-sponsored behavioral drug use research is predicated on this order of assumption.

Equally powerful in explaining the breadth of the drugs and criminal justice literature is the peculiar role of drug control policy as a subject of criminological inquiry. Drug consumption behaviors and drug control policies are cited frequently as archetypical examples of various criminological constructs.

The characterization of drug control as an example of "victimless crime" is familiar. Countless articles and papers describe the history and social policy implications of criminalization of drug use. The subject of drugs also serves a number of other criminological and criminal justice interests. Analysis of patterns of social deviancy, law enforcement practices, criminal lawmaking, judicial application of criminal sanctions, constitutional doctrines, social control theory, and rehabilitative practices are described amply in the drugs and criminal justice literature. These topics represent mainstream criminological foci.

This volume draws upon that fertile literature in a purposeful manner. Careful selection and integration of articles is intended to satisfy readers curious to examine the multifaceted drugs and criminal justice phenomena. To accomplish that intellectual goal, multidisciplinary perspectives including sociological, criminal justice, legal, and public health contributions are combined. The aim is to provide a systematic and elegant treatment of drugs and criminal justice relations.

A traditional educational anthology format is employed. Nine topical subjects are specified, each addressing a discrete aspect of the drugs and criminal justice phenomena. Each section is preceded by brief introductory comments. Although several sections feature only a single article, most contain companion articles.

The selection process has been painstaking. The editors have sought to include articles ranking highly in terms of being germane, incisive, and well crafted. A specific ideological approach has been eschewed in favor of directing emphasis toward maximization of the descriptive and analytical qualities of the volume. The major editorial obstacle has been the simple reality of limited space.

An unorthodox but increasingly popular stylistic method has been adopted to maximize inclusion of substantive materials within the volume. Footnotes and references have been deleted from the original articles. Readers seeking the eliminated material are referred to the original citations. This is a practical action which the editors and publisher hope will be understood by the readers.

Notwithstanding the temporal nature of certain dimensions of drugs and criminal justice phenomena, the editors feel confident that the selected articles highlight substantial and continuing issues. Saliency of the questions presented and quality of the analyses offered functioned as primary criteria meriting inclusion. Although fluctuations in social trends may alter the findings to a degree, a healthy residuum of intellectual durability should be associated with the contents of this volume.

CRIMINAL JUSTICE AND DRUGS

CONTRIBUTORS

Ronald Bayer, Ph.D., Institute of Society, Ethics, and Life Sciences, Hastings-on-Hudson, New York

Richard Brotman, Ph.D., Center for Comprehensive Health Practice, New York Medical College

Robert L. DuPont, M.D., Institute for Behavior and Health Inc., Rockville, Maryland

Gilbert Geis, Ph.D., Program in Social Ecology, University of California, Irvine

Kay Jamison, Ph.D., Neuropsychiatric Institute, The Center for the Health Sciences, University of California, Los Angeles

Weldon T. Johnson, Ph.D., Department of Sociology, University of Illinois, Chicago Circle

William H. McGlothlin, Ph.D., Department of Psychology, University of California, Los Angeles (deceased)

Patricia A. Morgan, Ph.D., Social Research Group, School of Public Health, University of California, Berkeley

George Nash, Ph.D., Department of Community Mental Health, Westchester County, New York

Robert G. Newman, M.D., Beth Israel Medical Center, New York City

Robert E. Petersen, Ph.D., Abt Computer Graphics, Cambridge, Massachusetts

Steven Rosenblatt, Ph.D., California Acupuncture College

Leonard D. Savitz, Ph.D., Department of Sociology, Temple University

Frederic Suffet, M.A., Department of Psychiatry, New York Medical College

James C. Weissman, J.D., Office of the District Attorney, Denver, Colorado

L. Edward Wells, Ph.D., Department of Sociology, Purdue University

Norman E. Zinberg, M.D., Department of Psychiatry, Harvard Medical School

Section 1

EPIDEMIOLOGICAL PATTERNS

Critical to understanding drugs and criminal justice relationships is familiarity with current facts associated with psychoactive drug use epidemiology. The study of drug use patterns is a controversial subject. The validity and reliability of epidemiological measurement instruments are widely criticized. Even more fundamental is widespread dissatisfaction with the accuracy of reported data interpretations. Professionals and public alike express skepticism toward reported drug use statistics.

The two selected articles address only a fraction of those concerns. Zinberg, a practicing psychiatrist, has adopted sociological investigative methods to advance his continuing examination of nonaddictive drug use patterns. Clinical contact with functioning users of various psychoactive substances stimulated his interest in this previously neglected subject.

The findings of Zinberg and his colleagues and other parallel investigators question basic public policy assumptions. The existence of sustained nonaddictive use of heroin, for instance, had been virtually inconceivable to most authorities. The article included in this volume describes available research bearing upon nonaddictive opiate use. Undoubtedly this provocative topic will attract intense scientific and policy attention during the remainder of the decade.

Savitz, on the other hand, considers a topic of continuing rather than emerging focus. His article outlines the popular "maturation hypothesis" and explores pertinent evidence. A criminologist, Savitz integrates criminological and drug use research in explaining the essentials of the maturation concept. Emphasizing the parallel nature of social deviance phenomena, he argues for a common analytic understanding.

To be sure, the Zinberg and Savitz papers highlight only a small segment of the fascinating set of questions pertaining to this threshold subject. A broad and constantly maturing literature seeks to accurately measure and interpret human drug use patterns.

Norman E. Zinberg

NONADDICTIVE OPIATE USE

Both the viewpoint and the data presented in this chapter are the outcome of my 4-year investigation of controlled opiate use, beginning with the pilot project sponsored by the Drug Abuse Council and continuing in the NIDA-sponsored project. The first section of the chapter will consider the evidence presented by the literature for the existence of extensive nonaddictive opiate use. Second, the chapter will describe several broad patterns of opiate use that have come to light during project interviews with a variety of users. Third, it will discuss the importance of the social setting variable; and fourth, it will briefly outline further areas of research that need to be undertaken, emphasizing the questions raised by my investigation. Finally, the fifth section will make some suggestions concerning public policy and education.

EVIDENCE OF NONADDICTIVE OPIATE USE

The existence of occasional or controlled opiate use has long been recognized by experienced observers in spite of the traditional view that chipping or chippying—that is, experimental or casual use—was a relatively brief way station leading either back to abstinence or quickly forward to habitual, chronic, heavy use, or regular abuse. The National Commission on Marihuana and Drug Abuse reported in 1973 that 90 percent of Americans disagreed with the statement, "You can use heroin occasionally without ever becoming addicted to it." The existence of hundreds of articles about heroin addiction as opposed to only a few on any other pattern of use attests to the research community's agreement with that

5

view. For example, Chein's group, while noting the existence of "long continued nonaddictive users," concluded that their numbers were insufficient to warrant investigation and that in all likelihood the large majority who continued use went on to addiction.

Lindesmith likewise had drawn a distinction between pleasure users of opiates, whom he called "joy poppers," and the prototypical addict. "A 'joy popper,'" he wrote, "is simply an individual who uses the drug intermittently and *who has never been hooked.*" He too suspected that most continuing "joy poppers" went on to addiction. By 1972 Goode was stating the same traditional position somewhat more ambivalently: "The occasional (weekend) heroin user is probably a good deal more common than most of us realize, although an extraordinarily high percentage of those who 'chippy' (experiment) with heroin eventually become addicted."

Of greater importance, however, is a rigorous retrospective study by Robins and Murphy of a normal population of young Negro males in St. Louis. They found that 13 percent of the total sample had tried heroin and that all but 3 percent had become addicted. All those who had used heroin more than six times had gone on to become addicts.

Any literature search that attempts to determine the extent to which observers have recognized long-term nonaddictive opiate use is hampered by the unwavering acceptance of this traditional view of chipping, which is reinforced by three factors: the concern that the mere recognition of such use might encourage experimentation by the unwary; the difficulty of arriving at any reasonable quantitative estimates of such use; and the multiplicity and impreciseness of the terms employed to describe drug-using styles. This last point caused Chein et al. to note as long ago as 1964 that the apparently specific term "heroin addict" had been used in so many different ways that "it is meaningless to identify an individual as an 'addict.'" In addition, and perhaps most important, the literature, because of the timelag both in the development and funding of studies of changing patterns of drug use and in publication, includes little up-to-date information on the swiftly changing patterns of drug use of the past 7 years.

Nevertheless, a careful literature review does indicate that patterns of long-term controlled opiate use have existed for some time. Although the literature does not provide quantitatively specific evidence, it does show that there is a considerably higher percentage of opiate users than had previously been supposed. This, however, has not been recognized by physicians and medical clinics other than those concerned with heroin use alone.

In 1961, while working at the Cook County jail, Scher reported on a group of heroin users whom he described as having *"what might be called a regulated or controlled habit."* Later on, when considering the life cycle of addiction, Alksne et al. noted with some surprise that "although no research reports are available for this kind of user, our own observations indicate that some persons continue in occasional or limited use for an indefinite period of time without going on to more regular use." These observations almost exactly parallel those reported in 1974 by Newmeyer of the Haight-Ashbury Free Medical Clinic in San Francisco, concerning individuals who, he said, could "be characterized as persons who sample heroin without becoming addicted."

A perspective different from the medical profession's excessive fear of addiction is presented by medical personnel who screen applicants for methadone maintenance programs. Even the 1972 guidelines suggested by the American Medical Association state: "The mere use of a morphine-type drug, even if periodic or intermittent, and/or violation of drug laws cannot be equated with drug dependency. In each instance a specific medical diagnosis is required." The same theme was brought up by Dobbs, who warned that some people applying for methadone maintenance should be rejected because they are only occasional users. It also led to a suggestion by Blachly that naloxone was useful in distinguishing between addicts and occasional users. Blachly noted that "a significant hazard exists in creating addicts to methadone hydrochloride, since a third of those applying to a methadone clinic without prior documentation of withdrawal in an institution showed no evidence of physical dependence." Glaser, too, suggested that 45 percent of the applicants to a Philadelphia maintenance program were not addicts, although he gave no data on their frequency of use.

The interesting and paradoxical recognition that there are occasional users who, for reasons of their own, present themselves as addicts is not new. Zinberg and Lewis reported on such a group in 1964. In addition, Gay et al. have published case histories of occasional users who presented themselves as addicts although urinalysis belied their claims. Such individuals were labeled "pseudo junkies" to indicate that they assumed the trappings of addiction without the necessary opiate use.

The reports mentioned so far have simply noted the existence of non-addicted opiate users. Several other reports, however, have introduced an experimental or quantitative dimension.

Hughes et al., while studying addicts, used 15 occasional users as a comparison group. Eleven of that comparison group, they stated, became regular, frequent users without progressing to addiction.

In 1971-72, Levengood et al. conducted a study of single white male heroin users between the ages of 15 and 24 who lived in a Detroit suburb. Although their sample comprised multiple drug users, they examined three distinct subsamples classified by frequency of heroin use. Of the 60 subjects interviewed, 22 individuals (or 37 percent) used "regularly or on a daily basis"; 24 (40 percent) used occasionally, with quantity and frequency of use varying widely; and 14 (23 percent), who had used within the last year but not during the month prior to study, were considered "former users." Some who had recently been using on a daily basis were included in this last group, but none of them had received any form of treatment.

Graeven and Jones, who examined adolescent heroin use in a suburban San Francisco high school between 1966 and 1974, reported that occasional use was almost as prevalent as addiction (49 percent as compared with 51 percent). Of the 143 "experimenters" identified, 33 percent had used between 3 and 30 times, 19 percent had used from 31 to 100 times, and 10 percent had used more than 100 times. Furthermore, by 1974, 24 percent of the addict group were using between once a month and twice a week, with only 47 percent using three or more times a week.

A 1975 study of Abt Associates Inc. on drug use in the State of Ohio showed that 1.39 percent of their respondents admitted having used heroin. If this figure were extrapolated to the general population of the state, the number of users would clearly be greater than any previous estimate of the number of actual addicts. Moreover, the survey indicated that among heroin users occasional use predominated: 8.7 percent used "several times per week or more"; 17.4 percent "a few times per month"; 34.8 percent "a few times per year"; and 65.2 percent "less frequently." The Ohio results are not drastically different from data reported by Abelson and Fishburne from their 1975-76 nationwide study, which showed that 0.5 percent of youth under age 18 and 1.2 percent of all adults had had experience with heroin. Although generalizations made from such data are hazardous, these findings together with the less comprehensive studies just described suggest that many more nonaddicts use heroin than has been supposed.

Bourne et al. made an interesting survey of heroin use in Wyoming, where, to their surprise, they found heroin use greater than expected, as well as many different use patterns, including occasional use. Their work contains few counts of the numbers of such users, but it is of particular importance that they take issue with the conventional view that most users are known to the authorities. They uncovered significant numbers of users and addicts who were unknown to the police or to the community health facilities responsible for treatment of drug problems.

Hunt, one of the participants in the Wyoming study, used these data along with other data collected with Chambers to place the heroin-using population of the United States at 3 to 4 million, of whom they claimed that only 10 percent were addicted.

Probably the most important study in this group is that which Robins made of Vietnam veterans 3 years after their return to the United States. Not only is it a more rigorously designed work than any described so far, but it specifically contradicts Robins's own previous work. She found in 1976 that 20 percent (114) of the 571 previously addicted veterans had used opiates occasionally after their return. Of these, only about 12 percent (14) had had any period of stateside addiction. In her study she concludes that this ratio of addiction to occasional use was consistent with patterns noticed in the general U.S. population. Furthermore, she explains that the discrepancy between these conclusions and her earlier St. Louis study is due to the changing patterns of drug use. While the earlier study had shown that nonaddictive use among blacks was infrequent between the 1930s and the 1950s, such use had become widespread by 1976.

Perhaps the most convincing data showing widespread nonaddictive heroin use come from studies reporting its appearance in other treatment modalities. Minkowski et al. found more than twice as many occasional heroin users as daily heroin users in a random sample of clients visiting the Los Angeles Health Department Youth Clinic. Excluding experimenters (those using fewer than 3 times), who constituted 12 percent of the 300 respondents, 4.6 percent used between more than once a week and less than once a month, while only 1.7 percent used once a day.

Health consequences usually associated with heroin addiction have been reported to affect occasional users. Kersh states that 70 percent of the narcotic overdose cases treated in a New York hospital emergency room were occasional users. Light and Dunham have reported on two cases of vertebral osteomyelitis due to septic intravenous administration of heroin in individuals who had not used heroin for at least 8 weeks preceding the onset of symptoms and who were "definitely not addicts." Lewis et al. reported that they encountered five occasional users in 1 year who had spinal chondro-osteomyelitis; they were not addicted, but all had used heroin intravenously within the week prior to their hospital admission. An independent medical biostatistician is currently studying all these medical figures more closely, and his initial response has supported the conclusions of Hunt and Chambers.

Before my work began, only one study, that by Powell seems to have been made that was specifically oriented to the occasional heroin user. Of the dozen subjects he recruited through placing advertisements in a counterculture newspaper, none reported previous addiction to heroin and each had used the drug for at least 3 consecutive years. Judging these scanty data by my standards, I would classify only a few of Powell's subjects as strictly controlled users and the others as having a more unstable or "marginal" use pattern.

Patterns of Use. As originally conceived, my DAC and NIDA studies were designed to deal only with individuals whose opiate use was carefully controlled. In selecting subjects, stringent criteria were used to define controlled use. Subjects were required to be over 18 and to have used opiates at least 10 times per year for more than 2 years and at least 2 times during the 6 months preceding the interview. They must not have had more than one "spree"—an instance of from 4 to 15 consecutive days of opiate use—in any of these years. With the exception of tobacco they must have been using all drugs, licit and illicit, in a controlled way and must not have been in a drug-free or methadone maintenance program, in jail, or in any other confining institution during their years of controlled use.

These conditions or standards were laid down to include regular weekend users, who often use 3 days in a row, as well as spree users, who may use for a number of days in a row on a vacation but then demonstrate equally prolonged periods of abstinence. The limit of one spree per year excluded users who might be intermittently addicted.

Finding controlled users who were willing to participate in the research project was at first a time-consuming process. But, as project workers grew more adept and also came across subjects who could help in finding other subjects by penetrating different social networks, it became clear that locating responsive interviewees was difficult not because they were so few in number but because under present social conditions, which condemn and punish any opiate use at all, they were terrified of being discovered. This secretive attitude and fear of discovery stand in sharp contrast to the attitude of the usual addict found in a drug treatment program.

So far the project has located and interviewed 90 opiate users who have been controlled for between 3 and 23 years. They have been found through advertising in newspapers (both regular and countercultural), through community agencies, by professional contacts, and by subject referral. All subjects have been interviewed for approximately 2 hours, 60 have been followed up between 6 months and 1 year later, and 25 of these have had still another interview 1 year after that. In addition, at least 1 friend of each of 45 of our subjects has been interviewed as a way of understanding these subjects' social interactions and as a check on the reliability of the data. The requirement that friends be interviewed has been added in the NIDA project only during the last 2 years; hence the smaller number of subjects so treated. Interestingly enough, two of the occasional users had participated in the study of controlled use made by Zinberg and Lewis 14 years ago. That they have continued their patterns of control over such a long period of time indicates the high degree of consistency such patterns can attain.

The following descriptive data are based on my combined DAC and NIDA samples. Because the NIDA Project is ongoing, these data are necessarily approximations.

Of the 90 controlled opiate users I have studied to date, some 30 percent are males and 70 percent are females. Their ages range from 17 to 50 years, with a mean of 27 years. Approximately 40 percent come from lower class or lower middle-class families, and the remainder are almost equally split between the middle–middle class and the upper–middle class. Of those subjects who are not currently in school, one-quarter did not complete 12 years of schooling, one-third did complete 12 years (high school), and the remainder completed more than 12 years. All those who are currently in school had previously finished high school.

As for my subjects' living situations and current activities, one-quarter are single and the remainder are divided almost equally between those who are married and those who are living with a mate. About 66 percent are working full or part time, approximately 15 percent are current unemployed, and 10 percent are in school either full or part time. Nine of the 90 (10 percent) are engaged in crime or drug dealing, more than half of them on a part-time basis, and these 5 are members of the middle class whose drug dealing is done to help out friends at little or no profit. Of those currently employed, 58 percent are blue-collar workers. The bulk of the white-collar workers hold either clerical or managerial positions. Only 10 percent of the employed are in professional positions, such as nursing. Concerns about confidentiality and about the consequences of disclosure of their opiate use seem to have discouraged the professional, well-educated, and upper-class users from entering my project.

Turning to the actual case of opiates by my subjects, heroin ranks first not only in current use but also as the opiate used most intensively during the subjects' using careers. Well over 80 percent of the sample use heroin. The mean current period of controlled opiate use is 5 years. Most subjects use opiates infrequently. About 20 percent use less than monthly (one to three times a month); 40 percent use monthly; 20 percent use weekly (once or twice a week); and the remainder use in various patterns, combining sprees with more regulated periods of use. More than 25 percent of my subjects have either a history of addiction to opiates or a history of compulsive use of another drug, or both. Their periods of compulsive use, however, have been significantly (at the 0.05 level) shorter than their current period of controlled use, a fact that underscores the importance of controlled use as a comparatively stable using style.

Despite the careful attention paid to personality description and personality formulation in the initial interview, and the additional data supplied by the followup interview and interviews of friends, correlations have not been found between occasional opiate use and specific personality types. At the same time, the interviews have revealed important similarities, which have served to indicate the problems users have in maintaining a stable chipping pattern. Surprisingly, with but three exceptions, my subjects have reported a greater fear of being forced into abstinence than of losing control and becoming addicted.

The chief difficulty in maintaining a pattern of occasional use seems to be the user's need to determine, either alone or in conjunction with a peer group, how to integrate the drug high into his or her regular pattern of work and social relationships. All of my subjects first tried an opiate as part of a series of drug experimentations and found the experience particularly pleasing. They all recognized that they had no social or psychological preparation for opiate use. Their anxious attempts to learn all they could about the drug's actions and effects from peers indicate that they had not gone through the kind of social drug education process that is available to alcohol users in our culture.

Although my sample of 90 controlled users is small, the interview material appears consistent. Taken along with the data obtained by Robins and other researchers, and with a growing body of conforming reports that I have received as personal communications, it reveals the existence of a category of people who have succeeded in setting up a stable pattern of controlled opiate use that does not necessarily lead to addiction. It is impossible to say what percentage of all opiate users this group represents. Some of the data mentioned in the literature review suggest that quite a high percentage of heroin users may not be addicts. But if this finding is correct, and I believe it is, it still does not mean that all of those who are not addicts fall into the category of stable controlled users, nor does it indicate which of the potential experimenters may be reasonably expected to be able to exercise the stringent sanctions necessary for controlled use. As an unexpected byproduct our research has uncovered several different patterns of use falling between the extremes of control and noncontrol.

In the course of recruiting controlled subjects, I unintentionally interviewed people who did not meet the stringent qualifications for controlled users. Rather than discarding these recorded interviews, I decided to analyze and use them as comparative cases. In this way I not only found out that even physiologically addicted users showed some evidence of control and reacted to changes in their social setting, but I also recognized a number of diverse using patterns that, while falling short of my definition of control, did not fit the addict stereotype. Of the 90 primarily opiate-using subjects who were rejected as controlled users by my standards, 18 (approximately 20 percent) reported addiction within the previous 2 years but were not currently addicted, 15 (roughly 17 percent) reported current daily use of a single dose but also did not regard themselves as addicted, and 13 (or about 14 percent) had used occasionally for less than 2 years. Others used different drugs, used them less frequently than my standard required, or had "speed" more frequently. Fourteen (about 16 percent) regarded themselves as currently addicted, and more than half of these addicts were not affiliated with a treatment program.

Thus my investigation revealed greater differentiation among the various levels of control and noncontrol than I had expected. First, some subjects used heroin several times a day, were physiologically addicted, and showed the stereotypical pattern of using as much of the drug as was available. (Most heroin users who at one time or another have been under treatment probably fall into this category.) Second, some, though physiologically addicted, placed limits on their use. (Sometimes this type is also found in the treatment population.) Third, there were those whose physiological addiction did not disrupt their functioning. (Although users of this type are rarely found in the treatment population in this country, they are found in England.) Fourth, some subjects were not addicted, but their history of addiction was so recent that they could not be considered controlled users. Fifth, some used heroin only occasionally but were more or less compulsive users of other drugs. Sixth, some users could not be defined as either clearly controlled or clearly addicted. These I called "marginal users," thus adding a third category to the two basic types of opiate users (controlled and compulsive) that I had been aware of originally. Not only have many professionals in the field overlooked stable controlled use as a basic category of nonaddictive opiate use, but they have also overlooked a complex and diverse group of "marginal users" who, while clearly at risk of addiction, must still be considered generally nonaddicted.

The Importance of the Social Setting Variable. Once it is recognized that responses to opiate use are far more complex and varied than has usually been assumed, the next essential is to consider those factors that determine the potential for controlled use. It is my contention that three variables determine the style and consequence, and therefore the degree of control, of drug use: drug (the pharmacological properties of the drug itself), set (the user's personality and his or her attitudes toward taking the drug), and setting (the characteristics of the physical and social setting in which use occurs). In theory each of these three variables can be manipulated to prevent abuse or to improve treatment methods. In fact, however, it is not easy to manipulate the first two.

In the case of the drug variable, attempts to prevent abuse by reducing the supply of opiates have proved costly and only partially successful because of the high demand for the drug, the windfall nature of black-market profits, and the permeability of national borders. Even if the supply is reduced, opiate users tend to substitute alcohol, barbiturates, pharmaceutical opiates, or other drugs instead of stopping compulsive use or going into treatment. Similarly, attempts to improve treatment methods solely through manipulating the drug variable, such as the use of methadone and other agents, have been only partially successful. Drug therapy programs appear to work well for only a portion of the client population, and those who enter such programs probably constitute only a small fraction of those who are genuinely addicted.

Prevention and treatment strategies grounded in the relationship between drug use and the set variable are also inadequate. Although some opiate abuse undoubtedly is related to personality disorders or social deprivation, it is difficult to see how those who are "addiction prone" by psychological makeup and social background can be identified and persuaded to remain abstinent. In addition, it is by no means clear how many opiate users are or have been deficient in these areas. When prospective work has been done with subjects who later turn out to be addicted, the personality aspects accounting for their addiction have not been clear.

Because of the difficulty in manipulating the drug and set variables in order to prevent abuse or improve treatment, my research has emphasized the importance of the third variable—the physical and social setting. This work has shown that embedded in the setting in which use takes place are a number of social sanctions and social rituals that influence individuals' decisions to use a particular drug and also the way in which they use it. Social sanctions are the norms and beliefs concerning not only the ways in which a particular drug should be used but also the ways in which its harmful physiological and psychological effects can be avoided. Rituals are stylized drug-using behaviors and practices, including the means by which the drug is obtained and administered, the physical setting chosen for use, the using circumstances and using companions selected, the user's activities when intoxicated, and any specific activities undertaken after intoxication that the user regards as part of the using process. For example, a primary sanction of controlled opiate users is "Don't use enough to become addicted," which is reflected by the rituals and behaviors related to frequency and time of use, such as use on weekends only.

Nevertheless, rituals do not act to control use unless they are based on limiting sanctions. Although addicts follow some of the rituals adopted by controlled users, deciding who "gets off" first, sharing "works," "tying off" with belts, or "booting," these rituals do not operate as controls because they are not grounded in sanctions. On the other hand, the controlled opiate users I have studied have internalized the social sanctions or precepts that tend to control drug use. They are even able to articulate these sanctions, sometimes explicitly and consciously, and sometimes in fragmented form, without conscious knowledge that they are following certain rules.

Thus social sanctions, internalized by the user, are the predominant sources of control, and rituals buttress, reinforce, and symbolize these sanctions. Rituals and social sanctions seem to function in four distinct ways. The following list explains these functions by referring to my research subjects.

1. Sanctions define moderate use and condemn compulsive use. (Most of my subjects follow sanctions that limit use to frequencies well below those required for addiction. Many have special sanctions, such as "Don't use every day" or "Never use on more than two consecutive days.")

2. Sanctions limit use to physical and social settings that are conducive to a positive or "safe" drug experience. (Some subjects refuse to use in the company of addicts from whom they have bought the drug, and most avoid driving a car when high.)

3. Sanctions and rituals identify potentially untoward drug effects and prescribe precautions to be taken before and during use. (Some subjects minimize the risk of an overdose by using only a portion of their drug and waiting to gauge its effect before taking more. Others avoid mixing certain drugs, boil their works before injection, or refuse to share works.)

4. Sanctions and rituals operate to compartmentalize drug use and support the users' everyday obligations and relationships. (Some subjects avoid using opiates on Sunday night so that they will not be too tired to go to work on Monday morning. Some carefully budget the amount of money they spend on drugs.)

The process by which controlling rituals and social sanctions are acquired varies from subject to subject. Most users come by them gradually during the course of their drug-using careers. But peer using groups seem to be the most important source of practices and precepts for safer use. Most of my subjects appear to require the assistance of other controlled users to construct appropriate and effective rituals and sanctions out of the folklore and practices circulating in the various drug-using subcultures.

Directions for Further Research. Because the samples studied in my DAC and NIDA projects were not random, and there is no assurance that they are representative, they do not provide generalizable data on five important topics: (1) the extent of opiate use; (2) the rapidity with which using patterns change; (3) the relationship of opiate use to other drug use and the stability of that relationship; (4) the connection between opiate use and demonstrable psychological difficulty; and (5) the leading demographic and social characteristics of users. The lack of such knowledge is serious; it would be extremely helpful both in identifying the difficulties that lead to and result from opiate use and also in deciding public policy issues. It is unfortunately true that the criteria being used in 1978 to determine the extent of opiate use, such as arrest rates, overdose deaths, and applications to treatment programs, relate only to the stereotypical addict and ignore the broad range of users.

The best way to provide information on the first four topics would be to construct and survey a carefully designed random sample of opiate users. The sample would need special construction because, even including the one-time experimenters, opiate users make up only a tiny fraction of the population. But such survey data would provide little information on the fifth topic, the main characteristics of users: who can use, their degrees of control over use, and how they maintain control. Only a qualitative and precise study of the concept of control itself could explain why some users do well at maintaining control while others control their use only moderately well, poorly, or very poorly.

To indicate and understand some of the ways in which control functions, and to test the general applicability of concepts of control, as well as the variations within the range of opiate-using types, information should be gathered on the extent to which all types of users have been exposed, knowingly or unknowingly, to sanctions and rituals and to what degree they have followed them. Information is also needed on the extent to which style of use is affected by background and personality and by the individual's decision to center control outside himself or herself, perhaps by letting someone else keep the drug supply. Groups of addicts both outside and within treatment programs should also be investigated, both for the purpose of comparing them with controlled and marginal users and as a potential measure of the social evolution of the drug using process. Interviews with addicts who have never been in treatment show that they feel greater concern about controlling their use than do those within treatment programs, who hardly believe that control is possible.

Long term longitudinal studies are needed to investigate these subtle aspects of control. At the same time, such studies could provide information on two other important topics: patterns of drug use and the ability of users to predict their future use patterns.

Longitudinal studies would be useful in measuring the stability of the various drug-using styles and detecting changes in the three basic variables of drug, set, and setting. In such a study the following kinds of life changes should be considered in relation to their impact on subjects' using patterns: death of mate, spouse, or other family member; change in health; change in job; geographic move; change in schooling; change in friends; change in drug supply; and change in using group or groups. A longitudinal approach, which would allow subjects to be interviewed during these life changes or soon after they had occurred, would elicit more reliable data than a strictly retrospective approach.

A longitudinal approach could also be used to test the subjects' own predictive abilities. It would indicate how correct subjects are in predicting what their future drug use will be and in projecting the effect of various changes on their use. Simultaneously it would permit observation of the extent to which subjects' rules for use (social sanctions and rituals) become more internalized and often more conscious.

Public Policy and Education. The review of the existing literature, the research described here, and a spate of personal communications show that not all groups of opiate users become addicts. Until longer term, more quantitative studies are completed, it is impossible to predict what percentage of experimenters will become addicted and what percentage will not. It is my impression that one of the most critical factors contributing to the development of controlled use, not only of the opiates but of any drug, is the attitudes and values of the larger social setting, which, in turn, are translated into social sanctions and rituals. In part, these attitudes and values are expressed in public policies and in the education about drug use that is offered by official bodies.

Until now, public policy has been essentially prohibitionist. Grounded in the conviction that all opiate use leads to addiction, and that addiction is the whole problem, it has dealt solely with the fraction of dysfunctional addicts in the population and has failed to take account of the range of users who are not addicted but are capable of stable, controlled use. Moreover, public policy has been almost exclusively directed toward the drug variable. Policymakers have recommended reducing supplies so that addicts cannot get their drugs and will be forced into treatment situations, an outcome that is expected to improve the set variable. So far policy has made only negative use of the setting variable, which admittedly can have either a reinforcing or a restricting effect upon the individuals's potential to exercise control. Policymakers, instead of considering the possibility that use can be controlled, have attempted to inhibit all use. While searching for methods of dealing with the heroin issue that would calm public fears, they have failed to realize that their own policy may be stimulating those fears.

If, as I contend, the use of opiates and other illicit drugs is indeed an evolving social process, the recognition that the social setting strongly influences the capacity for control offers an alternative to prohibition. Elements of potential control are active in all groups of opiate users, even among addicts. Many opiate users, representing many different styles of use, have precepts, however punitive, that dictate how they can use their drug without becoming addicted or suffering physical and psychological damage, or, at least, how they can use the drug in order to get what they desire from it. Is it not possible that using groups will gradually develop these ideas into social sanctions and rituals similar to those that govern acceptable alcohol use? Although the sample studied in my MIDA project is small, the fact that many of those who fulfilled the project's stringent criteria for controlled use had formerly been addicted suggests the need to consider approaches other than abstinence. For example, assisting the maintenance of controlled use could be a practical means of preventing drug abuse with the least social cost; and experimenting with this alternative in a careful and gradual way would not obstruct the effort to discourage the use of opiates generally.

If, as I contend, the use of opiates is a socially evolving process in which the social setting variable plays an important part, it is essential to reassess the current treatment programs for addicts. The bulk of these programs has grown out of the public policy decision implicit in the creation of the Special Action Office for Drug Abuse Prevention (SAODAP) in 1971. That policy decision to make drug treatment available to all who needed it may have been a forward step in 1971, but in 1978 it has very different implications.

Recently Nightingale reported that, while there are approximately 150,000 to 170,000 persons in treatment and another 100,000 in jail for opiate addiction at any one time, there are "another 300,000 to

400,000 not in treatment, the majority of whom have never been in treatment." This strongly supports the following conclusion of Bourne et al. regarding opiate use in Wyoming: "Very little is known about the characteristics of undetected opiate users," particularly by official bodies, such as the Drug Enforcement Administration, and treatment programs.

Another even more recent study of treatment programs also seems to suggest that the way in which opiate users view treatment has changed sufficiently to warrant a reassessment of treatment per se as well as of the public policies determining its form. In sharp contrast to earlier studies by Vaillant, who found few if any seriously emotionally disturbed clients in treatment programs, Millman and Khuri suggest that treatment programs are becoming wastebaskets for those addicts who have been remanded by the law enforcement system or who, because they are also in serious psychological difficulty, are incapable of functioning elsewhere.

If approaches to treatment were to be reassessed from the viewpoint of the social setting variable, it would first of all be necessary to combat the belief that heroin is "the devil drug." True, heroin is a powerful, highly addictive substance whose potential for individual destruction in this country, as it is now used and as it is now viewed, is enormous. But, like many other drugs used medically, it is deadly only when used improperly. In other countries, such as England and some of the European states, heroin is regarded as medically useful.

At this time, heroin maintenance is not a viable treatment alternative in this country because of the public attitude toward the drug, the well entrenched black market, the sheer numbers of addicts, and the difficulties of administration. But with a change in public policy I can imagine a series of small, carefully designed experiments intended to determine whether the many addicts now avoiding treatment could be brought into treatment. Those experiments would try to determine and give to addicts what they want from the street drug experience, such as getting their preferred drug on a weekend, in the morning, or at night, while maintaining them on oral methadone the rest of the time. It is a measure of our tremendous overconcern with heroin that during the last 10 years of high levels of addiction, not one small experiment of this kind has been carried out.

The National Institute on Drug Abuse has responded to the slight change in public attitude by funding a study of the efficacy of heroin as an analgesic. If heroin indicates any advantage over other available analgesics for even a small percentage of patients in pain, its use should be permitted. Also, the drug is much favored in other countries as an antitussive. The increased medicinal use of heroin along with its experimental use in drug treatment programs would not only add another substance that could be used humanely to alleviate suffering but would also begin to provide some knowledge of the drug's advantages, disadvantages, and side effects, as well as of individual differences in toleration. Objective knowledge about a drug, whether it is alcohol, strychnine, cortisone, or heroin, enables individuals to decide about its use in a more realistic way than when they are influenced by users who view it as a god or by the general public, which views it as a devil. The hyperemotional atmosphere surrounding the present use of heroin may actually be causing those to try it who can handle it least well.

The use of heroin in the ways just mentioned will only be possible if the prevailing view about drug use (abstinence versus addiction) can be shaken. The medical profession in particular must reassess its position because its cooperation will be critical in bringing about any change in heroin use and in the public understanding of that use.

My informal survey of medical teaching in this area in 1976 has shown why physicians feel insecure about the illicit drug issue. Every one of the medical lectures and courses I surveyed discussed the various addictions (opiates, barbiturates, alcohol), the noxious sequelae of use of certain drugs (psychedelics, cocaine, amphetamines), and the health hazards surrounding marijuana use. But none of them threw any light on the using patterns that lead to responsible use and even to beneficial relaxation.

Thus, medical education provides physicians with little of the information that they need when called upon to prescribe drugs now used illicitly. It prepares them inadequately for the frequent questions and requests for advice about the use of these drugs. The great majority of doctors seem to have accepted the abstinence-addiction alternative that has led to a prohibitionist public policy, and to be answering the public's questions from that position.

Such a response in the face of the constantly increasing use of illicit drugs has shaken public confidence in physicians. Their constant call for abstinence, except in the case of medical use, may even have led to a general weakening of their ability to promulgate social sanctions about drug use in general.

A good example would be the considerable misprescribing of amphetamines and barbiturates by physicians a few years ago. Physicians' overprescribing may well have occurred partly as a defense against patients seeking psychoactive drugs from other sources, or partly as an unconscious exaggerated response to the lessened power of physicians' instructions, or both. Whatever the specific reasons for the difficulty, the problem not only left the profession generally looking incompetent but, more important, exposed the extent to which most doctors did not understand the management of psychoactive drugs. Broadening physicians' education in this area and enhancing their role as purveyors of moderation rather than abstinence may help restore their reputation for wisdom in this field.

A new awareness of the existence of nonaddictive opiate use, of its complexity, and of the need for a broad study of control factors may bring about small changes in public attitudes and may help the medical profession and policymakers to see that the time is ripe for change and experimentation. An investigation of the exercise of control, particularly in relation to social sanctions and rituals, could have far-reaching effects. Long-term studies of controlled use, though considering primarily the opiates and other illicit intoxicants, may also have important implications for alcohol use and many other habitual behaviors.

Leonard D. Savitz

THE "MATURING OUT" OF DRUG USE (AND DEVIANCE): Hypotheses and Data

This paper examines a few selected publications containing recent data, speculations, and/or explanatory models relating to how a significant number of drug users/addicts move from a life of drugs into a more socially approved, conventional, and putatively, personally attractive life-style. No attempt has been made to enumerate, let alone closely analyze, all pertinent research and publications, though such would seemingly be extremely worthwhile.

The purpose has been to indicate the implicit assumptions and explicit amplifications of several research findings relative to the maturation concept.

For several reasons, which need not be gone into at this time, it would seem that the first major enunciation of the maturation hypothesis was related to criminality (rather than drug use) and was formulated by Sheldon and Eleanor Glueck in their early prospective, cohort study of 510 offenders whose sentences to the Massachusetts Reformatory expired in 1921–22. The subjects were followed through their first 5 postprison years in *500 Criminal Careers*, on through a second 5-year period up to 10 years after their release in *Later Criminal Careers*, to a final 5-year period encompassing the 10–15 years after prison release in *Criminal Careers in Retrospect*. The authors concluded that ages 25 to 35 were most crucial for those who mature "normally" and who will (or should) abandon a life of crime by age 36. By then, they postulate, a process of "benign maturation" causes all normal criminals to grow out of criminality. Those who remain criminals after that age are definitionally neurotic, psychotic, psychopathic, or homosexual. The Gluecks attributed these "organismal changes" to a biological, psychological shift involving loss or lessening of energy, diminishment of aggressiveness, a general "slowing-down" and a tendency to become less "venturesome." The many serious methodological flaws which characterized this multivolume study (e.g., the Gluecks demonstrated an unfortunate penchant for failing to age their study population as they moved from one 5-year period to the next) meant that most criminologists could not seriously consider any of their conclusions.

Regarding the five pieces of research which represent the primary focus of this paper, their sample populations, operational definitions, findings, and explanatory models vary enormously. A short summary of each is given first. Then a summary of the maturation concept is given in some detail.

Short Summaries of Five Studies. Winick used a list of addicts secured from the Federal Bureau of Narcotics. He clearly recognized the considerable problems associated with valid indications of permanent recovery. Believing that it was almost impossible to engage in regular drug use and avoid the attention of "authorities" for even 2 years, Winick used 5 years with no record of drug use as a measure of (maturational) success. He also indicated that not only abstention but also years of addiction and other "external" factors might be related to reaching a certain phase of the (drug-use) disease. Generally, he found about two-thirds of all addicts matured out of drug use. It was speculated that maturing out may be heavily related to reasons for the original entry into a life of drugs; some young people have seemingly insoluble problems and turn to drugs which permit them to avoid dealing with these problems (largely sex and legitimate occupation) and to become comfortably dependent on others. This stressfulness of youth diminishes, and by age 30 (Winick believes), life has become more stable, less fiery, less salient, and less urgent with problems; accordingly, there is a significantly lesser "need" for drugs.

DeFleur et al. examined a number of exaddicts who had been in Lexington Hospital and who were living in Puerto Rico. With extensive data from medical reports, field interviews, urinalyses, and FBI arrest records, maturing out was defined as having occurred if no record of drug use was found for 3 years or more. A maturing out rate of 22 percent was found for this restricted population. The study was also concerned with years of addiction as a factor in remission; 67 percent of the steadily employed subjects had matured out. Suggestions were made that continuous employment was related to cessation of drug use and that it was (somehow) easier for addicts with longer formal education and better previous employment records to permanently abstain from drugs.

Ball and Snarr also examined Puerto Rican drug addicts. Using medical and hospital records, FBI and Federal Bureau of Narcotics data, and field interviews, they defined 3 years of abstinence as the measure of success (cure). Within that definition, the data show 19 percent mature out; but the authors suggest that about one-third of all addicts will mature out (20–40%) by age 40. The possibility of remission of the (addiction) disease is considered somewhat distinct from simple maturing out (aging). The study dealt with maturation due to design, or persuasion (including treatment), or dint of circumstances. Maturation was found to involve separate dimensions of aging and years of addiction. The study found no evidence that criminality as well as drug use might have a maturational process.

Waldorf, using heroin addicts in New York City in 1968, dealt with varying periods of voluntary abstinence with the longest category of nonuse (8 months or more) having 21 percent of all subjects. The evidence, we are told, suggests that length of addiction is more important than aging to the cessation of drug use. (Data are not well handled, so the author's conclusion is not confirmed by his own data.) Waldorf suggested that perhaps a more likely explanation of nonuse was the "burning out" by heroin use rather than the maturing out by aging. Perhaps, he argued, the addict reaches a saturation point when life is simply too much (we are told that most addicts reach "rock bottom"). Abstinence brings regularity of employment, improved family relationships, and enhanced personal happiness. The principal "resource" in abstinence is education.

Brown examined three populations of District of Columbia drug addicts and asked *why* they voluntarily withdrew from drugs. This was a study, not of maturation but of articulated reasons for voluntary cessation. "Efforts to change life patterns" was the most common reason given by adult and juvenile male addicts. "Drug-related physical problems" was the most frequent given by female addicts and the second most common given by males. "Drug-related family problems" was also put forth frequently.

None of the above studies comes close to defining the maturation hypothesis. Most of the research was not designed primarily for that. The sample sizes were often too small to permit adequate statistical analyses; when the sizes were sufficiently large, the types of data were sometimes too restricted. Even when the number of subjects was adequate and the variables sufficiently detailed, the data analysis was often crude and inefficient; that is, a superior form of statistical analysis would have been appropriate and might have provided more valuable findings.

A Summation of the Maturation Concept. A significant number of persons are, and have been for a long time, engaged in behavior which is socially evil, bad, deleterious, and criminal. It is also widely assumed that the behavior is personally disadvantageous. (For this paper, illicit and illegal drug use/addiction is the form of behavior under analysis.)

A sizable percentage (20% to 67%) of all persons with serious drug problems will experience a major shift or change in this central characteristic despite bodily dependence on ingested drugs.

The shift or change in behavior is *not* thought to be the direct consequence of any (effective) treatment program, technique, or strategy directed at addicts by conventional society. It is assumed that the change is brought on by voluntary motivation of the addict.

For the addicted population, the dramatic change in this vital aspect of their lives is unanimously agreed to be socially desirable. The change in behavior is said to be (and some evidence supports this belief) associated with entry into a more conventional lifestyle involving better social relationships and greater legitimate economic productivity.

The changed behavior is thought to be psychologically advantageous to the individuals. These persons are expected to become happier, to exhibit less anxiety and tension, and to be in easier and more certain control of their environments.

The altered behavior is *abstinence from drug use/addiction,* not a *reduction* in drug use. Complete cessation from drug ingestion is a crucial element of the maturation concept.

Not only must there be complete avoidance of drug use, cessation must be judged to be (by varying operational definitions) *permanent;* that is, relapse into addiction must be an extremely unlikely possibility based on available data.

The definitions of permanent abstinence vary enormously, even within the few studies examined above. Some examine nondrug use for absurdly short periods of time (from which serious or realistic permanent recovery cannot be judged). Others examine longer (more persuasive) periods ranging from 3 to 5 years. The question is how long a period of complete cessation must be before researchers and policymakers can agree that the abstinence is permanent and the addict is "cured." (Using a disease model of drug use implies that physicians can recognize a cure with great accuracy and with consensus; the experts dealing with this disease—addiction—cannot make statements about cure with equal certainty and professional agreement.)

Little attention has been given to whether the decision to stop taking drugs must be completely voluntary or can be partially due to coercion. Some writers suggest that maturing out, by definition, must be completely voluntary in motivation, but *why* is difficult to fathom. Why the impetus of imprisonment or coercive diversion from the criminal justice system into a drug treatment modality could not be instrumental in persuading the addict to permanently continue the nonuse of drugs is not revealed.

The fundamental question is why some persons do mature out of drugs. Sometimes this is not dealt with at all. One is simply told that maturation has taken place and that the person has outgrown an addict's lifestyle.

One explicit explanation offered by some investigators points to the importance (sometimes the centrality) of the cyclical nature of drug use. After being an addict for a period of time and perhaps attaining a certain point in the more-or-less natural history of addiction, conditions are somehow right for an exit from the lifestyle. The precise number of years of addiction required and the exact moment in the cycle of addiction the magic moment occurs we are not told.

The simple attainment of a chronological age (usually in the thirties) is suggested by almost all investigators as being completely, primarily, or secondarily the cause of maturation.

There are suggestions that the impact of age is primarily sociological and involves the attainment of a certain level of social maturity which requires or permits the abandonment of "less mature," childish, or inappropriate social roles. The mature person will, consequentially, engage in more conventional roles with adult responsibilities and rewards. This is thought to be related to societywide, age-related changes in family life, friendship networks or, less clearly, legitimate occupational opportunities. It is believed that formal education is vitally important in causing (or predicting) maturation. Another belief is that employment somehow leads to abstinence from drugs.

There is some belief that age impact is primarily psychological—a certain age engenders major alterations in personality for appreciable numbers of drug-involved persons. These alterations encompass elements such as a reduction of extroversion, a diminishment of adventurousness, and the abatement of extrapunitive aggression. High "inner fires" are banked, and powerful driving forces are lessened. Also significant is the belief that the psychological problems which precipitated entry into a drug-taking lifestyle are no longer as serious and thus have far less impact on people in their thirties than those in their teens and early twenties. The chaotic maladjustments of youth are replaced by a greater psychological maturity which begins to express itself in the thirties.

One final, often implicit, belief is that age and aging involve some biological basis for the maturation out of drugs. Almost never clearly specified is *what* biological/physiological changes are involved or *how* these internal bodily changes direct or influence external behavioral changes. It is possible to argue that "lessening of energy," generally "slowing down," or more carefully husbanding personal (physical) re-sources are biological explanations for aging.

Generally, cessation of drug use (maturing out) includes factors which might *push* persons out of drugs. These factors include despair over one's current drug life (touching bottom), increases in drug-related physical and familial problems, and diminishment of energy levels needed to con-tinue a life of "ripping and running." There are also *pull* factors involving personal and social resources—formal educational and occupational ex-periences. To these must be added the crucial, if still unclear, age factor which cannot easily be classified as a push or a pull factor.

Finally, there is some belief (and some confirming data) that maturing out of drugs leads to an enhanced family life, improved relationships with friends, occupational capabilities, and personal satisfaction. Also, it is contended that dropping out of a drug life involves a concomitant aban-donment of criminality. This last assumption, while not central to the maturation hypothesis, is worthy of comment.

The idea that maturation eliminates the double problem of drug involvement and criminal behavior is intriguing, but it is not heavily supported by available data. A recent report by the Philadelphia TASC project demonstrates that exaddicts are often heavily involved in crime. Studying 6,800 arrestees in a 3-month period using several meas-ures of drug use (self-admission, urinalysis, and current criminal charges involving possessing or sale of narcotic drugs), TASC learned that 1,142 were current drug addicts; this number represented 16.8 percent of all persons arrested. The study also found, surprisingly, that an additional 9.5 percent of all arrestees (N=642) were exaddicts; that is, official records revealed narcotic drug histories, but the same records offered evidence that the arrestees were not currently involved with narcotics. Both current and exaddicts had similar age distributions (both groups were younger than nondrug-using arrestees). Exaddicts were more likely to have arrest histories than current addicts (averages of 8.4 and 7.3 arrests), and exaddicts were far more likely to have arrest histories involving weapon offenses, aggravated assault, and other assaults. Thus, exaddicts (even those in their thirties who perhaps had matured out of drugs) were heavily represented in the criminal population. They represented a significant percentage of all *arrestees* and contributed a disproportionate share of all *arrests* and violent (weapon/assault) offenses. These comments were not meant to prove or disprove the relationship of drug maturation and continued criminality; they were merely meant to indicate that the relationship is more complicated than some researchers seem to believe.

Section 2

HISTORY OF LEGAL CONTROLS

Although historical investigation is a promising tool of inquiry, it has been largely neglected by the social sciences community. Instead, complex quantitative methods and intricate quasi-experimental designs have nearly monopolized modern social science research attention. Only recently have sociology, criminology, and kindred disciplines begun to grant equal consideration to alternative investigative strategies.

Besides increasing interest in the application of finely tuned present-oriented methodologies (such as ethnography), social scientists have adopted historical techniques to examine social phenomena. Valuable insights have been yielded to sociology, psychology, psychiatry, criminology, and medicine through historical investigation. The capacity to predict future developments has been improved as social scientists have comprehended more precisely the evolutionary patterns of social phenomena.

Morgan's examination of California's initial opium regulation fits in that tradition. Reflecting a truly multidisciplinary approach (mostly economics and political science), her study offers notable findings. The enactment of a benchmark penal sanction is attributed to an interaction of political, social, and economic forces.

Patricia A. Morgan

THE LEGISLATION OF DRUG LAW
Economic Crisis and Social Control

Any close examination of legal prohibitions against drug use should include the law's historical development, those socio-economic forces which lay the foundation for legislative action. This study of the first opium laws enacted against the Chinese in 19th century California endeavors to do this. It explores the anti-opium crusade as part of the dynamics of both class conflict and symbolic/status dominance within the working class.

The case-study method employed here has often been the most appropriate way to examine the sources of drug law. Becker, Musto, and Helmer, among others, have shown that the case-study method offers the best possibility for in-depth analysis of the wide variety of conditions preceding legislative action. In addition, our study has made use of the abundant historical material available to the researcher in California. Although the economic and racial conditions in California were unique in the country during that time, its moral crusades and legislative action did represent later popular views linking immoral behavior with ethnic and racial minorities. This theme can be seen running through the works of Duster, Becker, Helmer, Lindesmith, and Gusfield. The interpretations of these events vary, however, according to the theoretical framework adopted by the researcher. This paper addresses the issue of moral reform via Becker's idea of moral crusades and Gusfield's notion of the symbolic function of the law.

In discussing Becker, we focus primarily on his notion that laws dealing with problems of moral order and deviance develop as a direct result of moral crusades waged by individuals or groups which inform the public of particular immoral conditions. Here Becker likens a crusader to a moral entrepreneur who develops through moral initiative a rule-making and selective enforcement enterprise:

> Wherever rules are created and applied, we should be alive to the possible presence of an enterprising individual or group. Their activities can properly be called moral enterprise, for what they are enterprising about is the creation of a new fragment of the moral constitution of society, its code of right and wrong.

There are two important questions, however, that Becker ignores. What acts as a catalyst to initiate such legal action by these moral crusaders? More importantly, how did these individuals receive the legitimation and power to effect change over other groups within the legal system? These questions will be addressed later in this paper.

Gusfield, in his work on moral reform, notes the importance of status in rule making. One function of the law is maintenance of control; a second is legitimation of a group's position in society. Gusfield terms these two functions the instrumental and the symbolic. The instrumental function lies completely with enforcement; "unenforced this function does not exist." The symbolic function of the law, however, does not depend on enforcement:

> There is a dimension of meaning in symbolic behavior which is not given in its immediate and manifest significance, but in what the action connotes for the audience that views it. . . . the symbol "has acquired a meaning which is added to its immediate intrinsic significance." . . . In analyzing law as symbolic, we are oriented less to behavioral consequences as a means to a fixed end: more to meaning as an act, a decision, a gesture important in itself.

Gusfield's conceptualization of moral reform limits itself, for the most part, to the realm of status. The law, however, can take on symbolic meanings which in themselves have instrumental force. The symbolic force behind moral reforms can reinforce basic divisions within the working class. The passage of these laws can be seen, then, as a means of coopting a segment of the working class, providing it with mere symbolic superiority over other "immoral" and economically threatening groups. This, in effect, can prevent a collective effort of combined work class interests.

The Chinese in California. The first law against opium use in California was part of a general anti-Chinese crusade in the latter part of the 19th century. The Chinese population in the U.S. was growing steadily from a little over 4 thousand in 1850 to over 107 thousand in 1890 with the overwhelming majority residing in California. Although hostility was present at the beginning of Chinese immigration, it did not develop into a full scale crusade until after 1870. The gold rush was a frantic era of rapid development and widely fluctuating economic conditions; it attracted people from widely different social, racial and economic backgrounds. Hostility against the Chinese was, at first, sporadic and based primarily on local labor competition. It was alleviated somewhat when construction began on the Central Pacific railroad employing over 9,000 Chinese workers.

After the Civil War, the labor picture changed as new discoveries of silver and gold brought thousands west—young men uprooted from the war and immigrants from Europe drifting into California looking for work. The labor situation worsened in the 1870s when the national panic of 1873 depressed local industries, and the completion of the railroad threw thousands of Chinese on the job market. White labor groups in California started forming loose coalitions in opposition to the growing competition of Chinese workers.

The Chinese were working jobs for cheaper pay that whites felt rightfully belonged to them. They were industrious and able to live on less than their white counterparts and "as they entered one field of activity after another it was claimed that they not only drove out American laborers but also tended to monopolize the industry." This claim has been documented for the cigar and shoe making industry as well as for certain types of clothing manufacture.

When the national economic depression hit the larger industries in California, the Chinese turned more toward small business and trade enterprises formerly under the control of the white middle class. Chinese competition in these areas drove thousands into the camp of organized labor. As McWilliams has noted:

The labor movement in California . . . has included elements which are not ordinarily thought of as part of labor . . . the small shop keeping element; a large section of the rural population; and a sizeable element of what today would be called 'white collar' workers.

Thus, both working and middle classes began to have a stake in organized anti-Chinese activities.

In September, 1877, many of the unemployed laborers in San Francisco organized the Workingmen's Party, which had a brief, but important, impact on California labor history. In a series of vacant lot meetings in the city, they denounced the Chinese as the cause rather than possible victims of capitalist prosperity. The California Workingmen's

Party, like its counterparts in the Eastern part of the country, was very much aware of the evils of "big business." They were therefore opposed to the large corporate and landholding monopolies which had continued longer than any other sector to encourage Chinese immigration. In their eyes, the corporations were similar to Southern plantations with the Chinese as "slave" laborers against whom no white worker could compete. This view was articulated in a Western newspaper which warned the white worker to "give California a wide berth, for the laborer is not worthy of his hire in that state, even when there is work for him to do."

The Workingmen's Party was aware of the connections between labor's problems and the monopolistic control of industry and railroads in the state. Their platform dealt with many economic and social issues unrelated to the Chinese. It stated, for instance, that the "object of the new party was to unite all of the poor and laboring men into one group for defense against the encroachment of capital." But poor and laboring men did not mean Chinese, because "Chinese labor provided the emotional drive and concrete motivation necessary for uniting the working men of the state." It was also the ideological mechanism which convinced workers that the elimination of the Chinese from the labor market would result in immediate economic improvement.

Agitating for Chinese exclusionary laws, the Workingmen's Party began to receive serious attention. The presence of the Chinese "menace" considerably strengthened the power of white labor:

It contributed more than any other one factor to the strength of the California labor movement. It is the one subject upon which . . . it has always been possible to obtain concerted action. . . . legislation prohibiting the further immigration of Oriental laborers has been the chief object of the organized activities of the working people of California for over fifty years.

In their crusade against the Chinese, the Workingmen's Party began to receive support from several different sources. First, the newspapers began to increase their campaign against the Chinese, and second, this was supported by the state legislature, which began official inquiries into every aspect of the presence of the Chinese population.

The Chinese had thus lost what little protection they had previously enjoyed. The corporate and railroad interests that had defended Chinese workers in the past now either joined the chorus of Chinese exclusionists or remained silent. The worsening economic picture and the large influx of militant unemployed white workers made the presence of Chinese labor problematic, as well, for big business in the state.

The State Legislature and the Chinese. After the panic of 1873, the legislature demanded more anti-Chinese reforms, and soon became a major force against the Chinese. Although earlier regional sporadic anti-Chinese sentiments had been addressed by the state legislature, they had been largely ineffective. Previous anti-Chinese legislation had focused primarily on Chinese exclusion, but those early laws did not receive much attention from the press, had almost no practical effect, and served primarily as "symbolic" reassurance that the state would not become overrun by alien Chinese.

The transition from those early Chinese exclusionary laws and later anti-opium laws is important for this analysis. Legal action that began with exclusionary measures helped to set the stage for the passage of laws which later harassed the Chinese on many levels. By 1885, most aspects of the Chinese presence suffered under some legal sanction. Thus, the common expression "he hasn't a Chinaman's chance" became very appropriate.

Starting in the 1850s, laws were introduced and passed by zealous legislators who wanted to limit or completely halt the immigration of Orientals to California. Many of these laws were later declared unconstitutional, but were often modified and reintroduced into the state legislature as the need dictated.

Chinese Exclusionary Laws.

1855   A state law prohibited Chinese and Mongolians from entering the state; later declared unconstitutional.

1858   A state law prohibited Asiatics from entering the state except when driven ashore by stress of weather or unavoidable accident, later declared unconstitutional.

1870   A state law provided a penalty of not less than $1000 for any person bringing an Asiatic into the state without first presenting evidence of good character. In 1876, this law was declared unconstitutional.

1879   After repeated resolutions to the federal government, Congress passed a bill limiting the number of Chinese who came to the U.S. on any one vessel to fifteen.

1880   The U.S. Congress ratified a treaty with China giving the United States the right to "regulate, limit, or suspend" Chinese immigration, but not to prohibit it.

1882   The U.S. Congress suspended Chinese immigration for ten years.

Several other laws provided economic or political sanctions against the Chinese within the state of California:

1850   The Foreign Miners Tax Act placed a monthly tax on non-citizens working the mines. This was later modified to pertain only to Orientals.

1854   The state Supreme Court included Chinese in an 1850 statute prohibiting court testimony of non-whites for or against whites.

1855   A head tax of $50 per person was levied on those who employed or brought into the country those "persons who could not become citizens." Although no legislation specifically named the Chinese, the tax was used primarily against them.

1862   A police tax required all Asians not already paying the Miners Tax and not engaged in agriculture to pay a monthly tax of $2.50.

1875   The California Supreme Court denied naturalization to a Chinese individual, thus establishing precedent denying legal citizenship to the Chinese.

These are merely examples of state legislative actions. The list does not include similar widespread local ordinances. Both state and municipal treasuries were made thousands of dollars healthier each year as a result of such tax laws.

After the economic depression of the 1870s the state legislature began inquiring into the "moral" aspects of the Chinese population. This helped to maintain an ideology, developing during this time, which transferred the onus away from the business class as cause of economic problems and became a moral attack against a race that could be perceived as the cause of a wide range of problems. Accordingly, the California legislature created several "fact-finding" committees which looked into every aspect of the Chinese lifestyle. The findings of these committees served both to legitimate the prejudicial actions of past legal sanctions and to form the basis for further legislation. Thus, the one subject that began to receive a large amount of official attention was the problem of vice found in Chinese communities. For instance, statutes were enacted against gambling and lottery. Although not specifically worded directly against the Chinese, they did, in fact, allow for selective enforcement. As one journalist observed:

The San Francisco papers recently recorded, with much satisfaction, the fact that the police had determined to suppress the Chinese gambling houses. . . . Considering the fact that the same laws which prohibit Chinese gambling prohibit monte, faro, and other sports of the superior race; and considering moreover that one faro game will do more actual harm in a month than a dozen Chinese hells would do in a year. . . . It is a matter of notoriety that there are some seven or eight old established faro banks on Montgomery Street alone. . . . The proprietors of them sport their figures on the fashionable prominades, redolent of essences and clothed in purple and fine linen. These are the men, and theirs the institutions upon which the sagacity and enterprise of the police authorities should be expended. But there is little hope for any such interference with them. They possess vested rights here and none dare meddle with them. The legislator who is asked to check their iniquitous practices looks coldly upon the petitioner, for he spent his last evening among them, and he thinks they are mighty good fellows.

Thus selective enforcement of vice laws against the Chinese was used without interfering with white middle or upper class gambling habits.

Inequitable rule enforcement went hand-in-hand with anti-Chinese legislative action. The success of this trend after 1870 is presented in the following statistics, which show that by 1900 over 80 percent of Chinese arrests in San Francisco were for crimes against "morality."

Offense	% of Chinese Arrests
1. Crimes against property	.96
2. Crimes against the person	1.03
3. Crimes against public health (includes opium)	15.95
4. Crimes against public policy and morals (includes gambling)	82.00

It seems safe to conclude that "moral reform" was an important motivation, during the last part of the 19th century, for the anti-Chinese crusade. It became an important component in exclusionary policies coming out of the state legislature.

The Chinese and Opium. The Chinese habit of smoking opium began to attract attention after the Civil War. This is because the earliest Chinese immigrants in California did not smoke opium. In China, opium use was concentrated primarily among the working class and peasant communities. The sale and distribution of opium within China was handled by the merchant and landlord classes, which were also the first groups to arrive in California. As John Helmer has pointed out:

The Chinese immigrants were typically the younger sons of landowners without primogeniture rights of inheritance. . . . They were not usually from laboring origins. . . . They paid for their own passages and brought capital with them to invest. . . . The number of wage laborers among the Chinese in the early period was low. As can be expected, if opium use was

confined to this class, there is no record of its use among the first generation of immigrants in California. . . . Indeed, there is no mention of opium-
smoking until the mid 1860s.

Thus, the first anti-opium crusade in U.S. history was directed against
working class Chinese brought over initially for use as cheap mass labor,
a function no longer needed by 1870. Consequently, the anti-opium
crusade begun in the 1870s was waged as an ideological battle in connection with the economic one to remove these workers from the labor
market. It was not the use of opium itself, but the smoking, a unique
Chinese habit, which became the focal point for legislative action. Most
importantly, opium smoking became a special problem when white men
and women in the state began to "contaminate" themselves by frequent-
ing the dens in Chinatown.

Direct action against Chinese opium smoking was first taken in 1875
when the city of San Francisco enacted an ordinance prohibiting the co-
mingling of the races in Chinatown's opium dens. Although the ordinance
had some success, it was soon found to be limited.

The vice was indulged in much less openly, but none the less extensively,
for although the larger smoking-houses were closed, the small dens in
Chinatown were well patronized, and the vice grew surely and steadily.

Finally, the San Francisco police department made an impassioned plea
before the California State Senate Committee on Chinese Immigration
in 1878:

These latter places were conducted by Chinamen, and patronized by
both White men and women, who visited these dens at all hours of the
day and night, the habit and its deadly results becoming so extensive as
to call for action on the part of the authorities. . . . The department of
the police, in enforcing the law with regard to this matter, have found
white women and Chinamen side by side under the effects of this
drug—a humiliating sight to anyone who has anything left of manhood.

The media soon became an important force behind this crusade, waging
a moral battle that placed the Chinese in an ever increasingly vulnerable
position. Essentially the media reinforced the idea that the Chinese were
responsible for opium smoking among Caucasians. They were portrayed
as sinister agents who lured young men and women into the opium dens.
Newspapers in the state daily saw to it that all "moral citizens" knew
the consequences of letting the Chinese remain in California. According
to the San Francisco *Post,* the Chinaman "has impoverished our country,

degraded our free labor and hoodlumized our children. He is now destroying our young men with opium." The Sacramento *Union,* among others, fanned the fire of incensed American manhood by printing lurid accounts of what went on inside these opium houses:

Upon a matting-covered couch lay a handsome white girl in silk and laces, sucking poison from the same stem which an hour before was against the repulsive lips and yellow teeth of a celestial. She was just taking the last pipeful; the eyes were heavy, the will past resistance or offense. She glanced up lazily, but was too indifferent to replace the embroidered skirts over the rounded ankles the disturbed drapery exposed.

The media, however, generally overlooked the possibility that reformers were observing fake Chinatown opium dens operated by whites:

Many of the places wherein opium was smoked, or was supposed to be smoked, were fakes, tourist shockers conducted by the professional guides to the quarter, who were licensed by the city and were organized as the Chinatown Guides Association.

However, the state legislature, in 1881, supported the media's charges against the immoral "anti-American" Chinese and enacted a law against opium smoking. Importantly, this law was aimed specifically at opium dens and opium parlors which then existed only in Chinese communities. As the law, itself, stated:

Every person who opens or maintains, to be resorted to by other persons, any place where opium, or any of its preparations, is sold or given away to be smoked at such place; and any person who, at such place sells or gives away any opium, or its aid preparations, to be smoked . . . is guilty of a misdemeanor.

Inasmuch as the only places where opium was being smoked were in the Chinese opium parlors, the legislation was clearly anti-Chinese.

A few years after the California law, the Federal government began discriminating between the different uses of opium in various tax measures. For instance, the government decided who, in fact, would control the importation and preparation of opium for smoking in this country. In 1890, Congress passed a law which stated that only American citizens were allowed to manufacture opium for smoking although the use of such was formally outlawed in the state where almost all opium smoking occurred.

The fact that the California law remained a misdemeanor and the nature of Federal tax measures concerning importation, point to serious questions concerning the actual prevalence of opium smoking among the Chinese. Helmer has estimated that no more than 6 percent of the Chinese population in California engaged in the habit regularly. In addition, the sketchy available records give no indication that legal enforcement of the opium law was important in ridding the state of the Chinese presence. The law's importance seemed to lie in bolstering California's claim to moral as well as economic reasons for Chinese exclusion.

Consequently, California's first opium law was directed only against those who smoked opium. The vast majority of those who used the drug by other means were not affected. Yet other forms of opium use were more common than the Chinese habit of opium smoking which California had declared both illegal and immoral. The influence of the patent medicine industry alone has led Troy Duster to observe: "In proportion to the population, addiction was probably eight times more prevalent then than now, despite the large increase in the general population." But these opium users were not considered deviant, falling under some morally evil influence, or anti-American. To the extent that their opium use was considered a problem at all, it was referred to as a medical and not a moral issue. This double standard remained until the passage of the Harrison Tax Act in 1914, and only later did all opiate use develop into a general moral issue. Those first Federal laws relating to the manufacture and regulation of opium were not crusades against immorality. The same economic and political factors which led to the moral crusade in California were not operating in the 1914 Harrison Act.

Thus, we conclude that the first opium laws in California were not the result of a moral crusade against the drug itself. Instead, it represented a coercive action directed against a vice that was merely an appendage of the real menace—the Chinese—and not the Chinese per se, but the laboring "Chinamen" who threatened the economic security of the white working class. Moral concern here took place on two levels. The first and more apparent level seemed to be aimed ultimately at removing the Chinese from the labor force. The moral battle could thus be seen as a supporting element to that end. However, on another more subtle level, the moral crusade against opium smoking could be viewed as an ideological mechanism diverting attention away from the real causes of the workers' problem—the economic power relationships in the state over which the white worker had little control. Those power interests were not harmed by a normative crusade which aimed hostilities back toward a segment of the working class itself.

When we try to fit Becker's idea of moral entrepreneurs into California's anti-opium crusade, a further analysis is needed. Moral crusades do not take place solely as a result of the appearance of deviant group behavior or of moral entrepreneurs. The enactment of moral reform laws is generally connected to particular historical conditions which act as catalysts to such action. Furthermore, these crusades usually receive legitimation from a source of authority within the system itself, in this case the media and the state legislature.

Similarly, Gusfield's analyses of the symbolic and instrumental functions of the law have to be broadened to include more than status maintenance alone. The motivation, which can stem from social or economic crises, behind quests for status dominance must be examined before either symbolic or instrumental functions of moral law can attain historical significance. In addition, symbolism in the law can affect groups in very instrumental ways. By agitating for normative control over Chinese moral habits, those crusading for status dominance also were in the process of instrumentally controlling the behavior of the Chinese vis-à-vis the labor market. By creating a diversion deflecting the more fundamental causes of the real economic issues, such drives for status maintenance also had the effect of insuring the continuance of basic power in the state—a real consequence. When this is understood, the historical significance of the first opium laws takes on a broader perspective than mere moral entrepreneurship or status maintenance alone.

Therefore, when studying the development of moral crusades leading to legal sanctions, one must look beyond the normative level of analysis to other structural processes during that period. There is a close symbiotic relationship between normative, economic, and political dimensions in any state system. One, therefore, cannot study crusades occuring on any one level without first examining the causal contributions of the others.

Section 3

DRUG–RELATED CRIME

Within the framework of drugs and criminal justice relationships, no subject has demonstrated more success in capturing the public fancy than the drugs and crime nexus. It may be forcefully argued that a singular conception of this relationship–viz., that drug use promotes street crime in a direct and inexorable fashion–explains national drug control policies. Abundant popular and scholarly evidence supports that conclusion.

In this encyclopedic treatment of the subject, Weissman systematically explores the parameters of the drugs and crime connection. This state-of-the-knowledge summary examines salient questions and available scientific evidence. Reported data are probed critically in an attempt to provide objective and accurate answers to fundamental research and social policy issues. The continuing investment of substantial government research awards demonstrates an uninterrupted commitment to further examination of this controversial but influential topic. The primer furnished in this article should aid understanding of the subject.

James C. Weissman

UNDERSTANDING THE DRUGS
AND CRIME CONNECTION

* * * * * * * * * * * *

HYPOTHESES

With regard to the nature of the relationships between drugs and crime, four general hypotheses have been constructed. Careful examination of the drugs and crime literature reveals a constant focus on these few questions. These hypotheses and their sub-questions are:

1. What is the precise relationship between consumption of psychoactive drugs and commission of criminal acts?
   - what is the probability that users of different psychoactive drugs will commit various types of non-drug crime?
   - what is the probability that criminals will use various types of drugs?
   - are there direct pharmacological effects of drug consumption which cause criminal behavior?
   - do addicted persons commit income-generating crimes as a result of their habits?
   - is there a definite temporal sequence between drug use and criminal behavior?
   - are drug use and crime patterns merely correlative or can cause and effect be demonstrated?
   - are there specific drug use and crime patterns associated with different age, race and sex groups?
   - are there other factors associated with drug use and crime, e.g., unemployment, which may cause a spurious correlation?

2. To what extent does the available supply of drugs affect consumption and related crime patterns?
   - as enforcement efforts reduce the supply of drugs and drive up prices, do drug users react by decreasing drug consumption?
   - if the price structure does affect consumption, do regular users seek treatment or substitute drugs?

- do rising prices deter marginal users from participating in the drug market?
- what are the income-generating habits of drug users?
- is treatment availability an integral component of the supply-crime rate equation?
3. Do treatment activities reduce drug-related crime?
- do individual drug users reduce their illicit activities as a result of treatment intervention?
- are community crime rates affected by treatment activities?
- is the effectiveness of treatment contingent upon user characteristics?
- are particular types of crime more influenced by treatment than others?
- does the effectiveness of treatment depend upon the level of intervention, quality of services and modality?
- are there factors other than the treatment itself which may cause a spurious correlation?
4. How effective are drug laws in achieving their penal goals?
- are drug laws capable of deterring drug consumption in a meaningful manner?
- are different types of drug users influenced similarly by the drug laws?
- do drug sanctions accomplish an incapacitative effect on a significant proportion of the drug-user population?
- does legal pressure advance the rehabilitation of drug users?
- do the instrumental and symbolic benefits of the drug laws outweigh the associated costs?

To the extent that probative data are available, these research questions are addressed in the following sections. Before proceeding to that inquiry, however, it is useful to review conceptual and measurement issues. The following section examines definitions and measurement questions pertinent to a valid understanding of the drugs and crime literature.

DEFINITIONS AND MEASUREMENT

Throughout this article references are made to methodological criticisms of drugs and crime research. Confidence in research findings requires that the researchers adhere to certain accepted standards and conventions. This is particularly true in social science research where investigation of phenomena is largely retrospective and unplanned.

Research accuracy requires uniformity in the application of conceptual definitions and measurement devices. In addition, to attach significance to research findings, it is necessary to be certain exactly what is being studied and what measures are being used to record the results.

Unfortunately, drugs and crime research has not adhered to principles of uniformity in a consistent manner; concepts have been defined inhomogenously. For instance, some researchers characterize criminal behavior as an all-or-nothing proposition, subjects being either law-abiders or law-violators. Other researchers, on the other hand, have adopted more precise standards refining the abstract notion of criminality into meaningful descriptive constructs. This latter line of inquiry classifies criminal behavior by type, severity and frequency.

Similar problems occur with respect to measurement techniques. Alternate methods are used for estimating the incidence of both drug use and crime. Individual criminal behavior may be assessed by reference to either official records or self-reports. Aggregate crime figures may be calculated by reference to either official reports, such as the FBI Uniform Crime Reports (UCR), or to victimization studies conducted by household survey methods.

Measurement of drug use patterns is subject to a similar order of choice. Both individual and aggregate counts may be derived by either official methods, such as urinalysis, or self-report methods, such as structured interviewing. The individual bias of a particular researcher generally accounts for selection of a particular method, although economics, time and related factors may contribute to the decision.

In reviewing the implications of the absence of uniformity in drugs and crime research, the 1976 Federal *Drug Use and Crime* report identified three elements requiring consideration. First, the types of drug use and criminal activity that appear to be of major social concern should be clarified. Secondly, drug use and crime phenomena must be defined in a non-simplistic fashion; terms should be capable of describing the nature, extent and seriousness of these behaviors. Finally, to the extent possible, measurements of drug use and crime should be related to the costs they impose on society.

Shellow has described a four-tiered typology of drug-related crime. The first type consists of criminal behavior which is a direct and proximate result of drug consumption, i.e., a pharmacological effect. Although the related phenomenon of criminal behavior as a consequence of drug intoxication is commonly reported, little hard evidence exists regarding the incidence of this type of drug effect. The primary relevance of this topic is to legal theory for purposes of applying the insanity and diminished responsibility defenses.

Drug-defined crimes represent a second entry in the typology. National crime statistics indicate that drug-defined crimes account for a substantial proportion of reported criminal activity. The 1976 UCR revealed 609,700 drug violations, ranking drug-defined crimes as the fifth most frequently occurring offense category. Only public drunkenness, larceny, drunken driving and disorderly conduct surpassed the drug violation total.

There are numerous categories of drug-defined crime. The following eleven offenses are the most frequently noted: simple possession or possession for personal use, sale or distribution; possession with the intent to sell or distribute; manufacturing or cultivation; obtaining by fraud or deceit; transportation of drugs; presence where drugs are being used; maintaining a disorderly place; loitering for purposes of unlawfully using or possessing drugs; disorderly persons or narcotics vagrancy; possession of narcotics paraphernalia; and driving under the influence of drugs. All of these offenses are the product of criminalization of drug use and would not exist but for that social-policy decision.

The third type of drug-related crime consists of criminal acts committed to maintain the functioning of drug-distribution channels. Manufacture and distribution of drugs is an unregulated form of commerce characterized by a potentially handsome return on investment but an equal risk of experiencing personal violence and financial loss. Access to data concerning the incidence of these secondary crimes is restricted by the surreptitious nature of the drug distribution enterprise.

The fourth crime type is that which most concerns the public—income-generating crimes committed by drug users to support their drug habits. Crimes against property (burglary) and crimes against person (robbery) aimed at income acquisition fit into this category. In addition, less serious public-order offenses, such as lottery, prostitution, wagering, etc., are committed to raise drug-purchase funds.

Drug use is also a complex, multi-dimensional concept. Occasional use must be distinguished from patterned abuse. A history of previous abuse should not be confused with current misuse. Accurate analysis requires distinction on the basis of the substance or pattern of substances consumed. This is a particularly important command in drugs and crime research. As indicated, drugs and crime data directly influence legal controls imposed on drug use behaviors. Studies which fail to draw these elementary distinctions are highly misleading as policy-making information.

Recent government policy documents have acknowledged the importance of achieving conceptual clarity. The second report of the

National Commission on Marihuana and Drug Abuse (1973) offered a typology of drug consumption patterns. By integrating the type of substance used the 1975 *White Paper on Drug Abuse* refined that paradigm and specified proposed national prevention priorities.

In terms of drug-related crime, the rank ordering of research priorities has been characterized by only a moderate degree of agreement. Although opiates are considered universally to be the most criminogenic substance and marijuana the least, the status of other drugs is less certain. The criminogenic properties of stimulants, depressants, hallucinogens and inhalants are disputed.

With regard to patterns of use, it is agreed that compulsive use is the consumption style most directly affecting serious drug-related crime. The focus of research and public attention is the income-generating drug-related crime and this is restricted, for the most part, to chronic abuse patterns. Drugs suspected of inducing acute criminogenic reactions (e.g., amphetamines) are of secondary research interest.

Accurate and reliable indicators are required to operationally assess the incidence of crime and drug use and to measure the relationships between these events. With respect to crime data, the most readily available source is official reports. The UCR furnish a national data base and comparable state and local records are generally available.

Official reports may be used to examine individual and aggregate criminal behavior patterns. "Rap sheets" record an individual's official arrest history and aggregate UCR data reveal crimes known to the police and officially recorded arrests. Although concerted efforts are made to standardize recording practices within and among jurisdictions, idiosyncratic law enforcement practices prevent attainment of this goal. Other deficiencies are associated with official reports and have been summarized by Inciardi.

The alternative method for measuring drug-related crime is the use of self-report data. At the aggregate level, victimization reports may be used to gauge the incidence of criminal events. Comparison of UCR and victimization reports may reveal systematic biases demanding official attention. Self-report methods are also encumbered by methodological weaknesses; in particular, veracity and memory retention of the respondents are frequently suspect. The skill level of the interviewer is also considered a critical element contributing to outcome variation.

Individual criminals may also be queried regarding their illegal activities. Developed for improving the measurement of delinquency, this method has proved capable of revealing a significant incidence of undetected criminality.

A number of drugs and crime studies have attempted to evaluate the superiority of the competing measurement methods as applied to individual criminal behavior. The conclusions are inconsistent, however. At times, official reports appear to be more inclusive, but a convincing body of evidence suggests that "rap sheets" seriously underestimate addict criminality. Advanced methodologies overcome the deficiencies associated with the individual methods by employing official records and self-reports simultaneously. Careful reconciling of these data may elicit an accurate description of individual criminal behavior.

Even more serious problems are connected with drug use indicators. At the aggregate level, although substantial progress is being made toward establishment of a reliable national measurement system, adequate indicators are yet unavailable. Official reporting systems such as DAWN, CODAP and STRIDE are primarily management information systems and are of limited drug-related crime research value. Annual self-report household surveys and related school population surveys sponsored by the government are unlikely to tap adequately the mobile criminogenic population. Valuable specialized offender population studies and surveys supplement these conventional data sources, but these activities have not been systematized. A critique of these methods is offered by Eckerman et al.

Individual drug-use indicators consist of urinalysis, self-reports and official records (e.g., narcotic registry entries). These methods are plagued by innumerable technical problems, especially when applied to criminal populations. Again, the literature is contradictory regarding the optimal method but the evidence attributes little confidence to reliance upon any single tool. The superior methodologies combine measurement techniques and attempt to reconcile apparent reporting disparities.

Studies investigating the social and economic costs of drug-related crime to society have appeared only recently. Such costs include more than a simple enumeration of the incidence and types of illegal acts. Cost experiences by the victim, the criminal justice system, the perpetrator and society are identified and subjected to sophisticated analytic methods.

The reported literature is sparse and inadequate with some studies including only a limited number of cost variables, emphasizing economic data. Other studies stress social costs but fail to accurately account for the full economic impact of drug-related crime. Actually, most of these studies measure not drug-related crime costs, but the costs associated with maintenance of existing legal strictures and enforcement patterns.

A comprehensive assessment of the social and economic costs of drug-related crime was recently commissioned by the federal government. That study reported estimated annual crime-related costs to society as between $3.9 and $5.2 billion in economic terms alone. Several other studies have attempted to measure the social costs of selected drug abuse prevention policy alternatives.

Despite the obvious advantages of the cost-analytic methodology in terms of generating data useful for structuring policy decisions, significant caution should be exercised in utilizing this approach. Cost studies can be used restrictively to justify adherence to existing policies rather than for assessing the merits of competing policy alternatives. The assumptions of such studies are critical and frequently predetermine the conclusions.

In summary, drugs and crime research presents substantial conceptual and measurement questions. The notion of drug-related crime is not a unitary construct but a multi-faceted concept requiring precise meanings and analytic methods. To appreciate the relevance of particular drug use and crime research findings, the consumer must approach data interpretation with an understanding of these complexities.

DRUG USE AND CRIMINAL BEHAVIOR

The initial substantive question is the relation between drug use and criminal behavior. Does the use of drugs promote criminal activities? If so, how is this influence manifested?

As indicated earlier, this is a complex question. Several dimensions of inquiry, e.g., types of substances, frequency of use and seriousness of criminality, are involved. Furthermore, methodological caveats and criticisms render understanding of the significance of the research findings a difficult task.

Simple Drugs and Crime Associations. Again adhering to the basic outline established by the *Drug Use and Crime* report, the first set of questions relates to the proportion of criminals using drugs and the proportion of drug users committing crimes. Although answers to these queries are not necessarily probative of cause and effect relations, they do provide outside parameters of drug use and crime connection. Thus, to the extent that data of this order are accurate and comprehensive, the overall incidence of drug-related crime may be defined.

What types of crime are associated with drug users? In determining the answer to this question, it is first helpful to distinguish by type of user, at least in terms of primary substance of use.

Much attention has been directed at marijuana users. It is a popular belief that alleged criminogenic effects precipitated the criminalization of cannabis, early advocates of marijuana controls arguing that the majority of marijuana users were also criminals. Using selective samples of hospitalized and incarcerated users, these researchers highlighted the marijuana habits of their subjects, implying an element of causality. This became known as "reefer madness" research—a body of pseudoknowledge which has been discredited.

The most systematic investigation of the marijuana and crime connection was undertaken by the National Commission on Marihuana and Drug Abuse. The Commission discovered that the majority of American adults (58 percent) associated marijuana use with the commission of crime. This belief was also voiced by two-thirds of American youth aged 12 to 17. Yet the Commission's independent assessment of the available research data rejected the criminogenesis hypothesis. Despite the presence of considerable evidence of manifestations of delinquency by some marijuana users, explanations other than drug use appeared more plausible. The Commission expressed its opinion lucidly:

We conclude that some users commit crimes more frequently than non-users not because they use marihuana but because they happen to be the kinds of people who would be expected to have a higher crime rate, wholly apart from the use of marihuana. In most cases, the differences in crime rate between users and non-users are dependent not on marihuana use *per se* but on these other factors.

Research findings reported since 1972 tend to substantiate that conclusion. On the one hand, data continue to show a clear association between marijuana use and crime. O'Donnell's et al. study of 2,500 young males indicates that marijuana users are significantly more likely to commit crimes than non-users. Dichotomizing the study's self-reported data on the basis of use vs. non-use (any lifetime marijuana use), the link to crime is as follows: breaking and entering, 18 percent vs. 6 percent; shoplifting, 56 percent vs. 29 percent; and armed robbery, 2 percent vs. less than 1 percent.

However, contradictory information is offered by an extensive longitudinal examination of youthful drug users. Johnston, O'Malley and Eveland found no evidence of association between marijuana use and increased delinquency. In fact, the delinquency patterns of marijuana users paralleled those of abstainers when followed over time.

The methodological superiority of this type of longitudinal method is convincing. It permits examination of the development of patterns over time rather than relying on associations detected at a single interval. Thus, Johnston, O'Malley and Eveland's data furnish persuasive evidence that, despite a clear statistical association between marijuana use and criminality, use of the drug does not contribute to the development of a delinquent career. Corroboration is reported in Gold and Reimer's 1974 *National Survey of Youth*. That study's data suggest that marijuana use may be evolving into a correlate of positive and well-adjusted social functioning.

Evidence regarding the extent of criminality among users of other non-narcotic substances is analogous but less certain. Again, drug users are found more often to commit criminal acts than non-users. Yet, as with marijuana, the relationship is static rather than dynamic. Few studies report increases in criminal behavior associated with patterns of non-narcotic drug use, just a higher incidence of deviancy among users as compared to non-users.

The *Drug Use and Crime* report examined data drawn from three discrete drug-user populations—treatment clients, arrestees and the general population. If opiate users are included, the percentages of drug users exhibiting arrest histories range from 55 percent to 91 percent. Unfortunately, however, the studies generally failed to make distinctions by type of substance, pattern of use and nature of criminality. Thus, precise understanding of drug use and crime associational patterns is not advanced.

In those studies which did distinguish between drugs of use, clear differences were found between opiate users and non-opiate users. Voss reported that nearly half of the non-opiate users lacked a criminal record, while more than two-thirds of the opiate users showed criminal histories. A like contrast was found among adolescents studied in the National Polydrug Research Project.

The previously discussed Johnston, O'Malley and Eveland longitudinal study once again provides methodologically advanced data. As with marijuana users, non-opiate drug users demonstrated no significant correlation between drug consumption and increased delinquency during the study period. The authors declared: "What we *do* conclude from these explorations is that nonaddictive use of illicit drugs does not seem to play much of a role in leading users to become the more delinquent persons we know them to be on the average."

Parallel methodologies have also been applied to examine the crime connection of these other non-narcotic substances. Tinklenberg undertook a comprehensive literature search of all studies investigating drug-related criminogenesis and he has initiated his own empirical investigations. Greenberg has conducted an exhaustive analysis of the criminogenics of amphetamine use.

The consensus of investigators is that although inadequate methodologies restrict firm conclusions, the weight of the evidence suggests no significant relation between non-marijuana, non-opiate use and criminal behavior. Correlative data are primarily of an indirect, associational nature. Representative of this view is McGlothlin: "It seems fair to conclude on the basis of currently available evidence that non-addictive drug use does not lead to crime in more than a very small percentage of current users."

Opinions differ markedly with respect to opiate users. Few researchers doubt that a substantial degree of criminality is associated with opiate use, at least chronic opiate use. Disagreement is limited to questions such as the relative influence of opiate consumption upon criminal behavior and the covariance of other factors, issues addressed later in this section.

Despite considerable variation among addict samples in terms of characteristics linked to criminologic identification, data yield an unmistakably consistent pattern. Criminal behavior histories are normative among addicts. Income-generating crimes appear to be a standard activity, albeit practiced in varying degree and frequency. Of course, knowledge concerning this subject is far from complete. Little is known regarding the undetected opiate addict for example. Reported data fail frequently to draw crucial distinctions between crime types and use patterns. Yet the overwhelming weight of the evidence confirms an associational relationship between chronic opiate use and criminal behavior. This finding applies regardless of the research method used or addict sample studied. Convincing ethnographic examinations have proved highly instructive in describing this phenomenon and dispelling skepticism.

The next issue to consider is drug use among criminals. What types and how much drug use occurs among offenders? Are there certain patterns unique to special groups of offenders?

As with the previous line of inquiry, the available data are incomplete and of questionable accuracy. Drug use statistics within offender populations have been collected in a random, piecemeal fashion. Data are highly fragmented and measurement is frequently inexact and idiosyncratic.

One approach to estimating the impact of drug use upon criminals has been to calculate the percentage of a particular offense category attributable to drug users. The Chicago Police Department, for example, examined thirty days of robbery reports and concluded that 18 percent were assignable to drug users. This tact has been adopted by numerous other locales attempting to define the parameters of drug-related crime.

Estimates of this nature are common and are typically associated with law-enforcement officials. Pomeroy's survey of police chiefs indicates that these officials believe that 30 percent to 70 percent of property crime is committed by addicts. Similar statements are reported in Sweezey's survey of a national panel of drug-abuse enforcement and treatment experts.

Interviewing and urine testing of arrestee populations has proven to be a popular method for estimating these relationships. Beginning with the District of Columbia in 1969, a number of jurisdictions have conducted jail studies to determine drug use patterns among detainees. Interpretation of these data yields inferences regarding the influence of drug use on particular offense categories.

Arrestee studies report widespread variation. Eckerman's et al. six-city study demonstrated significant differences geographically; the percentage of robbery arrestees identified as heroin users ranged from 11 percent in Los Angeles and San Antonio to 56 percent in Chicago. The percentage of positive urine samples (for any drug) recorded in the District of Columbia has fluctuated over time: January–March 1972, 32.6 percent; January–March 1973, 20.9 percent; January–March 1974, 22.7 percent; and January–March 1975, 17.8 percent.

Measurement of drug use among sentenced offenders has been less common. Barton's analysis of LEAA national prison survey data provides an important set of preliminary findings. Barton indicates that 61 percent of incarcerated offenders self-report some illegal drug use activity and 13 percent claim to have used heroin at the time of the arrest leading to imprisonment. Replication efforts are scheduled to test the stability of these findings among successive groups of inmates.

In addition to methodological problems already discussed, more fundamental limitations severely restrict the confidence attributable to estimates of drug use among recorded offenses and identified offenders. These studies include only reported and cleared crimes and offenders officially detected by law enforcement agencies. Yet UCR data state that less than 20 percent of known property crime is cleared by arrest, and victimization data suggest that UCR figures underreport the true incidence of property crime by several hundred percent. Inciardi and Chambers report that less than five percent of addict property crime may result in official detection. In short, the estimation methods manifest a bias. Perhaps, the drug-using offenders identified in the arrestee studies are the less skilled practitioners of drug-related crime. Or, they may be the object of police harassment due to known drug-use patterns. These are matters of conjecture, of course, and numerous other theses may be advanced.

The only certainty in this regard is the absence of proper tools to validly assess drug use among criminals. Adequate systematic data describing the drug-use patterns of identified offenders are not available and the representativeness of the information that is available is unknown.

Drug Use and Criminal Behavior Patterns. The next set of questions is considerably more straightforward and is of greater lay interest. In what ways are criminal behavior patterns affected by drug use habits? In other words, to what extent does the consumption of psychoactive drugs influence an individual's criminal activity?

This subject was considered indirectly in the previous materials with the probing of simple drug use and crime associations. The scrutiny becomes more focused at this point with assessment of the quality of these connections. Specifically, the following queries are examined: what is the temporal sequence between drug use and crime? does drug use intensify pre-existing criminal tendencies? how directly are associated increases in user criminality connected to changes in use patterns? and what types of criminal behavior are most influenced by drug consumption patterns?

Although these inquiries certainly apply with equal force to all substances and user types, research efforts have been largely restricted to the opiate addict. Knowledge concerning other substances and less than chronic use is sparse, and, in the interests of brevity, assessment of these topics is limited to materials already presented. The reader dissatisfied with this abbreviated approach is encouraged to examine the previously referenced data sources, particularly McGlothlin, Greenberg, and Tinklenberg.

An additional prefatory point requires acknowledgement. The focus of attention of the cited studies is that drug-related crime is associated with the costs of maintaining a drug habit. The other types of drug-related crimes, viz., pharmacological effects, drug-defined crimes and criminality associated with the maintenance of drug distribution channels, have received only secondary consideration. Of these other categories only the question of pharmacological effects has attracted significant researcher attention and few definitive conclusions have been reached. Except for alcohol and perhaps barbiturates, little evidence has been found supporting a pharmacological connection between drug use and commission of crime. As indicated earlier, however, reports of violent outbursts associated with PCP use are eliciting new interest in this subject.

The nature of the temporal sequence between drug use and criminal behavior has been of longstanding interest. For decades, this question was an important political issue. Alfred Lindesmith, a prominent proponent of drug-law reform, contended that opiate users became criminals as a result of the criminalization of drug use. Harry Anslinger, the influential federal narcotics enforcement czar, maintained that addiction is a result of criminal activity or association.

This dispute has been largely resolved as a result of numerous studies of addicts reported during the 1970s. The research data indicate that for the vast majority of addicts, delinquency precedes the onset of drug use. The relationship is neatly summarized by Greenberg and Adler:

In sum, it appears that the typical addict at present is not simply a confused, misguided but noncriminal adolescent who gets hooked on drugs by the neighborhood pusher or a middle-aged person who has become addicted through medical channels, but rather an individual who has been immersed in a criminal subculture and is introduced to narcotics as a result of his socialization into this subculture.

The impact of drug use upon pre-existing criminal tendencies is a critical policy concern. Drug control strategy is based in large part upon the belief that opiate addiction intensifies criminalistic behavior patterns. Addiction and the daily commission of income-generating crime are conceptualized as sequential activities. In general, evaluation of this thesis has been approached by retrospective examination of addict arrest histories. Self-reports and official records are scrutinized to determine the direction and extent of post-addiction criminality. Data reported by Nurco and DuPont, Weissman, Marr and Katsampes, and Hayim, Lukoff and Quatrone validate this thesis, revealing dramatic increases in income-generating crime subsequent to the onset of addiction.

Serious methodological limitations restrict the absolute validity of this genre of study, however. Rises in criminality may be the result of natural events in the development of deviant careers, rather than the product of addiction. Variables such as ethnicity, unemployment and social disorganization may be the true culprit. Although this question cannot be fully resolved without reference to suitable control groups of non-addict deviants studied over lifetime careers, methodological adjustments can increase the confidence imputable to such studies. Analyses which distinguish between different use patterns practiced during addiction careers refine understanding of the phenomenon. If criminal behavior is examined during daily use periods and abstinence periods, the influence of addiction may be ascertained in a more precise manner.

Assessments of this nature have been conducted by two investigators of national prominence. Using a California civil committee sample, McGlothlin, Anglin and Wilson employ both self-report and official records measurement techniques and rigorously analyze the generated data. During periods of abstinence, whether voluntary or involuntary, commission of crime diminishes, while daily use is associated with significantly increased criminal behavior. McGlothlin, Anglin and Wilson conclude:

The results are unequivocal in showing that, during the periods of addiction, individuals are more likely to report that they are engaged in criminal behavior, commit more crimes and acquire more money than when they are not using narcotics daily.

Using a similar research design, Nurco is still completing his parallel study of Baltimore addicts. Identification of his sample was accomplished by reference to a police narcotics registry. Preliminary results indicate agreement with the McGlothlin, Anglin and Wilson findings. Together, these data sets offer important clarification of the addiction/crime-intensification issue.

With regard to the types of offenses associated with addict criminality, reported research findings exhibit substantial consistencies. The data show that addict criminality is heavily biased in the direction of drug-defined crimes and income-generating offenses, particularly non-violent property offenses. This conclusion has been arrived at by a variety of research strategies. Eckerman et al. examined addict arrestees, Preble and Casey conducted an ethnographic analysis and Hayim, Lukoff and Quatrone studied treatment clients. Each method associates addict careers with income-generating crime. Violent crimes against person are not unknown but are nearly always related to the raising of funds or the acquisition and distribution of drugs.

Extraneous Factors Associated with Drug Use and Criminal Behavior. Notwithstanding the abundance of data supporting the drug use and crime connection, critical questions remain. Although a correlative association has been demonstrated beyond any reasonable doubt, the question of cause and effect has not been definitively resolved. As noted earlier, the possibility exists that drug use does not cause criminal behavior but that these are merely simultaneously occurring elements of a deviant lifestyle. In research terms, the correlation may be spurious. *Drug Use and Crime* underscores this possibility. The report suggests that numerous intervening variables may be distorting the drugs and crime data. On the individual addict level, factors such as chronological age, age of onset, gender, ethnicity, peer group affiliation, etc. are identified. Law enforcement practices and social program effects are designated as community level factors.

This contention deserves careful attention. To be sure, the enumerated individual addict characteristics have been associated with significant criminal behavior variation. Female criminality, for example, has traditionally been lower than that of male counterparts irrespective of age, ethnicity, addiction status, etc. In addition, community practices have also been shown to produce a measurable impact.

Social science research is plagued constantly by this type of gnawing question. In an environment characterized by the presence of numerous theoretically relevant intervening variables, cause and effect relationships are difficult to confirm. To a limited degree, sophisticated multivariate analytic techniques overcome this problem and hold significant promise regarding the drug use and crime dilemma. Yet, research in the imperfect real world, as contrasted with laboratory settings, presents many logistical, political and ethical obstacles restricting even the most advanced assessment methods.

There is little disagreement that improved methods offer substantial benefit in terms of clarifying the drugs and crime connection. The previously mentioned drugs and crime panel convened by LEAA is exploring this direction. The essential conflict, which is indisputable and widespread, is restricted to the level of confidence assignable to the reported body of research implying causality between addiction and criminal behavior. The following statements are illustrative of the difference in opinion regarding this issue:

Research using sophisticated models of human behavior, data collected in well-designed longitudinal studies and appropriate multivariate techniques hold the promise of providing answers to these key questions of causality. The questions are not academic.

Here, I think the phenomenon we are dealing with is that our research scientists have a standard of proof that we simply can't meet. . . . I can assure you, Mr. Chairman, that all members who have contact with heroin-dependent individuals have no doubt, on the basis of their personal experience with addicts, as I have had for several years with many thousands of heroin users about this relationship. It is clear and it is strong.

Of course it may be argued that the fact that criminality covaries with frequency of narcotic use does not necessarily establish a causal relationship. Both variables may be responding to other factors, e.g., being under parole supervision might suppress both narcotic use and crime, or life events such as getting married or obtaining rewarding employment might have a similar effect on both types of behavior. However, this possibility becomes largely academic in those instances where one behavior logically requires the other. When the individual spends large amounts of money for heroin, does not deal and has no source of legitimate income, then criminality is a necessary condition for addiction to exist.

DEMAND REDUCTION

Whatever the absolute incidence of drug-related crime, it is clear that there exists substantial societal support for reducing the phenomenon. Undaunted by the equivocation prevailing in the scientific community, public opinion adheres to the belief that drug-related crime is a premier social problem demanding effective remedial action. Furthermore, there is no question that American drug abuse policy is influenced by this mandate. Federal policy documents stress the goal of diminishing the social costs of drug abuse, especially drug-related crime. It has been forcefully argued that crime reduction is the principal objective of drug abuse prevention policies. This view, while surely debatable, has not been totally repudiated by the public servants directing prevention efforts.

The official government policy documents of the 1970s conceptualize the grand prevention strategy in terms of a reduction or abatement equation. One set of programmatic efforts (treatment, education and rehabilitation) is aimed at suppressing drug demand forces. Another grouping of activities (enforcement programs) seeks to minimize the available supply of drugs. In this section the performance of the principal component of demand reduction, drug abuse treatment, is examined. The ability of treatment to abate the criminal behavior of its clients and therefore to effect a reduction in community crime rates is assessed.

At the outset is must be acknowledged that the crime reduction mission of treatment is not universally accepted dogma. Opinion on this topic among public officials, treatment personnel and treatment clients varies. Some treatment officials have decried the emphasis on crime reduction, asserting an alleged impropriety of this goal for an essentially public health activity. Other drug-abuse figures acknowledge the legitimacy of the goal and encourage accommodation of this value to the more global rehabilitative task.

Irrespective of the views of individual officials, the public expectation is unambiguous. Drug-abuse treatment is expected not only to constitute a humane and enlightened approach for dealing with drug abusers but it is also intended to promote socialization, particularly as regards abandonment of criminal behaviors. Therefore it is entirely proper to assess the performance of treatment in achieving crime reduction. For purposes of such analysis, drug abuse treatment may be devided into health care treatment and correctional treatments. Health care treatment consists of medical-model rehabilitative programs operated by non-criminal justice public and private agencies. Correctional treatment, on the other hand, is administered by correctional agencies and eligibility is restricted to certain categories of offenders.

The regimens (e.g., ambulatory methadone maintenance with support services) may not differ, but there is a clear distinction in program identification. In many cases this distinction may be somewhat blurred if criminal justice referrals dominate a health care program's intake, but an important independence from the criminal justice system is preserved even under those circumstances. With regard to health care treatment a series of localized and national evaluation efforts have attempted to rate the crime reduction impact of such programs. In general, the results are mixed but indicate a limited capacity for crime abatement. As with the drug use and crime relation subject, serious methodological deficiencies limit the absolute validity of the measurements and cast the state of knowledge in a tentative status.

In a paper commissioned by the *Drug Use and Crime* panel, Nash reviewed a dozen of the better designed studies to determine the effects of health care treatment in reducing client criminality. This review included evaluations of methadone maintenance, residential drug-free and multimodality programs, as well as data reported by the national DARP program. Although each of these studies was methodologically advanced as matched with comparable efforts, none featured a randomly assigned control group. The results of the Nash review are summarized by Weissman and Nash:

1. Not all treatment programs are effective and even the more effective programs do not achieve favorable results with all types of clients.
2. The positive effects of methadone maintenance treatment are frequently limited to the during-treatment period.
3. Residential drug-free treatment tends to have a greater impact than methadone-maintenance treatment but addicts are reluctant to enroll in this treatment regimen.
4. The only three reliable predictors of the likelihood of post-treatment arrests appear to be pre-treatment criminality, sex and age; previous criminality and maleness are universally positively associated with post-treatment arrests, while the age correlation differs from study to study.

Other reviews have reached similar conclusions. *Drug Use and Crime,* for instance, declares:

From these diverse studies, it can probably be concluded that involvement with the criminal justice system, and possibly involvement in criminal behavior itself, is suppressed rather than eliminated while in treatment. Findings from the national follow-up study [DARP] suggest that criminal behavior increases after leaving drug treatment and many revert to pre-treatment levels.

Recent studies do not disturb the balance of these findings. Particularly noteworthy is Sechrest who reports on several years of data collected by the extensive evaluations of the Santa Clara, California, and Brooklyn ARTC programs. These studies, methodologically advanced in many respects, demonstrate only moderate abatement in client criminality. Declines in criminal behavior were not immediate, generally occurring only after two to three years of continuous treatment intervention. Furthermore, the reductions appeared most frequently with older clients who appeared to be naturally withdrawing from criminality as a result of declining age. Other more optimistic results may be cited to counterbalance the Sechrest data, or additional negativistic findings may be summoned to support the critical line of research. This would seem to be a futile exercise, however, in light of the tentative approval of this entire body of research.

The research community is unwilling to endorse the reported studies as firm evidence of the crime-reduction properties of health-care treatment. The methodological deficiencies are conceived as fatal limitations upon the confidence attributable to this research. Consider the comments of Greenberg and Adler:

Owing to all of the limitations outlined above, it is difficult to arrive at any conclusions, or even statements based on the weight of the evidence, about such vital issues as optimal length of time in treatment, type of addict best suited for particular modalities and specific variables in treatment that are most important in achieving desired results. The only conclusion to be drawn is that a great many more carefully controlled studies must be done before it becomes possible to make valid inferences concerning the impact of treatment on the criminal behavior of addicts. We believe it entirely possible that treatment may prove to have some effect on crime. At the present time, however, there has been no adequate research documentation of that effect and therefore, it remains an unproven hypothesis.

Drug Use and Crime expressly endorses this position and recommends methodological improvement in three critical elements—sampling, research design and measurement. A nearly identical cautionary posture was also adopted by the National Commission on Marihuana and Drug Abuse.

In addition to studying the crime patterns of treatment clients, another research stratagem can be applied to assess the impact of health-care treatment on community crime rates. Community crime indicators may be correlated with shifts in treatment enrollment to ascertain the existence of a statistical association. If community crime is affected by treatment participation, rises in the treatment roles should be correlated with reductions in the crime rate. Proponents of this thesis limit examination to property crime, theorized to be the most directly influenced by treatment. Researchers in a limited number of locales have explored this connection. Studies in the District of Columbia, San Antonio, New Orleans, and Detroit claim reductions in community crime concomitant with increases in treatment enrollment. Data from New Jersey and Brooklyn are contrary, however.

Methodological problems with this line of inquiry are nearly insurmountable. As was illustrated with drug use and criminal behavior relationships, a number of intervening variables may be operative. The community property crime index may be affected by changes in demography, unemployment patterns, law enforcement practices, social programs and conditions and numerous other factors extraneous to drug-abuse treatment. Furthermore, the property crime indicator is an overbroad and inexact measure without convincing evidence that the majority of property crime is in fact drug-related.

Assessment of the effectiveness of correctional treatment approaches is subject to the same constraints identified above. Evaluation designs are inadequate, relying on pre- and post-treatment measurement of client behaviors. Treatment practices are typically described superficially, providing insufficient information regarding the quantity and quality of rehabilitative efforts applied. And, as with health-care evaluations, the results are frequently skewed by client characteristics, age being a particularly influential factor.

In many respects analysis of the correctional modes is a much more complicated task. The lack of uniformity of treatment approaches renders comparison of data very difficult; activities cannot be categorized into a simple classification scheme such as methadone maintenance, therapeutic community, outpatient drug-free and hospital detoxification. Pretrial diversion, probation, halfway house, civil commitment, parole and institutional programs are all located under the correctional treatment rubric, but the differences in these diverse approaches frequently outweigh the similarities. McGlothlin recently conducted a systematic investigation of correctional treatment program performance. He divided the reported activities into three categories: (1) criminal justice programs—institutions, halfway houses, probation and parole; (2) noncriminal justice programs which admit clients both with and without criminal justice legal status; and (3) TASC (Treatment Alternatives to Street Crime) and other diversion programs.

With regard to criminal justice programs, McGlothlin offers a mixed assessment. He finds little evidence that institutions and halfway house programs achieve positive results. Encouraging evidence is noted in regard to parole practices, however, largely on the basis of his evaluation of the California Civil Addict Program. The Civil Addict Program is a civil commitment program featuring a combination of institutional care and parole aftercare supervision. The McGlothlin, Anglin & Wilson Civil Addict Program data are impressive. Comparing the outcomes of the Civil Addict Program addicts to a matched group of criminal addicts, the authors show significantly reduced drug use and criminal behavior. They attribute the positive results to intensive parole supervision, frequent urine monitoring and the availability of supplementary support services including methadone maintenance.

Other parole and community corrections data are less encouraging however. Bailey, for instance, reports that despite positive adjustments during parole supervision, a group of California parolees accumulated a substantial number of arrests during an eleven-year follow-up period. Much of the correctional treatment literature agrees with this finding including probation, parole and civil-commitment studies.

Comparison of the behavior outcomes of criminal justice referrals and voluntary clients also yields equivocal but basically negative findings. These analyses are typically indirect and of poor quality. Attribution of criminal justice referral status is frequently imprecise and of questionable validity. The more rigorous of these studies tend to question the crime-reduction capacity of legal referral mechanisms.

Diversion programs generally receive a qualitatively different assessment. To date, the principal drug-diversion program, TASC, has been credited with reducing client criminality and improving criminal justice-treatment linkages. Further evaluation of the TASC program confirms these initial findings. Other drug diversion efforts offer similar assessments. However many of these programs limit their scope to first-offenders requiring minimal rehabilitative services. Only the TASC program appears to deal uniformly with hard-core addict offenders.

In summary, the correctional treatment data are characterized by the same uncertainty associated with the health-care treatment reports. The methodological complications inherent in evaluating correctional programs reinforce this ambiguity. A positive crime-reduction impact is suggested under certain corrections as well as health-care situations but the specification of these circumstances has not yet been established.

SUPPLY REDUCTION

The federal drug-abuse prevention calculus assigns an equal emphasis to supply reduction as a means of abating drug-related crime. Theorizing that much of drug-related crime is the product of readily available drug supplies, the federal planners seek to reduce those supplies and thereby effect a reduction in community crime rates. As with the demand-reduction strategy this design is predicated on a series of key assumptions. It is conjectured that drug users respond to diminishing supplies by modifying their drug consumption and criminal behaviors in a predictable fashion. As supplies dwindle and prices rise, it is expected that drug users restrict their illegal activities and search for rational alternatives, principally abstinence, drug substitution or entry into treatment. By establishing a national network of community drug-treatment centers, the federal strategy seeks to maximize this avenue by attracting significant numbers of drug users into treatment as drug supplies diminish. Simultaneous emphasis is directed toward insuring a reduction in those supplies by including activities aimed at every dimension of the drug distribution system.

Proponents of this stratagem further assume that significant reductions in property crime may be effected. Attributing much of urban property crime to drug users it is argued that to the extent that decreased drug supplies influence reduced drug consumption patterns, either by abstinence or treatment enlistment, property-crime rates will also decrease. The focus of this strategy, of course, is the opiate addict. It is his/her behavior which the planners hope to modify by reducing supplies and driving up retail drug prices. It is the addict whose income-generating needs are believed to account for the high incidence of urban property crime.

By now the reader will detect certain obvious question marks pertaining to this strategy and its underlying assumptions. As already noted, the evidence of a direct connection between addiction and property crime is equivocal. To be sure, there is substantial evidence that addicts do commit a significant amount of property crimes during addictive states. Yet the impact of addiction upon the total incidence of property crime is unknown, and it is unwarranted to assume that community property crime rates are aggregately responsive to addict behavior.

In addition, descriptive data regarding addict income-generating behavior show that property crime is *not* the modal activity. Hughes et al. report that only 38 percent of a sample of Chicago addicts relied on property crime as a source of income, 34 percent participated in the drug-distribution system and 28 percent were gainfully employed. In his examination of New York addicts, Moore found that nearly half of drug-acquisition funds were raised by drug-trafficking activities. The property crime connection appears to be even more attenuated for female addicts who stress prostitution and drug distribution.

Nonetheless, even if the addiction and property crime relationship is tenuous in terms of its global applicability, the evidence does support a degree of relation between the two phenomena. Accordingly it is appropriate to at least consider reported variations between opiate availability (measured through the surrogate indicators of market price and purity) and community property crime rates. Such data may offer useful exploratory information.

The reported studies have been conducted in locations associated with a rapid expansion of treatment capacity. The prototype research tact has been to measure the direction and strength of associations between changes in heroin availability, treatment enrollment and property crime. Official aggregate statistics, i.e., DEA price and purity indicators, CODAP treatment statistics and UCR property crime data, are used to examine these relations. In the District of Columbia and San Antonio, rising heroin prices accompanied by expanding treatment programs have been correlated with a decrease in property crime incidence. Since elements of both increased law enforcement and treatment efforts were present, it is impossible to identify the exact crime reduction contribution of each.

More precise analyses aimed at isolating the impact of reduced heroin supplies have been reported. Starting with the hypothesis ". . . if addicts must consume a fixed quantity of heroin each period, then to the extent that addicts support habits through criminal behavior, a rise in the price of heroin may be expected to lead to an increase in criminal activity," Brown and Silverman examined heroin price and property crime data drawn from nine cities. After rejecting data from eight of the cities as ambiguous, the researchers focused on the New York City results which supported their hypothesis. The New York City data were interpreted as indicating that:

. . . [a] 10 percent increase in the price of heroin is predicted to lead to a 3.6 percent increase in robberies, a 1.8 percent increase in burglaries, a 2.0 percent increase in larcenies under $500, and a 2.5 percent increase in auto theft.

This singular interpretation of the data has been subjected to searching and persuasive criticism. Objecting to the Brown and Silverman conclusions, Goldman illustrates that additional and equally plausible interpretations of the findings may be made. Among the alternative hypotheses is the familiar possibility that independent variables other than the heroin availability may have affected the crime rate.

Goldman also demonstrates that the Brown and Silverman model is too simplistic to determine the effects of these other independent factors. Baridon's appraisal of the analogous District of Columbia data indicated a similar assessment. Baridon succinctly notes:

The following summary seems warranted by the facts. The powerful association observed between the price of heroin and gainful crime is somewhat deceptive. Heroin costs and quality are not the only significant independent variables. Other factors have been found likely to contribute to the strength of the observed relationship. The substantial increase of law enforcement resources in a stabilized population, the arrival of a massive methadone maintenance-detox program in a deteriorating narcotics market, and a changing social environment in the city have combined with rising heroin costs to produce a corresponding decline in property offenses.

Using several years of Detroit data, Silverman, Spruill and Levine conducted another study of a similar methodological nature. Again, rising heroin prices were associated with increased property crime incidence. Similar criticisms are applicable to this study. The basic problem remains the likelihood of spurious correlation in the absence of more sensitive design and measurement. The research methods and assumptions applied in these studies do not insure that the correlations between heroin prices and property crime rates or between heroin prices, treatment enrollment figures and property crime rates are not the result of the influence of other social, economic and criminologic factors.

This subject, the relationship between heroin availability and criminal activity, raises a number of important questions regarding drug consumption and criminal behavior patterns. In addition to those already mentioned, there is the related issue of addict lifestyle and general consumer habits. Awareness of these behaviors may assist in fashioning effective prevention strategies. Improved understanding of the drug marketplace and its impact on addict behavior may facilitate new intervention approaches. By combining economic, ethnographic and sociological methodologies, this research strategy may contribute significantly to the drugs and crime knowledge base. At the moment, however, conclusive information is lacking.

PENAL EFFECTS

The remaining substantive topic concerns the effectiveness of the drug laws in achieving their intended penal effects. This subject, similar to the earlier areas of investigation, is characterized by ambiguous data and conflicting opinion. In essence, advocates of the status quo affirm the utility of existing penal sanctions while reformers disparage the value of such efforts. Central to this discussion is a fundamental need for doctrinal clarity in regard to the use of the penal sanctions concept. Analysts as well as the lay public tend to merge two discrete elements inherent in the criminal law approach.

First, the general impact of a criminal law remedy for the prevention of drug use must be considered. This concerns the existence of penal sanctions as opposed to other social control methods, e.g., public health regulation. The utility of this framework must be assessed in terms of achievement of its multiple objectives which include punishment as well as deterrent and rehabilitative aims. In addition, the influence of the operational components of the penal system, viz., law enforcement, judiciary and corrections, commands evaluation. For instance, the ability of law enforcement agencies to restrict drug supplies is a critical ingredient of the criminal law drug-control approach. Application of the penal sanctions is surely a distinct subject with a separate set of policy implications.

Unfortunately analysis of these inputs as separate and distinct influences is a very difficult task. Methods of enforcing penal sanctions may overshadow the impact of the strictures, or conversely, the nature of the laws may mute enforcement practices. For the most part, major drug-law evaluations have treated these topics as the same phenomenon—the legal approach—and it is difficult to ascertain severable effects. To the extent that data permit such distinctions, they are noted in the following materials.

In general terms success of drug-control efforts is evaluated in terms of accomplishment of the goals of restricting the availability of drugs and preventing the use of drugs. These appear to be consensus values of American society and at least theoretically, are the aims of the drug laws. As a penal control measure, however, the drug laws command evaluation in an orthodox criminal law framework. Sanctions are assessed according to their achievement of four penal objectives— retribution, incapacitation, general deterrence and rehabilitation. Although general deterrence may be superordinated, as is certainly the case with drug laws, attainment of these other objectives may not be disregarded.

According to retribution theory, the purpose of the criminal law is to realize society's interest in law abidance by exacting punishment and expressing moral disapproval of law violators. Incapacitation, as a goal of criminal law, seeks to remove and isolate miscreants from the community. General deterrence applies criminal sanctions to identified lawbreakers in order to discourage other potential violators from disobeying the law's commands. Rehabilitation is intended to serve as a corrective device and is applied to lessen the offender's probability of returning to criminal activity.

Few analysts have evaluated drug control sanctions in terms other than general deterrent effects. Measurement of retributive and incapacitative effects is subject to substantial ideological distortion and researchers have generally refrained from such analyses. This caveat, appreciation of ideological influence, is an important element in reviewing the drug-law literature and its primacy should not be overlooked.

The basic conflict regarding retributive and incapacitative effects is associated with interpretation of enforcement patterns and application of drug sanctions data. In the main these data show a minimal probability of being detected and sanctioned for drug-law violations. Parenthetically, this is hardly a unique finding in criminal justice research as all crimes exhibit a funnel effect from violation to punishment.

Yet this pattern is fairly dramatic for drug offenses. Grizzle analyzes drug arrest data from New York City, California and Mecklenburg County (Charlotte), North Carolina. Of those arrested, approximately 10 to 20 percent serve sentences and one-third to one-half escape prosecution altogether. Similar results are reported for the District of Columbia and six other major metropolitan jurisdictions. Restricting her analysis to Mecklenburg County, Grizzle computes estimated probabilities for arrest, conviction and imprisonment by selected drug offenses. Over a one-year exposure period, the drug distributor faces a .06 probability of arrest and a .04 probability of incarceration. The addict faces a .37 probability of arrest but only a .04 probability of incarceration. The experimental drug user faces a $< .02$ probability of arrest and $< .001$ probability of incarceration. To the ideological conservative this is persuasive evidence that the drug laws fail to punish and incapacitate. Data such as these are cited by law enforcement officials in requesting tougher penalties and increased budgets.

Advocates of reform, on the other hand, focus on the aggregate statistics of arrest and imprisonment. The fact that more than 600,000 drug law arrests are recorded annually and scores of thousands of drug offenders are incarcerated is offered as proof that the drug laws do punish and isolate. This situation is declared unjust, inhumane and wasteful.

The rehabilitative potential of the drug laws has received an even more amorphous scrutiny. The majority of the relevant review concerns the effectiveness of rehabilitative treatment programs: these data have already been discussed in the demand reduction section of this article. Such data reflect indirect effects of drug sanctions insofar as the legal disposition is integrated into the treatment practices.

A small body of studies considers another aspect of the rehabilitative objective, however: the ability of drug laws to effect eradication of illegal behaviors as a result of the legal sanctioning per se. This intended capacity of the law is known as specific or special deterrence. Specific deterrence doctrine contends that the labeling and unpleasant effects associated with the sanctioning process should discourage the violator from further deviations.

Within the drug-law literature, probably the most direct examination of specific deterrence is reported by Erickson, who interviewed a sample of convicted cannabis violators in Toronto to determine their subsequent cannabis consumption behaviors. She summarized her findings as follows:

In summary, the research has shown that more severe penalties and higher perceived certainty of punishment do not have the effect of reducing the likelihood of subsequent cannabis use among a sample of persons who have been officially criminalized for the offense of simple possession.

Drug use and availability control-measures are assessed primarily on the basis of their ability to deter the general population. Does the legal sanctioning system deter non-users from experimentation, experimenters from advancing to chronic use or chronic users from self-destruction? In short, do drug law controls work?

The initial difficulty encountered in responding to this important query is the conspicuous and disheartening lack of precise data. The federal Strategy Council on Drug Abuse acknowledged this fact in stating, "At present, we cannot determine the best way to distribute resources among the various drug enforcement activities in order to achieve the maximum impact." McGrew offers a more damning assessment declaring, "What is known about the effectiveness of individual aspects of the federal regulatory system could be written on a toenail."

A series of conceptual and measurement difficulties is also associated with the assessment task. First, general deterrence is a complex criminal law concept requiring application of sophisticated analytic methods. The absence of this level of analysis extends to nearly all criminal phenomena. A very comprehensive critique including remedial prescriptions was recently prepared by the National Academy of Sciences.

Additional complications are reflected in drug-law deterrence research. As noted earlier it is difficult to distinguish between the effects of the prohibitions per se and the patterns of applying the sanctions. Are the laws inadequate or do the enforcement practices impair their potential social utility?

Ideological factors are a conspicuous influence upon the assessment process. The majority of the general deterrence drug-law studies are global qualitative judgments which either reject the utility of the criminal sanctions or affirm their wisdom. This order of inquiry features selective interpretation of data based in large part on the analyst's politics. Wilson and Glaser, for example, review the identical District of Columbia 1970s data and arrive at opposite conclusions regarding the effectiveness of the control measures.

Finally, the available aggregate measures for interpreting the impact of legal sanctions are inadequate. With few exceptions the official reporting systems, such as UCR, DAWN and STRIDE, are imprecise and of questionable applicability. Although these limitations have been discussed earlier, they are raised again in this context to underscore the difficulty of assessing drug-law effects with any degree of exactitude.

Notwithstanding these limitations, assessments may be drawn from several different perspectives. First, qualitative global evaluations may be reviewed to gain a basic understanding of the diversity of opinion. Second, and more important, case study reports may be examined. Finally, social costs or cost-benefit methodologies may be analyzed.

With regard to the impressionistic global assessments, as may be expected, judgments vary markedly. Wilson and Moore, influential social scientists of the right, find a vitality in the penal law approach. Packer, on the other hand, summarized liberal opinion in declaring that "A clearer case of misapplication of the criminal law would be difficult to imagine."

The case studies provide more fruitful data. In this classic treatise *Licit and Illicit Drugs,* Brecher systematically evaluates claims of drug law successes. With respect to curtailment of drug supplies, he finds a single instance of significant abatement, the temporary World War II shortage of illicit drugs.

Hunt and Chambers recently conducted a comprehensive investigation of heroin epidemiology. They conclude that arrests, seizures and fluctuating price and purity have little effect on the spread of heroin use.

McGlothlin, Jamison and Rosenblatt's study of Operation Intercept, a Nixon-era marijuana interdiction program, is revealing. McGlothlin and his associates document that marijuana availability did decrease during the program but college students responded by substituting other, more potent drugs.

Wheat's study of Boston indicates that the level of law enforcement is correlated with the number of addicts. Related studies were reported in the supply reduction section of this article, correlating, in selected cities, indices of enforcement pressure with crime and drug use measures.

Grizzle's evaluation of Mecklenburg County data provides a useful analytic model. She develops estimates of the prevention results alternative enforcement policies can be expected to achieve. Fiscal and social costs are attached to the estimates.

A cross-national review of the reported case study material was undertaken by the Canadian researcher Smart. After acknowledging the significant limitations of available data, Smart declared:

From the evidence currently available it can be tentatively concluded that:
(1) Successful attempts to reduce the supply of heroin, by means of seizures and crop reductions have produced reductions in illicit heroin availability, heroin addiction and deaths from heroin. However such reductions are sometimes small and so far no set of legal restraints has reduced the heroin problem to a negligible level.
(2) The effectiveness of the British heroin clinic system cannot be stated with any certainty.
(3) Large reductions in cannabis availability can probably reduce cannabis consumption, at least temporarily but probably with the substitution of other drugs.
(4) Legal restraints may have their greatest impact when they are combined with educational and rehabilitative efforts as in the Japanese amphetamine epidemic.
(5) The greatest successes in legal restraint appear to involve legal drugs. The British, American, and Swedish amphetamine epidemics probably represent the best documented cases where legal restraints alone led to the virtual disappearance of a drug problem. In all cases concerted action was taken to get legal suppliers and/or physicians to modify their practices.

The study which has attracted the most recent notoriety is the New York Drug Law Evaluation. This $959,000 project examined the effects of the harsh Rockefeller Law over a three-year period. From a policy perspective this study is of great importance, as numerous states are considering penal law schemes based on the New York model. However the Final Report concludes that the 1973 New York drug law did not achieve its intended purposes of deterring drug use and reducing drug-related crime. According to the report, "The available data indicate that despite expenditures of substantial resources neither of the objectives of the 1973 drug law was achieved. Neither heroin use nor drug-related crime declined in New York State."

Although the New York evaluation is subject to valid methodological criticism, the principal conclusion of no significant impact upon drug-use patterns is beyond reasonable dispute. The data also demonstrate conclusively that the mandate of imposition of lengthy penalties was systematically undermined. Despite the optimism of Governor Rockefeller and the New York legislature, this latter outcome should have been anticipated. A similar fate befell earlier "get tough" drug laws; evaluation of a 1950s Michigan mandatory law revealed that only twelve of 476 persons charged with the sale of narcotics were convicted of that offense. Mandatory penalty laws restricting the discretion of criminal justice institutions appear to inevitably undergo a neutralization or negation effect blunting their intended impact.

Returning to the more general issue of the effectiveness of the drug laws in deterring drug use, a further line of inquiry requires examination. The social cost or cost-benefit method offers a potentially valuable tool for assessing the utility of the penal approach.

This method entails a weighing of the social and economic costs and benefits associated with a particular policy. The social profit or loss caused by the policy is identified enabling policymakers to accept, reject or modify the particular approach. The advantage of this promising method is that important externalities of policy decisions are exposed. The principal disadvantage is that many of the cost and benefit measures, particularly the qualitative indicators, are value judgments subject to ideological manipulation. Further, these paradigms offer the appearance of scientific certainty by reducing their findings to a definite social profit and loss statement which in many cases may be a deceptive conclusion.

With regard to the penal drug law approach, a number of social cost analyses have been reported. Moore, Grizzle, the National Commission on Marihuana and Drug Abuse and Kaplan offer competing models and conclusions. Weissman reviewed these findings and stated:

Results yielded in the social costs models are problematic. The ledger of social profit is governed by the threshold assumptions of the architect. . . . The strength of the social cost model is its ability to identify applicable costs and benefits. Interpretation of the meaning of the social cost data becomes a judgmental exercise, however. Is maintenance of anti-drug symbolism worth the current investment in fiscal and social resources? Cost analysis raises this line of questioning but does not provide a satisfactory means of answering these issues.

In summary, the pertinent data are once again incomplete and ambiguous. Despite application of several different research strategies, analysts are unable to assess definitively the effectiveness of drug laws in achieving their intended penal effects. Perhaps as fair a conclusion as may be reached on the basis of this contradictory evidence is offered by Weissman:

An informed and reasoned judgment is possible on the basis of the adduced evidence, however. At a visceral level, it is apparent that the prohibitionist policy has failed in accomplishing its goals. Drug use has not been effectively deterred. . . . The Drug Enforcement Administration calculates the existence of at least one half million bona fide addicts and less conservative estimates, such as the Hunt and Chambers report, increase that figure substantially. Use of other drugs is widespread. . . . Furthermore, the unacceptably high toll in social costs associated with the current policies is beyond dispute. . . .

On the other hand, data demonstrating a valuable return for the investment are hard to find. The majority of the evidence reported in the literature and in government documents fails to show anything but inconclusive results. . . .

To be sure, when the costs of a social policy have been unequivocally documented but the existence of benefits is in doubt, continuation of the policy is contraindicated. This is especially the case with regard to drug use and availability controls where the social and fiscal costs are significant. As the National Commission on Marihuana and Drug Abuse [1973] noted, symbolic effects may temporarily suffice but eventually, these forces must coalesce with instrumental effects or lose their vitality. As the symbolic value of drug control rapidly wanes in American society, the day of final judgment approaches.

FUTURE AGENDA

By this point certain conclusions are painfully evident. First, although the drugs and crime literature is abundant, knowledge of the exact dimensions of the drugs and crime connection is limited. Cumulatively the many research reports do indicate firm directions but conclusions are rated as tentative.

This assessment raises an additional set of issues. The most obvious issue to this researcher is that of logic and common sense. The evidence is quite convincing that drug users, at least opiate addicts, do commit a significant amount of non-drug crime, primarily of an income-generating nature. Furthermore, their lives are pervasively associated with antisocial activities, be it drug distribution or predatory crime. Is this outcome the product of the social decision to criminalize drug use or do the drug laws prevent more serious harms by the socially deviant addicts? Although the research rules prohibit definite statements in this regard, application of common sense appears to override the technical methodological restrictions.

It is this writer's opinion that the available evidence, notwithstanding the legitimate methodological concerns, indicates that: (1) under our prevailing criminalization of drug-use system, society forces addicts to practice income-generating criminal behaviors; (2) addicts and, to some extent, other drug users exhibit generalized deviant behavior independent of drug use; (3) treatment does tend to decrease the pressure for committing crime but in an oblique manner; and (4) the drug laws are relatively impotent in achieving their articulated principal goal of deterring community drug use.

To be sure, these statements are more limiting than the conclusions announced by public officials interested in drug-related crime prevention. The lay public continues to support the notion that drug use and crime are inextricably intertwined in a singular and pernicious relationship. That assessment is premature and perhaps incorrect however. The body of research discussed in this article demonstrates that knowledge of drugs and crime relations is limited. The methodological deficiencies are real rather than illusory. Sweeping imprecise statements such as 50 percent of urban street crime is committed by addicts are inaccurate and misleading. These interpretative issues pertain to more than aggrandizement of individual researchers' reputations or the continued economic well-being of academic research. The nation's drug-abuse prevention policies are in large measure based on a simplistic set of beliefs regarding the drugs and crime connection. Federal documents and public officials' rhetoric reveal this fact.

Accordingly, it is critical to inculcate a more exact understanding of the drugs and crime research knowledge. Politicians and the public alike must be made aware of the reported data and their significance. Then perhaps more enlightened, or at least better informed, social policy decision-making can be expected in regard to drug-abuse prevention.

Thus, two sets of agenda may be identified. First, drugs and crime research must be refined and strengthened. Excellent ideas for improvement have been systematically developed by the *Drug Use and Crime* panel. If implemented, those suggestions will reduce much of the uncertainty associated with the drugs and crime literature. Of course a residue of uncertainty will always remain, as social science research methodology is not capable of measuring and assessing complex social phenomena with complete certitude. Yet considerable progress can be advanced. This progress is already occurring. As noted earlier, under the leadership of LEAA, a new multidisciplinary drugs and crime panel has been established to explore the unfinished research agenda. Additionally, individual researchers continue to score contributions to the drugs and crime knowledge base.

The other agenda relates to education. Reported research findings must be disseminated in a manner which insures utilization by public decision-makers. Symbolism dominates drug policy and a great deal of the symbolism is associated with an incomplete and erroneous understanding of drugs and crime relationships. The real challenge to the research community is to develop a strategy for translating the body of drugs and crime findings into a format which will be understood by public officials and their constituencies. Hopefully, sensitive appreciation of these issues may stimulate more cautious and rational social policy.

Section 4

ENFORCEMENT PRACTICES

The inclusion of only a single article shortchanges this important topic. The manner in which drug prohibitions are enforced against citizen violators is of critical significance to the maintenance of social equilibrium. Enforcement decisions reflect the ideological values of a community, and the resultant social consequences are durable and pervasive.

Space limits preclude the presentation of additional material focused directly upon the observation and empirical analysis of enforcement practices. The coordinate topics of enforcement philosophy, culpability of violators, and penal effects are considered in sections 5 and 6, however; a parallel examination of these interrelated subjects is recommended.

The Johnson et al. article represents one of the few reported major empirical analyses of drug arrest data. Several jurisdictions are included in the study, and an adequate methodology is employed. The general applicability of these findings to enforcement of other drug prohibitions and to other communities is uncertain, but the results of this valuable study demand careful examination and policy consideration.

Weldon T. Johnson
Robert E. Petersen
L. Edward Wells

ARREST PROBABILITIES FOR MARIJUANA USERS AS INDICATORS OF SELECTIVE LAW ENFORCEMENT

It is generally recognized that most instances of deviance are not sanctioned. In this sense, the relationship between deviant actions and social reactions, because it is incomplete, is probabilistic rather than deterministic. This observation implies that in accounting for the likelihood of sanctioning, the deviant act is to be regarded as only one relevant factor; other factors that influence the probability of sanctioning include certain characteristics of the actor, the sanctioning agency, and the community within which social control occurs. Attention to the differential but organized processes of recognition, sanctioning, and labeling encourages a sensitivity to how reactions to deviance may be themselves normatively regulated. Presumably, these reactions are not random because there are rules for identifying, sanctioning and labeling deviance. The issue of selectivity in law enforcement directly implicates this normative element.

In the context of reactions to crime, the specific standard which is ostensibly violated by selective enforcement—selective detection, arrest, prosecution, conviction, and sentencing—is the constitutional prescription of "equal protection" specified in the Fourteenth Amendment. This standard suggests that the elements of criminal law are to be viewed as generally applicable rules of conduct and ought to be applied equally to all. In broader terms, there seems to be at least partial identity between the ideas of "justice" and "equality of treatment." This suggests one essential meaning of "equal justice under law": if the distribution of enforcement outcomes (arrests, convictions, incarcerations, etc.)

across relevant social groups is not equal, the standard of equal protection has been violated.

But an adequate test for selectivity in this context presumes a basic analytical framework. It requires, first of all, conceptual specification of what is meant by "selectivity" in enforcement. Further, it requires an operational identification of the appropriate null model—that is, a specification of what things would look like if selectivity were absent. On the surface, the equal protection prescription may be interpreted as a "no difference" or equal outcomes null model: all persons or groups should have equal frequencies of being apprehended, sanctioned, and labeled; *any* difference indicates something anomalous. While basic, this model is too simplistic in its assumption that the likelihood of apprehension or sanction should be directly and solely determined by the direction or magnitude of deviance control reactions. Sanctioning outcomes are clearly dependent on a variety of factors in addition to the actions of deviance control, factors such as the nature of the offensive behavior, the manner in which it is enacted, its visibility, the setting in which it occurs, the extent to which it is viewed as "offensive," the kind of publicity needed to prosecute offenses formally, and the cooperation of the community in detecting or prosecuting the offense.

A more appropriate alternative to the null model is an "explicable differences" model, involving the explicit recognition that differences in reactions to deviance may occur for a number of reasons—appropriate as well as inappropriate according to specified normative standards. Thus, differences per se cannot automatically be regarded as indicators of selective enforcement but those differences which cannot be reasonably accounted for can be so regarded. Here, the analytic implication is to explain observed enforcement outcome differences by considering extraneous but relevant variables which may have produced such differences. These variables may involve certain characteristics of acts or actors which also affect legitimately the probability of detection, apprehension, and prosecution.

Recently, several studies have invoked, at least implicitly, explicable difference models. The research reported here explores the question of explicable differences in an analysis of variations in estimated arrest probabilities according to certain social characteristics of suspected offenders and features of the jurisdictions in which those arrests occurred. Attention is directed toward one criminal offense where the disparity between the occurrence of an initial act and an enforcement reaction— and hence the opportunity for selective enforcement—is generally thought to be extreme: illicit use of marijuana.

DATA AND METHODS

The data utilized here were collected for the National Commission on Marihuana and Drug Abuse in two separate but related studies of the characteristics of marijuana users and arrestees. In the first study, marijuana use data were collected by Response Analysis Corporation as part of a national survey of licit and illicit drug use in 1971. The survey involved face-to-face interviews, a self-administered questionnaire, and a national probability sample of noninstitutionalized adults age 21 and older. The use data we analyzed involved three subsamples—corresponding to three jurisdictions which differed in the statutory penalties for conviction of marijuana offenses at this time. In anticipation of the analysis reported here, three jurisdictions were oversampled within the larger national survey: a high-penalty area (Cook County, Ill.), a low-penalty area (Douglas County [Omaha], Nebr.), and an intermediate penalty area (Washington, D.C., metropolitan area). The oversampling produced a total sample of 637 (Cook, N = 216; Omaha, N = 206; Washington, N = 215). A technical discussion of sampling, field, and weighting procedures is provided by Abelson et al.

Arrest data were retrieved from police files in a second study conducted for the commission. The data analyzed here pertain to the three jurisdictions that were oversampled in the use survey. In these three jurisdictions, the total marijuana arrestee population was first defined by an enumeration of police log entries between July 1 and December 31, 1970. From this enumeration, all cases involving at least one marijuana offense charged by the police at custody were included in the sample (except in Cook County where one-in-10 cases was sampled due to the volume of total cases). These procedures produced the following (unweighted) subsample sizes: Cook County (N = 431), Douglas County (N = 113), and Washington metropolitan area (N = 678).

Estimating outcome probabilities. Estimation of arrest probabilities involved aggregate-level computations, yielding ratios rather than actual proportions to estimate the jurisdiction-specific probabilities. Rates of both marijuana use and marijuana arrest (each expressed per 100,000 persons, 18 years or older) were computed from the two data files for each jurisdiction overall and for selected demographic subgroups within each jurisdiction. These separate estimated user and observed arrestee rates were then combined computationally to estimate the proportion of persons having used marijuana who have also been arrested for such use. Specifically, the "risk of arrest" was computed by the *ratio* of the arrest rate to the estimated user rate (the value of the ratio expressed per 100,000 marijuana users, 18 years or older). Two marijuana user rates were computed for this analysis. In addition to computing user rates for those persons who reported use of marijuana at least once (ever users), we also estimated rates for persons who reported present use of marijuana in the month of the interviews (current users).

An arrest rate for these same jurisdictions was estimated by establishing the number of marijuana arrests for the area and computing the ratio of this quantity to the population and specified subpopulations of that jurisdiction as given in the 1970 census. The arrest rate used here pertains only to arrests in which possession of marijuana was the only offense charged by the arresting officer(s).

Calculation of arrest probabilities involved certain measurement considerations. Here, it was necessary to establish roughly comparable category systems or operationalizations of variables in two data files. The compatibility of the two data files generally was not problematic for the measurement of these variables. Gender was coded dichotomously, as was race—black and nonblack. Age was dichotomized into less than or equal to 25 and greater than 25 years, the approximate split at the median for the various samples (i.e., users, arrestees, and the jurisdictional populations). Occupation, originally treated as a nine-category code, was coded as blue collar, white collar, and student.

Comparing Outcome Probabilities. The logic of our analysis of arrest probabilities is implied by the equation specifying the relationship between arrest rates and rates of self-reported marijuana use (ostensibly the violation rates):

$$\frac{\text{Arrestees}}{\text{Users}} \quad \text{X} \quad \frac{\text{Users}}{\text{Population}} \quad = \quad \frac{\text{Arrestees}}{\text{Population}}$$

$$(A) \qquad\qquad (B) \qquad\qquad (C)$$

$$\text{(Arrest} \qquad \text{(Violation} \qquad \text{(Arrest}$$

$$\text{Probability)} \qquad \text{Rate)} \qquad \text{Rate)}$$

As suggested by its position in the equation, the arrest rate (term C) is the phenomenon ultimately to be explained: it represents the social control outcome. More specifically, the analytic task is to account for the distributions of such outcomes across different sociodemographic categories. In the analysis that follows, we focus first on the arrest *probability* (term A) as that portion of the outcome rate which is distinguishable from variation in the distribution of sanctionable behavior and which reflects the contribution of the enforcement context other than, or in addition to, variations in sanctionable behavior. In this sense, our estimation of term A (by construction of the arrest/use ratios) is an attempt to "peel apart" arrest rates and focus on that component of these rates which reflects more substantially on the input of law enforcement systems.

TABLE 1: Arrest/User Ratios, User Rates, and Arrest Rates by Four Sociodemographic Groups for Cook County

| Sociodemographic Group | Arrest/User Ratios (per 100,000 Users) | | User Rates (per 100,000 persons) | | Arrest Rates (per 100,000 Persons) |
	Possession: Ever Use	Possession: Current Use	Ever Use	Current	Possession
Gender:					
Male	653 (542–816)	1,864 (1,398–2,815)	17,670	6,190	115
Female	107 (90–132)	238 (179–359)	11,470	5,160	12
Employment Status:					
White collar	123 (101–156)	—	26,777	—	33
Blue collar	1,055 (802–1,551)	—	8,903	—	94
Student	294 (200–553)	—	47,300	—	139
Race:					
Black	665 (519–918)	1,686 (1,146–3,203)	22,980	9,060	153
Nonblack	298 (259–352)	723 (564–998)	12,200	5,030	36
Age:					
25 or less	632 (556–733)	1,368 (1,081–1,888)	44,070	20,370	279
26 or more	123 (98–164)	377 (245–675)	8,140	2,650	10
Overall total	277 (244–321)	694 (562–909)	14,500	5,790	40

NOTE. The range specified in parentheses with each arrest/user estimate in this and other tables is the "range of plausible variation" in the estimate, described in the text. This range indexes the variability of the ratio estimate resulting from sampling variability in the user rate estimates. The width of the interval reflects the relative stability of each ratio estimate. In comparing observed ratios for different social units, the overlap, or near overlap, of the intervals for the two ratio values indicates that any observed difference may not be reproducible with different samplings.

Supplementary Data. In addition to the basic data used to estimate total and group-specific arrest probabilities, the analysis ultimately required additional data concerning the arrest encounter itself. That is, the explication of differences in arrest/use ratios directed our attention to the circumstances of detection and arrest. From the arrest data file, we retrieved police reports on the circumstances of the arrest, as well as the antecedents of the encounter. These supplementary data included information about the number of persons included in an arrest

TABLE 2: Arrest/User Ratios, User Rates, and Arrest Rates by Four Sociodemographic Groups for Washington, D.C., Metropolitan Area

Sociodemographic Group	Arrest/User Ratios (per 100,000 Users)		User Rates (per 100,000 persons)		Arrest Rates (per 100,000 Persons)
	Possession: Ever Use	Possession: Current Use	Ever Use	Current Use	Possession
Gender:					
Male	229 (190–289)	393 (307–546)	15,340	8,940	35
Female	48 (39–62)	120 (88–191)	11,110	4,410	5
Employment status:					
White collar	32 (26–42)	—	20,381		7
Blue collar	487 (331–901)	—	6,471	—	32
Student	61 (45–93)	—	61,630	—	37
Race:					
Black	120 (88–190)	247 (146–823)	13,420	6,540	16
Nonblack	148 (127–178)	291 (236–381)	13,400	6,820	20
Age:					
25 or less	152 (134–176)	264 (219–335)	46,790	27,020	71
26 or more	112 (77–200)	1,152 (576–115,520)	2,680	260	3
Overall total	96 (84–113)	192 (156–248)	13,190	6,630	13

(group vs. solo), the spatial location of the arrest (a private area, a public off-street area, a public street area, a vehicle), the type of police officer involved, the occurrence of a prior drug-related investigation, the type of enforcement activity leading to detection and arrest (e.g., proactive, reactive, routine patrol), and prior arrests.

FINDINGS

Tables 1-3 show arrest rates and user rates as well as the arrest/use ratios for gender, occupation, race, and age within and across jurisdictions. Small cell size precluded the simultaneous breakdown by occupation

TABLE 3: Arrest/User Ratios, User Rates, and Arrest Rates by Four
Sociodemographic Groups for Douglas County

Socio-demographic Group	Arrest/User Ratios (per 100,000 Users)		User Rates (per 100,000 persons)		Arrest Rates (per 100,000 persons)
	Possession: Ever Use	Possession: Current Use	Ever Use	Current Use	Possession
Gender:					
Male	255 (207–332)	754 (558–1,176)	15,950	5,400	41
Female	87 (66–129)	304 (179–1,012)	4,280	1,230	4
Employment status:					
White collar	83 (63–120)	—	15,303	—	13
Blue collar	419 (277–884)	—	9,086	—	38
Student	214 (143–428)	—	16,350	—	35
Race:					
Black	195 (131–390)	325 (198–930)	24,730	14,840	48
Nonblack	214 (178–270)	791 (577–1,258)	8,710	2,360	19
Age:					
25 or less	268 (220–343)	591 (443–875)	31,000	14,050	84
26 or more	89 (67–134)	1,429 (715–142,900)	4,010	250	4
Overall total	137 (102–170)	420 (319–622)	9,740	3,180	13

and any second variable. Thus, although age, race, and gender were analyzed not only singly, but also with each other variable two at a time, and all three variables simultaneously, occupation was treated singly. This process was repeated for each of the three jurisdictions and their aggregate total, although the results of these analyses are not shown.

The tables include component rates (marijuana use and marijuana possession arrest) as well as their computed ratios, so that the contributions of components to differences in arrest/use ratios can be examined. These tables also show the estimated "range of plausible variation" for each ratio. The relevant comparisons are discussed in turn.

Interjurisdictional Patterns. Tables 1–3 show that both arrest/use ratios are higher in Cook County and lower in Washington; Douglas County is intermediate. That is, the probability of arrest for marijuana users is higher in Cook County than in Douglas County and lowest in Washington. The relationship of the magnitude of the arrest/use ratios for these jurisdictions is approximately: 2½ : 1½ : 1. When each jurisdiction's arrest rates and estimated user rates are examined separately, the basis for the observed ordering of ratios becomes apparent. Cook County has the highest arrest rates; the arrest rates in Washington, D.C., and Douglas County are about one-third as large. In estimated drug use, Washington and Cook County are similar and have higher user rates than Douglas County. Thus, the difference in ratios is produced by a substantially higher arrest rate in Cook County. In this respect, a question that is raised by these data is why arrest rates are so much higher in Cook County than in Washington or Douglas County.

Effects of Gender. Tables 1–3 also show the relevant arrest/use comparisons by gender. Overall, larger gender differences appear in Cook County than in Washington: gender differences are smallest in Douglas County. The relationship between gender and the arrest/use ratios is consistent across all three jurisdictions: males have substantially higher arrest/ use ratios than females; overall, male ratios are about five times larger although this varies across jurisdictions. The gender differences in arrest/ use ratios are attributable primarily to *arrest rate* differentials.

Effects of Occupation. Tables 1–3 also show that arrest/use ratios vary by occupational status, and these relationships are sizable and consistent across jurisdictions. Of all occupational groups, the blue-collar group has the highest arrest/use ratios; student ratios come next, and the white-collar group has the lowest ratios. This pattern is apparent in each of the three jurisdictions, although intrajurisdiction differences are less striking because of small sample sizes and, hence, less stable estimates.

The large arrest/use ratios for blue-collar persons are produced by this group's high arrest rates coupled with relatively low estimated user rates. The student group also has a high arrest rate but the arrest/use ratios are lower than those for the blue-collar group because student user rates are the highest of the three occupational categories. The white-collar group has a moderately high user rate but it is coupled with the lowest arrest rates.

Effects of Race. In contrast to the arrest/use ratio differences associated with gender and occupation, the effect of race is not consistent across jurisdictions. Tables 1–3 show arrest/use comparisons by race. Racial differences are largest in Cook County and relatively small in Washington and Douglas County (except for current users). In Cook County, blacks have substantially higher arrest/use ratios than nonblacks—at least twice as large. These differences are attributable to a striking difference in arrest rates (black rates are about four times larger than those for nonblacks) which offsets small differences in estimated user rates. In contrast, Washington and Douglas County show no appreciable racial differences.

Effects of Age. Arrest/use comparisons by age are also shown in tables 1–3. Like the racial comparisons reported above, the effect of age is not consistent across jurisdictions. The largest age differences are again found in Cook County; the differences in Douglas and Washington are generally smaller. In Cook County, the age effect is consistent across both ratio indices and is substantial. In this jurisdiction, persons 25 and under have higher arrest/use ratios than do persons over 25. Although the rates of both marijuana use and arrest are higher for the younger group, the age differential is greater for arrest rates than for use rates, and the younger group has correspondingly higher arrest/use ratios.

EXPLICATING ARREST DIFFERENTIALS

The data presented above show that the probability of arrest for marijuana users varies by certain sociodemographic categories across and within jurisdictions. One general pattern of apprehension risk is a gender effect: males have substantially higher arrest probabilities than do females. This pattern is clear and consistent across all jurisdictions. A second general pattern of apprehension risk is an occupational group effect: the probability of arrest is generally higher for blue-collar persons than for others; students show higher arrest probabilities than do white-collar persons. Third, age patterns of apprehension risk are more clearly jurisdiction specific. The age effects observed in Washington, D.C., and Douglas County arrest/use ratios differ visibly from those of

Cook County. Finally, the effect of race on arrest probability involves one of this study's more interesting findings: a race effect is apparent only in Cook County where blacks have higher arrest/use ratios.

As indicated earlier, such differences do not necessarily constitute evidence of selectivity. The general question they raise, however, pertains to their explicability: What can be made, sociologically, of these differences? The question of explicability directs attention to three possible components of the sanctioning episode: (1) the distribution and characteristics of sanctionable acts—or actors; here, differential sanctioning is explained in terms of "differential violations," including the kind or number or seriousness of those violations; (2) the organization and focus of sanctioning agents; here, differential sanctioning is explained in terms of "differential enforcement," including the harassment of, or discrimination against, certain presumed offenders. It is assumed that the sanctionable acts, both kind and number, are constant across sociodemographic groups; and (3) the intersect or interaction of sanctionable acts or actors and the organization or focus of sanctioning; this latter approach explains differential sanctioning in terms of "differential visibility."

In exploring these alternative explanations, we reject a *simple* differential violation interpretation of the arrest rate differentials for marijuana possession. The data show that the most frequently arrested groups also have generally higher estimated user rates. At the same time, the differences in the violation rates are insufficient to account for the arrest rate differences (which are typically much greater in magnitude); indeed, this differential between the arrest differences and the marijuana-use differences is sufficiently large and robust to preclude possible effects of measurement or sampling errors in our estimation procedure. The explanation we wish to explore is the third—differential visibility. Our analysis focuses on the conditions under which violations come to be "suspected," that is, come to the attention of enforcement agents and prompt a response from them.

Prior research indicates that, for most criminal offenses, the likelihood of detection is affected to a great extent by the behavior of citizen complainants and victims who decide whether or not to contact the police. However, except for a small percentage of drug offenses which are reported by nonparticipant third parties, citizens play a relatively small role in determining whether or not drug violations are detected. In contrast to most other crimes, the detection of drug offenses—which do not produce victims or complainants—virtually always arises from police-initiated contacts with the violator.

In *drug* law enforcement, virtually all criminal arrests are produced by one of two policing styles. First is the police-initiated investigation in which police actively seek out violations of drug laws, especially those involving commercial distribution. This style involves the use of undercover agents, drug buys, stakeouts, and informants. A second drug law enforcement style encompasses residual policy activity: drug violations are "spontaneously" detected in the course of preventive patrol, traffic control, or general "peace keeping" activity. Here, the primary determinant affecting the detection of drug violators is whether the police conduct a search during the citizen encounter.

In marijuana arrests generally, it is estimated that about two-thirds of all arrestees are apprehended spontaneously without any prior investigative activity; furthermore, these arrests usually are made by general patrolmen in the course of the routine policing of public areas, often after a seizure involving less than one ounce of marijuana. We attempted to further illuminate the observed arrest probability differences by examining data pertaining to the circumstances of detection and arrest for the various demographic groups within and across jurisdictions. Supplemental analyses of additional data in the arrest files involved reported information about the number of persons included in an arrest, the location of the arrest, the type of police officer involved, the occurrence of prior drug-related investigation, and the type of enforcement activity leading to detection and arrest.

In examining these data, we found the following patterns: (1) males, compared to females, were more often arrested by general patrolmen, often in vehicles, more often arrested alone, and more often had prior records. Conversely, arrest of females more often involved investigative or proactive policing where the apprehension occurs in an indoor non-public location. (2) Student arrestees in all jurisdictions were less often targets of prior investigation than other persons. Arrests involving students appear to involve spontaneous or routine general patrol-citizen encounters, often in connection with a vehicle stop. Similarly, arrests of blue-collar persons (in Cook County and Washington), compared to arrests of white-collar persons, were somewhat more likely to result from spontaneous police contact and to involve persons with prior arrest records. (3) In all jurisdictions younger persons (25 and under) were generally more often arrested in vehicles or groups than older arrestees, while the older group more often involved persons with prior records and arrests in an indoor context. (4) Racial differences are evident in the circumstances of detection only in Cook County. In this jurisdiction, the apprehension of blacks, compared to arrests of nonblacks, was less often the result of prior drug-related investigations, and more often occurred in a "street" context as a result of either spontaneous police contact or the detection or suspicion of simultaneous nondrug events or offenses.

To further scrutinize the relationship between arrest probability and certain arrest circumstances, we dichotomized the arrest sample into high and low arrest probability groups. The high probability group includes nonblack males 25 and under, black males 25 and under, and black males over 25. The low probability group includes all females and nonblack males over 25. The two groups were compared, for each jurisdiction, with respect to a prior arrest record, an investigation prior to the arrest, the prevalence of group arrests, the public or private arrest location, and the recorded cause of police presence.

TABLE 4: Dimensions of Detection and Apprehension by High and Low Arrest Probability Groups for Three Jurisdictions (%) (Partial Table)

	N	Prior Arrest	Investigation	Single Arrestee	Public Area	Spontaneous	General Patrol
Cook County	(3,813)	54.42	21.32	29.35	72.36	50.38	86.81
High	(3,091)	56.84	15.95	30.93	80.69	55.61	89.52
Low	(653)	45.02	47.01	19.14	32.62	23.74	74.27
Missing	(69)	(168)	(101)	(24)	(21)	(625)	(81)
Douglas County	(108)	47.22	34.26	22.22	54.63	19.44	41.67
High	(89)	49.44	34.83	23.60	58.43	21.35	41.57
Low	(18)	33.33	33.33	16.67	33.33	11.11	38.89
Missing	(1)	(0)	(1)	(5)	(0)	(15)	(0)
Washington, D.C.	(712)	25.70	35.25	31.32	67.70	42.13	42.28
High	(547)	29.43	33.27	35.28	71.66	43.88	45.16
Low	(135)	14.07	40.74	19.26	51.85	35.56	29.63
Missing	(30)	(147)	(3)	(41)	(7)	(30)	(7)

NOTE. This is a partial table insofar as percentage distributions are shown for only the variable category of interest, i.e., the proportion of the arrest group—with a prior arrest record, apprehended after an investigation, apprehended alone, apprehended in a public place, apprehended spontaneously, arrehended by a general patrolman. The rows designated as "missing" display the number of cases for which arrest circumstance data were unrecorded or unknown.

These comparisons are summarized in table 4. The data show that in *each* jurisdiction arrests of persons in the high arrest probability group, compared with those in the low probability group (1) more frequently involved persons with a prior arrest record; (2) less often resulted from a prior investigation, except in Douglas County; (3) more often involved apprehension of a single suspect (rather than a group "bust"); (4) more often occurred in a public ("street") location; (5) more often involved spontaneous contact with police (rather than either reactive or proactive policing), especially in Cook and Douglas Counties; and (6) more often were carried out by general patrolmen than by officers with a limited or specialized jurisdiction, especially in Cook County and Washington.

These relationships between arrestee characteristics and arrest circumstances suggest to us two considerations for explaining the observed differences in marijuana arrest probabilities. First, the data indicate that the number and kind of marijuana users who enter the criminal justice system depend largely on the nature and scope of police detection activity. In particular, the substantial role played by general patrol officers in generating "spontaneous" arrests is remarkable. Our characterization of these arrests as spontaneous and resulting from fortuitous police contact is consistent with Black's description of typical proactive police activity, that "in the average case proactive detection involves a simultaneous detection of the violative acts and of the violative person." The discovery of drug offenses may vary from a proactive but noninvestigatory search for drug crime to an essentially reactive style associated with the ordinary patrolman who routinely encounters "suspicious behavior," "suspicious circumstances," and traffic violations in which drugs are serendipitously discovered.

The second consideration pertains to how behavior or circumstances come to the awareness of police as suspected violations. Although the data presented are not sufficient to determine unequivocally what specifically triggered the police attention or suspicion that preceded these arrests, several explanations are plausible. The first is the importance of the *social location* of suspects and suspected activity. The data analyzed here suggest that the context and manner in which marijuana is used render it more or less susceptible to detection. The sociodemographic groups examined may differ in the extent to which marijuana was used in publicly accessible settings and this difference may in turn lead to differences in detectability. Stinchcombe notes the importance of police access to private (vs. public) places including those situations or settings whose penetration by law enforcement agents is formally limited by statutory or constitutional specifications. Stinchcombe suggests that private places are differentially distributed across various social groupings and that arrests dependent upon public discovery are correlated with the distribution of private places. Similarly, Chambliss and Seidman have speculated about the legal consequences of differential access of social classes to the "institution of privacy." The public context of marijuana law enforcement (where general patrol officers play a major role in generating spontaneous arrests during routine patrol activity) implies that variations in detection and apprehension should correlate with the distribution of access to private places (and corresponding use of public places for otherwise private activities). The data examined here are consistent with this interpretation. The groups most liable to arrest were also those groups with least access to privacy and whose arrests most frequently involved discovery in a public context (i.e., in vehicles, in the street, or in off-street, on-view settings).

The social location of suspects and suspected activity also directs attention to the sociological importance of "territoriality." Aside from the question of differential access to privacy, the location of sanctionable actors may determine the *kind* of social reaction they prompt. Werthman and Piliavin conclude that areas regarded by some persons as "home space" (suitable for activities that might otherwise violate the public order if enacted in public places) may be regarded by others, such as police officers, as public areas subject to maintenance of public order. In this regard, we note that in Washington, D.C., arrests of young blacks frequently occurred in an urban street setting while arrests of young whites often occurred in parks. One implication of this finding is that public territories frequently provided the "testing ground" of challenges to authorities. In these contexts, a behavior whose propriety or whose relationship to the public order is in dispute may be enacted openly in public to generate confrontation; and, indeed, the marijuana controversy seems to have involved this kind of symbolic interaction. The large number of arrests of young nonblack persons in Washington, D.C., may reflect precisely this phenomenon: a substantial number of these arrests were made in park areas where, it may be recalled, the protest rallies of 1970 and 1971 were also located. Many of the arrests associated with these events involved drug charges.

Beyond accessibility to public view, the visibility of deviant activity also involves the coding of behaviors and persons into "suspected" categories. This interpretive component implicates a second explanation—the potential significance of *cues* in the apprehension of suspects. In this regard, the general overrepresentation of young, blue-collar males may reflect either a greater visibility of these persons and their marijuana use to the police or a police predisposition to search persons with these characteristics. Matza's discussion of the role of categorical resemblance within the "method of suspicion" indicates that not all social categories of persons and activities are equally "suspect." Organizational pressures for efficient policing inevitably encourage police reliance on resemblance to "known" categories of suspected persons. Suspicion is neither randomly directed nor incidental, but rather methodical and involves the application of existing category systems of suspects. Certain characteristics of actors and action may signify such categories and, therefore, serve as cues that affect police perception, focus police attention, and direct police investigation. Although we are without direct observational data concerning these dimensions of police activity, the available data do suggest certain patterns of police suspicion. As we have indicated, the most frequently arrested groups—young males, often black—more often involve general patrol officers and a police-citizen encounter where the marijuana violation was not initially or directly seen. Instead, arrests of these groups often result from police stops for other purposes, often "suspicious circumstances" after which a search produced marijuana evidence. Many of these arrests imply a methodical application of suspicion to persons with reputations for "making trouble."

Finally, we note that although the police harassment hypothesis is often associated with drug law enforcement, it is also apparent that the context of much marijuana use is one where such activity is visible. In these circumstances, the probability of police-offender contact is greatly increased, a condition that is largely determined by marijuana users. The data presented here are compatible with both interpretations—differential enforcement or differential visibility—and, therefore, with either inappropriate or appropriate selectivity. We wish to emphasize, however, that an empirically based choice among them requires observational data concerning the arrest event, including the detection process by which citizens are linked to a violation.

SUMMARY

The preceding analysis estimated arrest probabilities for marijuana users by combining arrest data with marijuana user estimates for three jurisdictions. Sociodemographic variations in the estimated arrest probabilities show two general effects: arrest probabilities are higher for males than for females and higher for blue-collar persons than others in all three jurisdictions. Other effects are more clearly jurisdictionally specific: in two jurisdictions, persons under 25 have higher arrest probabilities than older persons; in one jurisdiction, arrest probabilities are higher for blacks than nonblacks.

Because a simple differential violation explanation for these differences can be ruled out, alternative interpretations were explored. This subsequent analysis involved examining additional data pertaining to the circumstances of marijuana arrests and certain characteristics of the law enforcement activity that preceded the arrests in these three jurisdictions. Here, we explored the plausibility of both "differential enforcement" and "differential visibility" explanations for the observed arrest probability differences. It was concluded that *both* interpretations are consistent with the available data; that is, the social *location* of much marijuana use as well as the suspicion *cued* by certain sociodemographic characteristics of marijuana users are equally tenable explanations of these arrest probability differentials.

Despite the common assumptions concerning the prevalence of inappropriate selectivity in policing, it appears that its documentation is more difficult than imagined. There *are* some alternative explanations for selectivity in law enforcement.

Section 5

SOCIOLEGAL QUESTIONS

This hybrid topic, sociolegal questions, reflects the predominantly mixed quality of drug control policy. Drug prohibitions activate the legal system to accomplish social policy aims. The policy aims involve controversial and debated notions of efficacy and propriety as regards human choice and social welfare. Separation of the "legal" and "social" aspects is an impossible and futile task.

This section is intended to underscore the centrality of this dimension of drug control policy. Articles have been selected which illustrate the prevailing suppositions of national policy. The articles describe the social deviancy attributed to drug users and the basic policy values associated with prohibitionism. Although both selections assail the rationality of the governing doctrine, a contrary opinion may result from an analysis based on a competing ideological perspective. It is the analytic framework of each article which represents its primary intellectual contribution.

Bayer's article summarizes succinctly and accurately the basic legal culpability doctrine and applies those principles to the heroin addiction phenomenon. Weissman reviews dominant drug control theories within a popular sociological paradigm. Certainly, numerous other analytic approaches are available and equally valuable and may be utilized to expand awareness of the sociolegal tenets of drug control policy.

Ronald Bayer

HEROIN ADDICTION, CRIMINAL CULPABILITY, AND THE PENAL SANCTION
The Liberal Response to Repressive Social Policy

Several years have passed since Nelson Rockefeller's drastic proposals for controlling drug abuse in New York State precipitated intense public dispute. Though his proposals—for the lifetime incarceration of anyone found guilty of selling even the smallest quantities of drugs—were ostensibly directed against those who "trafficked" in drugs, most agreed that the target of repression was, in fact, the drug user. The nature of the debate, which raged in the first months of 1973 and aroused considerable national attention, has been analyzed elsewhere, as has the character of the legislation that emerged from the controversy. This paper examines the intense opposition aroused among liberals by Rockefeller's proposals, with the purpose of showing what appears to be the growing incoherence of contemporary liberal social policy with regard of social deviance. Also considered are the limitations of contemporary liberalism's exculpatory ideologies and its support for "therapeutic" intervention as a form of social control.

BACKGROUND AND OVERVIEW

In his discussion of law and Western moral thought, H. L. A. Hart observed that rules regulating behavior generally assume the capability of compliance. A person cannot be held morally culpable if he cannot do what he ought to do, nor can he be blamed if he cannot refrain from doing what he ought not to do. If the criminal sanction is morally appropriate only in situations of moral culpability, then those who cannot control their own behavior cannot be punished. Exclusion of the "insane"

94

and certain minors from the sanctions of criminal law is based upon this relationship between personal responsibility, guilt, and punishment. Belief in the utility of the criminal sanction as a technique for controlling behavior rests upon the assumption of free will. Only if a person can freely determine his own behavior can punishment deter transgressions or prevent the recurrence of such behavior.

The rise in the nineteenth century of deterministic theories of social and individual behavior, often modeled on the natural sciences (e.g., Comte's positivist sociology), together with the emergence of professional medical groups claiming the ability to explain the causes of human behavior, had an enormous impact on the understanding of criminality. Classical criminology, as typified by the work of Beccaria, had reflected the individualistic assumptions characteristic of early liberal social thought. The abstract individual, a free agent, was free to choose among competing behavioral options, both legal and illegal, just as the firm was free to complete in the economic marketplace. In sharp contrast to this ideology was the work of Enrico Ferri. Founded upon the emergent deterministic social theories, his writings challenged both the moral and practical bases for the use of the criminal sanction. If persons were compelled to violate the law because of forces—social, psychological, or biological—beyond their control, then there was no longer a moral basis for punishment. Without freedom, there could be no blameworthy action. If behavior was determined, punishment or the threat of punishment could not act as a deterrent.

The adoption of determinist social theories—and the consequent abandonment of the philosophical premises of radical individualism—marked the transformation of classical liberalism into modern, social welfare liberalism. Commenting on this "assimilation of a collectivist" understanding of the nature of human action, Robert Paul Wolff stated:

The collective character of social action is the universal presupposition of the social sciences, and modern liberals who have wholeheartedly adopted the theories of sociology and social psychology are accustomed to view society through the eyes of conservative social theorists like Weber and Durkheim and radical social theorists like Marx.

Obviously, this transformation had a profound impact on the liberal understanding of the problems of crime and social deviance. The abstract individual of classical liberal thought was replaced by the social individual; the individual capable of free choice was replaced by the individual whose behavior was largely the outgrowth of a complex of social forces.

And liberalism found it increasingly difficult to grapple with the problems of blameworthiness, guilt, and punishment. Conservative social thought, which continued to extol the virtues of competitive individualistic capitalism and which rejected determinist theories of human behavior, became the repository for these concepts. Support for the moral, exemplary, and utilitarian functions of punishment fell to the conservative thinkers.

In spite of their difficulties with the concepts of guilt and blameworthiness, liberals have recognized the necessity of isolating, for purposes of social defense, persons who pose some threat to the prevailing order—even though those persons are victims of forces beyond their control. However, the sole justification for such incarceration is "rehabilitation." This belief underlies the liberals' zealous support for prison reform and for such innovations as the indeterminate sentence and the inclusion of psychiatric clinics in penitentiaries. Liberals have also supported the use of closed-ward hospital treatment for "mentally disturbed" criminals—those for whom prison could not be rehabilitative. The rise of institutional psychiatry in the United States can be partially attributed to liberalism's ideological and political force.

Clearly, a faith in the ability of social institutions to achieve their purported aims was a necessary part of the commitment to rehabilitation. In treating the deviant as *personally* deformed, although still a product of the *social* process, liberal social policy turned to the increasingly sophisticated technology available to the medical profession, psychiatry, and social work and psychology.

Recently, however, that faith in rehabilitation has weakened. Professionals are now taking a close look at what actually occurs in "rehabilitative" institutions—both prisons and hospitals—and are concluding that the goals of enforced rehabilitation and treatment are illusory. Further, rehabilitative technology is perceived as representing a threat to individual freedom (a condition portrayed in the recent film *A Clockwork Orange*).

Faced with the failure of rehabilitation and recognizing the enormous costs of long-term institutionalization, the liberal response to deviancy has begun to founder. Liberals today are offering two solutions for the problem of crime. In instances of victimless crime—what might be termed a *symbolic* attack on the social order—liberals propose to extend legal tolerance, a solution consistent with early liberal notions of radical individualism. However, where the deviant activity involves an assault on the community—on persons or property—liberal policy makers have begun a flirtation with the concepts of personal responsibility, guilt, and punishment. Given the social understanding of human behavior, the return to these concepts represents an irresolvable contradiction in contemporary liberal thinking.

HEROIN ADDICTION: The Liberal Concept

Having briefly outlined the development of liberal thought with regard to crime, it is now possible to examine the issue of heroin addiction.

The Addict as Victim. Social scientists have advanced numerous theories to explain the prevalence of opiate addiction among poor and minority groups, as well as to explain the nature of the addiction itself. While these theories often sharply conflict, they tend to share a perception of the addict as in some way the product of social, psychological, or physiological forces beyond his immediate control. The analyses suggest that to a greater or lesser degree the addict's behavior is determined, an explanation compatible with the liberal understanding of human deviance. As a consequence, America's punitive narcotics policies became a natural target for liberal thinkers. Eschewing notions of blameworthiness and guilt, liberals regarded the heroin user as a product of social deprivation, a victim of psychological disturbance and of physiological illness. Of course, most liberals did not propose that we tolerate the heroin user's aberrant personal behavior, which might well become a social threat. Rather, they advocated treatment-oriented social intervention and control, as a replacement for punishment.

The perception of the addict as victim of blocked opportunity was derived from the many sociological studies of heroin addiction produced during the last two decades. Like the problem of juvenile delinquency, addiction suggested to liberals the need to "finish the work of the New Deal." Discussions of heroin use published during the 1960s and early 1970s in journals of liberal opinion are consistent on this point. Thus, the *Nation* stated:

Society must come to realize that it is a cause—perhaps the major cause— of the affliction that it now observes with such fear and revulsion.

Dr. Joel Fort, writing in the *Saturday Review of Literature,* underscored the extent to which addiction was perceived as a signifier of social distress by referring to heroin use as a "barometer" of society's affliction with "poverty, segregation, slums, psychological immaturity, ignorance and misery."

Typically, those accepting this point of view called for the full range of social programs to combat the "root causes" of deviancy—programs designed, within a liberal capitalist framework, to attack poverty and chronic unemployment. The *Nation* asked:

Why . . . doesn't President Nixon devote more resources to the elimination of the social and economic problems which permit large scale drug abuse to take root?

Supporting such programs was the same alliance of groups that provided the social basis of welfare liberalism—the trade unions, liberal intellectuals, and, with increasing force, the black and Hispanics of the American ghettos.

The psychopathological theories of addiction, like all such theories of proscribed behavior, explained the behavior of the heroin user in terms of forces beyond his rational control—and therefore beyond the possible influence of the threat of the criminal sanction. The notion of addiction as a reflection of a psychological disease was exculpatory, for it denied the possibility of freely willed action. The victim of the disease of addiction was in need of "cure" rather than "punishment" precisely to restore his capacity for freely willed behavior.

Given liberalism's openness to deterministic theories of behavior, the arguments of those who put forth psychopathological theories of heroin use seemed particularly congenial. The influence of mental health professionals—psychiatrists, psychologists, and social workers (all of whom would gain considerable prestige and power from the adoption of the psychological-disease model of addiction)—on liberalism's perception of drug use cannot be overstated. Not only did they offer to explain the user's discordant behavior in terms which avoided notions of personal guilt, but they could also provide a technology of rehabilitation untainted by punishment. The disease concept of addiction provided liberals with a mechanism for achieving the corrective ends that more conservative law enforcement approaches had failed to attain. With addiction defined as a psychological disease, liberals could offer, instead of prison confinement, a full range of programs related to social welfare and public health projects, including outpatient clinics, hospital-based treatment, as well as other medical approaches to drug addiction.

The perception of addiction as a psychological disease or as the symptom of a psychological disorder was not, however, the most significant element in the liberal critique of prevailing social policy toward heroin use. Rather, it was the adoption of a position, by virtually all liberals, in favor of narcotic maintenance. This set liberal opinion at odds with the federal and local authorities, which had imposed a regime of abstinence and which regarded narcotic maintenance not as medical care but as a pandering to depravity.

Liberalism launched its attack on enforced abstinence by placing the responsibility for the harmful social consequences of heroin use upon an unreasonable prohibitionist stance. Enforced abstinence ignored or distorted the history of the American narcotics clinics of the 1920s and the comparative social studies of England. Instead, narcotic "drugs" should have a central role in the treatment of addiction. Proposals for drug treatment such as these can be attributed in part to the successful efforts of physicians and other scientists to "prove" that narcotic maintenance was no different than the prolonged chemotherapeutic treatment of those with other chronic ailments. In both instances, the goal must be the return of the patient to "normal productive functioning." Given its tendency to avoid concepts of blame and its commitment to the provision of medical care, free if need be, for those who were "sick," liberalism found the arguments for maintenance attractive. The addict could be relieved of responsibility for his drug-seeking behavior, and the costs to society of addiction-related crime could be eliminated by the legal distribution of narcotic drugs.

Throughout the 1960s, liberal reform efforts, supported by a wide range of professional and social groups, attacked the authority of the law enforcement model of addiction. What emerged from these efforts was a model for the treatment of the heroin addict that was incompatible with traditional law enforcement practices. Now, the addict was viewed and treated as a person in need of therapeutic social intervention *and* as a criminal subject to the full force of the criminal sanction. The coexistence of rehabilitative and punitive orientations was at the basis of the confused social practice regarding heroin users in the late 1960s and early 1970s.

Impact upon the Criminal Sanction. The liberal conception of the problem of addiction had a significant impact upon views of the utility and function of criminal law. This is clear from a reading of law reviews published between 1960 and 1973. Many professionals seriously reconsidered the basic premises of criminal law as they related to problems of social intervention with regard to heroin users.

As early as 1960, many recognized that the criminal law had failed to stop the flow of narcotics into the United States and to stop the addict from seeking those drugs. In addressing this issue, Donald J. Cantor turned to a physiological explanation of the addict's behavior:

The addict is like an insane man in that his craving deprives him of any *rational capacity* and leaves him impervious to the threats of *deterrent* legislation.

Since the addict could not weigh the consequences of his own behavior, application of the criminal sanction could not be justified on utilitarian grounds. Criminal law's only function under such circumstances was retribution, a concept anathema to liberal jurisprudence.

The landmark Supreme Court decision of *Robinson* v. *California,* in which it was held that an addict could not be punished for the *status* of addiction—which was defined as an illness—stimulated much controversy in legal reviews across the nation. The extent to which the notion of the "sick" addict had taken root among legal writers is reflected in many of the comments at that time. Typical of these is a statement that appeared in the *Texas Law Review:*

The impact of the decision should be to direct the states toward both a more effective and humanitarian treatment of drug addiction and to serve as a general warning that *no state may constitutionally ignore the findings of medical science in the construction of its criminal law.*

The most problematical issue raised by *Robinson*—and the issue which engaged the legal commentators—concerned the Court's distinction between the "status" of addiction (which could not be punished) and the "acts" of addiction (which might be subject to the criminal sanction). Those who addressed the inadequacy of the Court's ruling generally held that the logic of *Robinson* required that those acts that were "symptomatic of the disease" could no more be subject to criminal sanction than the disease itself. If a person could not be imprisoned for having a common cold, in the Court's analogy, then certainly imprisonment for sneezing was not permissible. If one could not be imprisoned for *being* an addict—for the uncontrollable *craving* for opiates which was part of that status—how could one be imprisoned for the possession of narcotics? Clearly, if one accepted the definition of addiction as a disease, then the criminal sanction for the acts of addiction could not be justified either on moral or theoretical grounds.

Addiction was thus an instance of the general problem of "diminished responsibility." Between the mid-1960s and 1973 the discussion of that issue took two forms. A number of commentators sought to include it in the more general category of mental illness and insanity—thus, addiction was a symptom of mental illness and the acts of addiction were symptomatic of that underlying psychopathology. One commentator stated:

Because narcotics addiction in most cases is symptomatic of an underlying mental illness and because the compulsion of narcotics addiction eventually subjugates all aspects of the addict's life to the goal of obtaining a steady supply of drugs, a "new" test of criminal responsibility for the drug addict would not appear to be a radical departure from the traditional insanity defense.

Others suggested that since the link between underlying psychopathology and addiction was not always easy to substantiate, a stronger argument could be made by establishing a direct relationship between the "disease of addiction" and the inability to control proscribed behavior—regardless of factors antecedent to the onset of physiological dependency. The argument, which was implicit in some earlier discussions, took on explicit form after the mid-1960s. In 1967, the *Harvard Civil Rights–Civil Liberties Law Review* suggested that an argument founded on the "duress" caused by the physiological disease of addiction could be the basis for defending an addict charged with the possession of heroin. Duress would serve as an exculpatory factor in criminal prosecutions.

That argument was advanced in the early 1970s by the United States Circuit Court in Washington, D.C., which suggested the plausibility of a defense based on "pharmacological duress." The fullest discussion of the "duress" defense appeared in 1973 with the publication of Richard M. Goldstein's "The Doctrine of Pharmacological Duress: A Critical Analysis." Reviewing related decisions by the district courts of appeal, he stated:

If the compulsion is sufficiently great, the addict should be exonerated regardless of the presence of any underlying disease or disorder ... [because] ... the influence of a physical dependence, and the cognitive fear of withdrawal and a need to prevent it, produces a compulsion to use and possess narcotics which *overwhelms the exercise of free will*. The commission of such offenses is merely an involuntary submission to the compulsion.

Because of the physiological-chemical basis of this argument, all implications of moral failure, weakness, blameworthiness, and, hence, guilt could be avoided. In its narrowest form, "pharmacological duress" was invoked as an argument with regard to the "paraphernalia" of addiction. Some commentators, however, were willing to extend the doctrine to property crimes committed to obtain narcotics on the black market.

The extensive support, in the early 1970s, for the doctrine of pharmacological duress—and its most extended interpretations—is ironic. After the last narcotics maintenance clinics closed in the 1920s, opiate users were subject to the ruthless enforcement of abstinence. With only a few stalwart reformers supporting the concept of maintenance, the suggestion that addicts might be able to claim their addiction as an exculpatory factor in a criminal defense could scarcely have been seriously considered. It was only after the successful pioneering efforts of Dole-Nyswander and the widespread acceptance of their approach to narcotic maintenance that the doctrine of pharmacological duress received thoughtful and substantial support. Yet at the same time the doctrine lost its critical force. By 1973, virtually any heroin addict in the United States could gain admittance to a methadone program in a matter of days. No longer could the defense argue that the state had coerced the addict into illicit activity by its unreasonable deprivation of access to narcotics.

THE ROCKEFELLER PROGRAM

Given this context, the liberal response to Rockefeller's drug law proposals in 1973 becomes clearer. Liberals had argued that "treatment" was more appropriate than prohibitionist policies as a social response to the problem of addiction and addiction-related property crime. By 1973, the liberal program had been actualized. Yet the demand for treatment by narcotics users indicated that many "sick" addicts were uninterested in therapeutic intervention. At this point, calls for more treatment seemed hollow. Liberalism had attained its ends and had exhausted its capacity to counter the conservatives "law and order" policies. The inadequacy of the liberal position in New York State in 1973 was stunning.

During the debate regarding the Rockefeller proposals, and in subsequent years as well, some liberals argued that the only position consistent with the needs of social defense and the rejection of the notion of culpability involved large-scale civil commitment of drug users into therapeutic settings. Such an approach recognized that voluntary treatment had not proved adequate but rejected the premises of the effort to recriminalize addiction. Widespread civil commitment represented the substitution of the state's "rational judgment" for the addict's flawed capacity to choose in his own behalf—the addict remained, in liberal terms, the victim of a disease. However, support for compulsory treatment, in institutional settings if need be, involved a self-deception of significant proportions. A decade of investigations into the course of treatment in closed settings indicated that confinement in therapeutic settings differed only marginally from incarceration in penal institutions.

Some liberals, however, opposed "therapeutic" incarceration as an assault on individual freedom. They viewed the use of drugs, including narcotics, as at most a tragic rejection of convention posing no palpable threat to the social order. The only policy option acceptable to this group was one founded upon libertarian principles. They argued that both the conservatives' penal proposals and the thinly veiled therapeutic proposals of liberals who favored compulsory treatment were logically linked to the effort to deny adults, in the name of the state's superior reason, the right to make fundamental life choices, even foolish ones. Heroin use should be tolerated; each adult should be permitted to purchase narcotics under conditions of control not very different from those relating to alcoholic beverages. In proposing such a course—in substituting an individualistic perspective for the social understanding of human behavior so characteristic of contemporary liberal thought— the libertarians were suggesting that conduct, which formerly had served as the basis for a critique of the prevailing order, be integrated into the social fabric. Clearly, libertarian tolerance may serve a profoundly conservative ideological function.

For those liberals who found in neither option an acceptable solution to the problem of drug use and addiction, the characteristic response in recent years has been a turning away from the issue. It is remarkable, given the salience of the problem of drug abuse in the 1960s and 1970s, that the issue has vanished as a subject of serious discussion in the journals of liberal opinion. The problem continues, however, as a potent symbol of liberalism's failure in treating the full range of socioeconomic problems. Indeed, liberalism's silence is but the other side of the periodic efforts by avowedly conservative political forces to rely upon repression in dealing with crises of the social order.

James C. Weissman

DRUG CONTROL PRINCIPLES
Instrumentalism and Symbolism

Efforts aimed at control of drug use and availability proceed on the basis of certain principles regarding the rationale and potential effectiveness of such efforts. Applying the analytic framework developed by Gusfield in his classic study of Prohibition, the principles can be distinguished according to their association with "instrumental" and "symbolic" functions of the law. The symbolic function pertains to the designation by the political majority of norms determined to be socially desirable. The instrumental function is the dimension of the law intended to effectuate the articulated action goal of the law (e.g., prevention of drug use and availability).

The instrumental vs. symbolic framework is useful in evaluating the operative principles of drug control measures. The enactment of drug use and availability strictures is a societal attempt to fulfill both functions. Instrumentally, control sanctions are designed to prevent drug use and symbolically, the sanctions condemn drug use behavior.

Five major instrumental principles are discernible. The threshold instrumental principle concerns the ultimate aim of drug control efforts. Traditionally, in American society, the announced goal has been the total elimination of non-medical drug use. Superordination of this goal has been maintained until very recently.

Evidence of the dominance of this principle is obtained by examination of government expressions of drug control policy. Enactment of the Drug Abuse Office and Treatment Act of 1972 mandated publication of an annual catalogue of federal policy. These reports have been issued as the *Federal Strategy for Drug Abuse and Drug Traffic Prevention* (hereinafter *Federal Strategy*). Assessment of the *Federal Strategy* reports

104

and other related government documents illustrates the evolving government position in regard to the ultimate aim of drug control policy.

Federal Strategy (1973) characterized the incidence of drug use as directly proportionate to the availability of drugs and affirmed government policy as restriction of drug use to medical and scientific purposes. The succeeding report, *Federal Strategy* (1974), went even further calling for complete abolition of trafficking in heroin.

This doctrine was advanced despite thorough condemnation of the position by the prestigious National Commission on Marihuana and Drug Abuse. In its final report, *Drug Use in America: Problem in Perspective,* the National Commission advocated a policy calculus based on the relative social cost of the various substances to be controlled, the costs of the controls themselves and the importance of the availability decision as a symbol of control. The National Commission stressed the companion concepts of variability in the levels of harm associated with differing psychoactive drugs and distinguishability in drug consumption styles creating variable personal and social risk elements. *Drug Use in America* asserted that eradication of drug use is unfeasible and public policy goals must be readjusted to achieve the more socially productive objective of minimizing harm associated with drug use and availability.

In 1975 at the request of the President, the Domestic Council Drug Abuse Task Force prepared the *White Paper on Drug Abuse.* The *White Paper* was intended to serve as a blueprint for future drug abuse policies. Previous federal policies were critically reviewed and a fairly dramatic alteration of policy objectives was recommended. With regard to control of drug use and availability, the *White Paper* declared:

Unfortunately, total elimination of illicit drug traffic is impossible.... Sufficient resources are not available to eliminate all illicit drug traffic; nor would a free society tolerate the encroachment on civil liberties which such a policy would require. The realistic goal of supply reduction efforts, then, is to obtain and disrupt the distribution system, and hopefully to reduce the quantity of drugs available for illicit use.

The *White Paper* announced new drug abuse policy themes. Recognition of differential medical and social risk variables was achieved. Priority in both treatment and enforcement efforts was reserved for the highest risk drugs and treatment availability was targeted for the most compulsive users of those drugs. Supply reduction programs were designed to make drugs difficult to obtain, expensive and risky to possess, sell or consume. The basic assumption of supply reduction efforts became "that if taking drugs is hazardous, inconvenient and expensive, fewer people will experiment with drugs, fewer who do experiment will advance to chronic intensive use of drugs and more of those who currently use drugs will abandon their use."

Essentially, the *White Paper* adopted the approach advocated by government consultant Mark Moore. Moore labels his paradigm the "inconvenience model"; he uses the phrase effective price of heroin as an index for all things that make heroin difficult, inconvenient, risky or otherwise "costly" for individuals to consume. Moore suggests that with respect to heroin, enforcement policy should be designed to create two different effective prices—a very high, effective price for experimental users and a moderate, effective price for current users. The "inconvenience model" is based on Moore's interpretation of heroin use experiences on the East Coast (1972-1973 decline), among Vietnam veterans, in post-World War II Chicago and among physician addicts.

Embracement of this revised policy approach represents acknowledgment of a vast body of accumulated scientific evidence concerning the nature of drug use patterns and drug distribution networks. The detailed studies of Hunt and Chambers regarding the spread of heroin use and substitution of other drugs in the absence of heroin availability, for example, are given partial credence. The unitary prohibitionist policy of drug control is eschewed for a more flexible and realistic control system aimed at less unobtainable outcomes.

The *White Paper* themes were accepted by the Ford Administration and appeared as official doctrine in *Federal Strategy* (1976). In its first major pronouncement on the subject, the Carter Administration has espoused similar stratagems. The President's Message on Drug Abuse of 2 August 1977 supported the altered assumptions regarding the mission of drug abuse control. Summarizing his views, President Carter declared that "no government can completely protect its citizens from all harm— not by legislation or by regulation, or by medicine, or by advice . . . but the harm caused by drug abuse can be reduced."

Thus the revised policy, still in its embryonic stages, proposes containment of use and development of supply reduction resources in accordance with specific minimization of social cost objectives. The greatest disruption of the most costly distribution systems has become the articulated goal of federal drug control efforts.

Skeptics regard the change in announced policy goals as simply rhetoric. Critics of government policy predict that in terms of actual program activities, the impact will be negligible. To be sure, dramatic changes have not yet occurred, but compliance with the new dogma will have to be monitored in the context of years, not months. In any event, the rhetoric has changed and previous eliminationist doctrine has been formally replaced with reductionist language.

A second instrumental principle involves another element of the drug control equation. As drug enforcement becomes effective, drug prices rise (application of the rule of supply and demand). Rising prices create a dilemma for drug users, particularly for compulsive users of heroin whose demand remains constant and who engage in risky behavior to acquire funds for the purchase of drugs. If treatment is made readily available in community settings, it is conjectured that the drug users will resolve the dilemma by volunteering for treatment. At a minimum, this will temporarily reduce illicit drug use and drug-related crime in the community and it may achieve long-term reductions if treatment is successful in achieving rehabilitation.

This paradigm has been an integral element of the drug control policy of the 1970s. In 1971 there were no less than 50,000 persons enrolled in drug abuse treatment. By 1977 after an investment of over a billion dollars in federal funds alone, estimates of enrollees neared 300,000. The Drug Abuse Office and Treatment Act of 1972 catalyzed the process and it has remained an axiom of national policy.

A specific federal diversionary program, Treatment Alternatives to Street Crime (TASC), has been designed to facilitate this referral to treatment objective. Communities instituting federally-funded TASC projects are able to identify criminal addicts and efficiently direct them into treatment programs. Over thirty million dollars has been invested in TASC and the sixty projects have processed approximately 38,000 drug abusers.

Public support for this feature of the overall control strategy is generally favorable. Elected officials and community leaders view this mechanism as a humane and effective means of reducing the costs of drug abuse. There is even some hard evidence validating this perception. Studies of Washington, D.C., and San Antonio, Texas correlate increased enforcement efforts, drug prices and treatment enrollments, but methodological limitations restrict the level of confidence attributable to those findings.

Civil libertarians have criticized not the substance of the principle, but the procedures for safeguarding rights of drug users channeled into diversion programs. Few critics have questioned the fundamental appropriateness of this dimension of the control strategy. The National Commission on Marihuana and Drug Abuse did carefully consider the issue and sanctioned its propriety after raising considerable doubt. This is in contrast to the conclusion of the Canadian Le Dain Commission of Inquiry into the Non-Medical Use of Drugs; the Le Dain report concluded that the criminal coercion model deters treatment candidates risking recognition as illicit drug users and serves as an impediment to reduction of drug use.

The treatment linkage serves as a fundamental principle of American drug control policy. Crime and drug use abatement objectives are advanced through the simultaneous application of supply and demand reduction forces. This strategy joins social protection and humanitarian values.

Reduction of social cost is a third principle of drug control. As with any social policy, the populace favors that set of policy objectives which offers the maximum social cost savings (i.e., highest social benefits at the lowest social costs). The principle is a fundamental proposition beyond reasonable dispute. Application of the principle, however, is a difficult task. Social costs and benefits are largely qualitative and value-laden. What price should society pay for reduced drug use and availability? Is a 10 percent decrease in drug use incidence worth a 20 percent increase in law enforcement costs accompanied by significantly impaired civil liberties? Weighing of the social costs and benefits is a critical component in the determination of national drug control policy despite the formidable measurement problems inherent in the process.

The *Federal Strategy* (1975) attempted to develop a baseline of the social costs of drug abuse. Analyzing the current system of drug control, the report projected annual social costs of ten billion dollars. A recent National Institute on Drug Abuse report refined that measurement methodology and projected the annual costs as between 8.4 and 12.1 billion dollars. Actually both studies measure not the costs of drug abuse, but the costs of controlling drug abuse under the existing framework. Negative costs of current policies (e.g., the expenses involved in arresting hundreds of thousands of user-possessors annually) are erroneously conceived of as costs of the drug use phenomenon rather than as costs of reacting to that phenomenon. Costs of alternative policies are not considered.

The 1975 *White Paper on Drug Abuse* also examined costs of drug abuse. In contrast to the *Federal Strategy* report, negative costs of current policies were identified and analyzed. With respect to supply reduction efforts, the following costs were noted: money outlays for enforcement; side effects, such as arrest stigma, impure drugs/health hazards, creation of a black market, increases in associated crime rates; and the inability of the efforts to reduce casual use of licit drugs. Benefits balancing these costs are alluded to, as the task force summarily concluded that "the effort to control availability through supply reduction should remain a central element of our strategy."

Critics of national drug abuse policy have been more imaginative and generous in describing costs of the prevailing supply reduction policy. Glaser has noted the prominence of organized crime in drug distribution activities and the widespread presence of official corruption. Kaplan has added alienation of societal elements, effects on police morale and selective enforcement patterns. Zinberg and Robertson introduce further costs of diversion of scarce resources, erosion of the rule of law, invasion of privacy, reduction in personal freedom and police-citizen hostility. Hellman cites police perjury and official deception and betrayal.

These types of qualitative descriptions have dominated social costs analyses of drug control policies. Few analysts have attempted quantified comparisons of competing policies. The McGlothlin and Tabbush study, commissioned by the federal Bureau of Narcotics and Dangerous Drugs, undertook an investigation and quantification of policy alternatives. That study was of high scientific quality but limited its scope to comparison of traditional treatment modalities and a heroin maintenance regimen. Alternative supply reduction strategies were not examined.

Another exception is Grizzle who, in a series of Law Enforcement Assistance Administration funded reports, examined the social cost of policy options. Comparing various law enforcement strategies, Grizzle finds that the most cost-effective course is arresting the addict and confining him to the maximum term and the least cost-effective course is arresting the seller and treating him similarly. Comparing education, treatment and law enforcement approaches, Grizzle finds education to be the most cost-effective strategy and law enforcement to be the least cost-effective. In the latter study the criterion measure applied is "years of addiction prevented"; for an expenditure of 100,000 dollars, drug education will prevent 240 years of heroin addiction as compared to 47 years for the most effective enforcement strategy and 29 years for the most effective treatment strategy.

Grizzle's studies are limited to regional data and are subject to valid methodological criticism. The latter deficiency is universal with regard to the social cost studies. As McGlothlin and Tabbush note in prefacing their conclusions: ". . . the calculations obviously include a number of speculative assumptions. The major intent has been to provide a framework of *reasonable* internal consistency in order to examine the various approaches to addiction treatment and control" (emphasis added).

Clearly, social cost analyses are becoming an important factor in the development of drug control policy. Examinations of public policy should not displace that principle. The important caveat underscored at the outset must also be remembered, however. Many costs and benefits are simply not quantifiable. Value judgments and subjective assumptions will continue to influence the outcome of social cost analyses. Costs assessments will serve as a helpful tool but will not substitute for ideology and social judgment.

The next principle summarizes the direction of the previous principles. The fourth principle holds that economic models have become the consensus framework for assessing the value of drug control policies. Reliance on economic paradigms has become the prevailing practice of liberals and conservatives alike. Beginning with the 1970 Hudson Institute study *Economics of Heroin Distribution* authored by Moore, influential reports have utilized economic organization. Prominent studies conducted by Moore, Goldman, Grizzle, McGlothlin and Tabbush, Heller and Holahan have applied economic methodologies.

The significance of this fact relates to the degree of importance attached to these reports. The use of economic models in areas of social policy must proceed only with extreme caution. Social values are still the principal ingredient and economic analyses serve only as supporting data bases. Further, as intimated earlier, the threshold assumptions of the selected model may easily predetermine the outcome, and choice of the particular paradigm is to a large degree a philosophical rather than a scientific decision.

The previously mentioned social costs of drug abuse analysis in *Federal Strategy* provides an excellent example of the potential for tautology and abuse. The report aggregates the social cost of drug abuse as reflected by property losses attributable to drug abuse, health costs, criminal justice system costs, lost productivity costs and direct treatment costs. The total bill reaches ten billion dollars, an impressive mark. Policy-makers confronting this figure might be expected to react by allocating more drug abuse control dollars to ameliorate this tremendous social-economic loss.

In actuality, however, as noted earlier, the ten billion dollar figure represents not the social cost of drug abuse, but the social cost of controlling drug abuse in accordance with current policies. Not arresting a half million drug offenders per year would dramatically diminish the criminal justice system cost, for example. Similarly, according to a Drug Abuse Council, Inc. sponsored study of the relationship between heroin supply and urban crime, reduction of the vigor of drug enforcement would most likely diminish rather than increase the property loss attributable to drug abuse. Other examples of the tautology may be cited.

Of course, on the other hand, reduction of enforcement, prosecution and incarceration might magnify the social cost in the form of heightened drug use and increased costs associated with that fact (e.g., loss of productivity). The point to be emphasized by this discussion is the precariousness of reliance upon the seemingly scientific economic model.

Economic analysis is probative, powerful and precise, but the formulation of drug control policy remains a socio-political judgment.

The final instrumental principle concerns selection of the control mechanisms. Notwithstanding the uncompromising dogma of invested bureaucrats and opinionated academics, a fairly wide panorama of drug control strategies is available. Within each broad category of drug control programming (e.g, border interdiction), alternative devices may be selected. International cooperative control efforts, for instance, may stress bilateral agreements or multilateral pacts. Preemptive purchase of cultivating nations' crops competes with direct controls of crop production. Domestically, trafficking prevention resources may be directed at large-scale wholesalers or at street-level retailers. User-possessors may be ignored, strictly prosecuted and incarcerated or diverted to treatment programs. Civil remedies, such as the proposed Emergency Civil Drug Control Act, may also be creatively employed.

The variables pertinent to the selection of drug control sanctions are difficult to catalogue. In general, drug distribution networks have been resistant to traditional control devices. The consensual and commercial features of drug distribution have impeded regulatory efforts. The resiliency of the industry is beyond dispute; when Turkish-European trafficking routes were closed by enforcement agencies in 1972–1973, distribution entrepreneurs relocated their enterprises without a serious interruption in business.

Political, economic, social, moral and constitutional factors affect the choice of control tactics. Traditionally, American policy-makers have been conservative in their selection of techniques. Orthodox law enforcement methods have served as the primary weapon. Increasingly, however, American officials are contemplating experimenting with alternative strategies. The availability of innovative methods is being realized and the possibility exists that creative drug control sanctions may be applied.

With regard to drug control, the symbolic function of the law demonstrates an importance at least equal and arguably superior to the instrumental function. At times the symbolic functions are deceptive. Enactment of a drug control measure may appear, at first blush, to be aimed at restriction of drug usage and availability. Further inspection might reveal, however, a prevailing symbolic purpose (e.g., designation of a disliked behavior as blameworthy and deviant).

Scholars examining drug control history have unearthed numerous examples of symbolic influence. Racism has been a pervasive theme. Early efforts to control opium consumption were aimed at Chinese laborers who committed the sin of being more productive than their American counterparts. Opium smoking episodes were believed to cause Chinese men to engage in sexual intimacy with American women whose will was weakened by the lure of the opium den. As King has noted: "Spectacular raids on Chinatown 'dens' raised the specter of helpless America seduced and betrayed by inscrutable Orientals organized into 'tongs' and fronting for the Yellow Peril."

Between 1877-1911 eighteen states passed anti-narcotics laws, ten of the states being western states with high concentrations of Orientals. Although the defamation of opium was associated with the Chinaman, that defamation has far outlived its origin.

Cocaine has experienced a similar history fraught with racial overtones. It was believed that cocaine stimulated sexual excitation of southern Blacks leading to the rape of white women. Not only was cocaine hypothesized to cause Blacks to forget their prescribed bounds, but it was conjectured that the drug's extraordinary excitatory abilities would immunize the Black from the lethality of ordinary firearms, necessitating use of .38 caliber pistols in the South.

Similar deviancy myths linked marijuana use to Mexican-Americans and aberrant behavior. Bonnie and Whitebread have shown that by 1930 sixteen western states experiencing large increases in Mexican-American migration enacted anti-marijuana laws aimed at racial repression. Enactment of the Federal Marihuana Tax Act was intended to placate the Southwest and its fear of the alien Mexican-American custom.

The evidence is convincing that racial animosity was associated with each of the major drug control movements of the nineteenth and twentieth centuries. Blumberg comments that "In each instance the zenophobic fear of some threatening minority associated with the use of a particular drug precipitated the quotient of outrage necessary to justify legal intervention."

Racism, however, was only one ingredient in the symbolism formula. Fear of violence and the criminality of drug users was a significant influence. The infamous "Marihuana Crimes" reports of the Federal Bureau of Narcotics alerted Americans to the alleged criminogenic effects of cannabis. Reasons speculates that an impassioned national fear of the drug user, fear of the "immoral, vicious social leper," facilitated passage of drug control legislation.

Zinberg and Robertson adopt a more psychoanalytic approach. The drug laws, inter alia, permit American society to define evil. "We need evil in order to define good, and we love evil with a truly ambivalent love." The characterization of drug use as an evil furnishes non-users with a psychological defense protecting them from their ambivalent attraction to the forbidden pleasure.

Applying a social conflict frame of reference, Musto reaches a similar conclusion. Drug control is conceptualized as a vehicle for affirming social stratification. "Customary use of a certain drug came to symbolize the difference between that group and the rest of society; eliminating the drug might alleviate social disharmony and preserve old order." Kaplan expanded this thesis in exploring the rationale of the marijuana laws. Social conflict arose from polarity concerning lifestyle choices, radicalism, permissiveness, authority, intercultural conflict and generation gap.

Szasz utilizes a religious-moral analysis. The drug laws are characterized as a collective judgment against personal autonomy. Numerous commentators have stressed this finding, attributing moral indignation to the drug use regulators. Blumberg has labeled this phenomenon the "true believer" syndrome; "the true believer is confirmed in his certitude and sanctity of his beliefs and is ready to impose his doctrines on others for their own good." According to this paradigm the drug user became firmly characterized as a "degenerate, invariably dishonest, constantly seeking to debauch others, brutish, and absent any moral sense at all." Chein et al. traced this mood back to the nineteenth century anti-opium laws, opium smoking being identified with the opening of the far West where gambling, abandoning families and swindling were commonplace.

Fear that youth would be proselytized into drug use also explained the tenacity of drug control efforts. The image of the ubiquitous "pusher" maintained that American youth were in constant danger of indoctrination to the drug culture. Success in the efforts of the pusher would lead to immobilization of young people and destruction of the productivity ethic.

The second half of the twentieth century has witnessed an update in the drug control demonology and symbolism. Communism and the Mafia, unlikely allies, have been associated with drug trafficking. More prominently, social conflict theories have stressed the class strife inherent in the drug control process. The emergence of radical or critical criminology has trained a new cadre of behavioral scientists skilled in describing social conflict, and the extreme cultural conflict of the 1960s and early 1970s has provided rich material.

To be sure, there is also ample proof that the moral crusade has not ended. At the start of 1974 Senate hearings regarding marijuana control, Senator Eastland declared that, "I consider the hearings which are the subject of this record to be among the most significant ever held by the Senate Internal Security Subcommittee, or, for that matter, by any committee of Congress." The Eastland hearings were decidedly anti-marijuana and proponents of reduced control were not invited to testify. In an era of waning support for marijuana criminalization, a fiercely loyal adherent of the moral enterpreneur camp attempted to rally support for maintenance of the status quo.

Despite diminishing public support for rigid control of drug use and availability, public opinion remains anti-drug in nature. Only extremely moderate changes in drug laws are countenanced and old myths are still held in esteem. Recent public opinion polls reveal, for instance, that 58 percent of the adult American public still believe that "Marihuana users often commit crimes that they would not otherwise commit" and 89 percent favor retention of criminal penalties for the use of heroin. The cumulative evidence indicates unequivocally that symbolism continues as a potent and perhaps dominant influence in the modern force field of drug control politics.

Instrumentalism and symbolism coexist in a delicate and unstable balance. To date, drug control efforts have been largely evaluated in terms of symbolic effects. Maintenance of an anti-psychoactive drug norm has served as a central organizing principle of American drug control activities. Increasingly, however, policy-makers are beginning to change focus by questioning the instrumental effectiveness of drug control measures. Social cost and economic tools are gaining acceptance as valuable decision-making aids.

For the "true believers" instrumentalism is of no consequence. The moral entrepreneur is impervious to the disappointing realities of his lack of success in achieving the instrumental objective. For the rest of society, however, symbolism and fact must eventually join forces. Policy-makers are demonstrating an increased appreciation of this connection and the next decade should experience a heightened awareness of the importance of the instrumental effects of drug control.

Section 6

PENAL EFFECTS

The effectiveness of the prohibitionist approach to drug control has not been subjected to rigorous and satisfactory assessment. Evaluation efforts have been conducted on an ad hoc basis and usually have suffered from poor design and faulty execution. Of course, this negative report is not unique. Few examples of adequate social control evaluations exist. Design and execution defects flaw most reported undertakings, and many social control activities have escaped critical scrutiny altogether.

A constant peril intrinsic to penal policy assessment is the confounding effect of ideological bias. Evaluators are influenced by personal values, the expectations of their sponsors, and prevailing social dogma. Occasionally, research designs are conceived to validate a predetermined result favorable to the interests of the program proponents instead of being designed to serve the traditional function of truthseeking. Caution is therefore indicated in weighing the results of reported social policy evaluations.

The selected articles, representative of the more credible assessment efforts, offer different approaches to drug control policy evaluation. The McGlothlin et al. study capitalized on a naturalistic event, a particular drug trafficking interdiction project exercised by the Nixon administration. Geis, on the other hand, compares time-equivalent drug use patterns occurring in distinct cultural milieus.

Also probative to the issue of penal effects is the Weissman article appearing in section 3. He presents a detailed state-of-the-knowledge summary within the related topics of demand reduction, supply reduction, and penal effects.

William H. McGlothlin
Kay Jamison
Steven Rosenblatt

MARIJUANA AND
THE USE OF OTHER DRUGS

It is well established that the use of marijuana by young people is positively correlated with at least the experimental use of other drugs. The probability that an individual uses the strong hallucinogens such as LSD and other drugs rises sharply with increasing frequency of marijuana use. Such associations are not, of course, sufficient to establish causal relationships between the use of one drug and another. It seems quite likely that important sociological factors contribute to the progression from marijuana to more hazardous drugs. Goode has found that frequent marijuana users tend to limit their social life to persons in the illicit drug subculture and thus frequently have the opportunity of trying other drugs. Chronic marijuana intoxication may also contribute to the generally poor reality orientation manifested by many adolescent drug users. This, in turn, can lead to poor judgment concerning the use of the more dangerous drugs. On the other hand, it has been found that older users of marijuana, introduced to the drug about 20 years ago, contain a much higher than average proportion of heavy alcohol users, which suggests that personality and other pre-existing variables are also related to the use of multiple intoxicants.

An unexplored aspect of the interaction between the use of marijuana and other drugs is the effect of suppressing the marijuana market. A shortage of marijuana was reported during the summers of 1968 and 1969. The United States administration sought further to diminish the supply by means of Operation Intercept during the autumn of 1969. Some of the rumoured effects of the shortages were higher prices, the sale of poor grade marijuana grown in the United States and an increase in the use of other drugs as substitutes for marijuana. We have investigated the effects of these shortages during the summer of 1969.

In October 1969, during Operation Intercept, we surveyed 478 students from a university in Los Angeles, and 116 patients from the Los Angeles Free Clinic which specializes in treating drug users. The students were members of one graduate and two undergraduate psychology classes.

TABLE 5: Incidence of Drug Use for Student and Free Clinic Samples

Drug	Students		Free clinic	
	Male (N=245) Percent	Female (N=233) Percent	Male (N=44) Percent	Female (N=72) Percent
Tobacco (current)	29	21	68	57
Alcohol ($>$2 drinks/day)	6	1	24	9
History of heavy alcohol use*	20	5	43	31
Marijuana (1 or more times)	73	49	95	89
Daily	3	0	32	26
3–6 times/week	11	5	25	24
1–8 times/month	30	20	23	22
$<$1 time/month	29	23	16	17
Hashish (1 or more times)	53	35	90	89
Any non-medical use of:				
Sedatives	16	15	57	60
Stimulants	32	21	80	67
LSD	24	8	82	69
$\geqslant$5 times	13	1	54	48
Other strong hallucinogens	30	16	79	74
Opium, morphine or cocaine	14	3	65	41
$\geqslant$5 times	3	1	40	20
Heroin	3	0	37	24
$\geqslant$5 times	1	0	18	11
Methamphetamine (injected)	3	0	20	29

*Heavy alcohol use defined as five or more drinks during 3–4 h, two or more times per week for a minimum of 1 year.

Because we were primarily interested in the interaction between the use of marijuana and other drugs, we included a large (335 members) somewhat unorthodox class in human relations which we thought would contain a fairly high proportion of marijuana users. Thus the results are not representative of the incidence of drug use in the overall campus population. The mean age of the sample was 20.1 years, and it was 51 percent male, 91 percent white, 94 percent single, and had completed 13.6 mean years of school.

The patients were people attending the clinic on two successive nights. Their mean age was 20.9 years and they were 38 percent male, 97 percent white, 86 percent single, having completed 14.8 means years of school. Of these people 51 percent were in full or part-time employment, 28 percent were unemployed and 21 percent were students.

Data were collected by means of an anonymous, self-administered questionnaire requiring about 5 to 10 minutes for completion. Items were designed primarily to reveal the incidence and frequency of use of

TABLE 6: Drug Using Behaviour as a Function of Frequency of Marijuana Use: Student Sample

Behaviour Drug Use	Marijuana use by males 0-10 times >10 times			Marijuana use by females 0-10 times >10 times		
	(N=122) Percent	<1 x/ wk (N=61) Percent	≥1 x/ wk (N=62) Percent	(N=161) Percent	<1 x/ wk (N=44) Percent	≥1 x/ wk (N=28) Percent
Tobacco (current)	16	34	50	13	43	32
Alcohol (>2 drinks/day)	2	2	16	0	2	4
History of heavy alcohol use	13	20	34	3	5	11
LSD	2	17	72	0	17	39
Opium, morphine or cocaine	2	12	41	0	7	19
Heroin	1	2	10	0	0	0
Marijuana* Has had own supply	—	39	85	—	25	50
Prefers hashish to marijuana†	—	39	48	—	32	32
Experienced marijuana shortage	—	38	53	—	34	54
Substituted other drugs (inc. alcohol)	—	33	44	—	11	46

*These questions were only asked of those who had used marijuana more than ten times.
†Percentage of those having experience with both hashish and marijuana.

various drugs; whether those using marijuana had reduced their use during the previous 5 months as a consequence of its unavailability; whether the frequency of use of other drugs had increased as a result of the shortage of marijuana. We also compared the prices paid for marijuana during the spring, summer and autumn of 1969.

Students completed their questionnaires during a class and the response was virtually 100 percent. The study was simply described as a survey of patterns of drug use being conducted as a graduate student project. In the Free Clinic questionnaires were passed out in the waiting room with the approval of the administrators. Virtually everybody attending agreed to complete the form.

As with other surveys of this type, the validity of the results depends on the cooperation of the respondents. It might be argued that some answers would be biased so as to reflect unfavourably on the current drug laws, and our only safeguards against this were the usual pleas that the validity of the study depended on the accuracy of the answers, plus the fact that it was a student project rather than one conducted by the school

TABLE 7. Drug Using Behaviour as a Function of Frequency of Marijuana Use: Free Clinic Sample

Behaviour Drug Use	Marijuana use by males		Marijuana use by females	
	≤2x/wk* (N=12) Percent	≥3x/wk (N=25) Percent	≤2x/wk* (N=23) Percent	≥3x/wk (N=36) Percent
Tobacco (current)	58	72	57	61
Alcohol (>2 drinks/day)	50	12	14	6
History of heavy alcohol use	50	48	32	33
LSD	75	96	67	83
Opium, morphine or cocaine	30	90	43	51
Heroin	0	54	33	24
Marijuana				
Has had own supply	50	87	50	81
Prefers hashish to marijuana	60	57	43	64
Experienced marijuana shortage	50	72	35	47
Substituted other drugs (including alcohol)	42	64	17	44

*Does not include respondents who reported using marijuana less than ten times.

administration. In addition, there is the advantage of a virtually 100 percent response. (The difficulty of obtaining accurate self-report information on drug use has probably been overemphasized—most investigators find that people are remarkably candid in providing such data.)

Table 5 shows the percentage of students and patients who have used various drugs, and the current frequency of marijuana use. The incidence of use among the ninety-seven members of the second undergraduate class in introductory psychology was much lower than in the large, atypical class (for example, LSD or other strong hallucinogen, 10 percent; and opiates or cocaine, 0 percent). It is interesting that fewer students than patients used tobacco and alcohol.

Tables 6 and 7 show the incidence of other drug use as a function of frequency of marijuana use for the two samples. It was necessary to group the data differently for the student and Free Clinic samples because of the much higher frequency of marijuana use in the latter. The use of other drugs is strongly correlated with the frequency of marijuana use in the student group, and to a lesser extent in the sample of patients. For the latter group, there is a reversal in terms of alcohol use—frequent marijuana users report less use of alcohol; subsample sizes are relatively small, however.

Tables 6 and 7 also detail other behaviour related to marijuana use for people using it ten or more times. The information about supply gives the percentage of respondents who sometimes, or generally, have their own supply rather than depending on marijuana provided by others. The preference for hashish over marijuana is more common among patients

TABLE 8: Percentage of Respondents Experiencing Marijuana Shortage Who Substituted Other Drugs

Drug	Students		Free clinic	
	Male (N=56)	Female (N=30)	Male (N=24)	Female (N=25)
Hashish	52	37	54	44
Alcohol	55	23	50	48
Sedatives	9	10	29	24
Stimulants	11	7	21	16
LSD	16	7	50	48
Other strong hallucinogens	23	13	37	28
Opiates or cocaine	2	3	25	24

than students. Of those using marijuana ten or more times, 44 percent of the students and 51 percent of patients reported that their frequency of marijuana use was below normal at some time between May and October, 1969, as a consequence of the unavailability of marijuana. Of those reporting a shortage of marijuana, 76 percent of students and 84 percent of patients reported that they increased their consumption of one or more other drugs (including alcohol) because of the unavailability of marijuana.

Table 8 shows the drugs which were substituted. For the students, an increase in the consumption of other drugs was largely limited to hashish, alcohol and the strong hallucinogens. The patients had a similar preference, but a significant number also reported substituting sedatives, stimulants and opiates.

During the spring of 1969 the mean cost of marijuana per ounce reported by the respondents was $10.13. In October 1969, the mean reported price was $11.87 per ounce—an increase of 17 percent.

In countries where cannabis (marijuana) has been regulated by the Government, its relative popularity with respect to alcohol has been manipulated by varying the respective taxes. Similarly, suppression of opium availability in India resulted in increased use of cannabis. It is not surprising that reduced availability of marijuana in the United States results in the substitution of both licit (alcohol) and illicit intoxicants. The current marijuana epidemic is too new, and too much in a state of flux, to permit an assessment of the net consequences of reducing its availability solely in terms of the substitution of other drugs. The effective suppression of marijuana might well decrease the number of adolescents who start to use illicit drugs. On the other hand, the results of our survey indicate that there is a need to consider how social policies directed at controlling one drug affect behaviour with respect to competing intoxicants.

Gilbert Geis

ILLICIT USE OF CENTRAL NERVOUS SYSTEM STIMULANTS IN SWEDEN

It is generally agreed that the world's most serious problem in regard to heavy intravenous use of amphetamines and their congeners is found today in Sweden. This is a distinction that plagues authorities in a country which deservedly enjoys a reputation for deep concern for the financial and social wellbeing of all its citizens. Little, if any, real poverty exists in Sweden, and generous unemployment allowances, liberal sickness benefits, nearly free medical and hospital care, and a wide array of similar subsidies provide a comfortable cushion against the consequences of bad luck, poor judgment, and other kinds of untoward misfortune. It is almost as if (as Americans antagonistic to the Swedish welfare emphasis would like to believe) the drug users were japing at the "good life" established in this Scandinavian outpost.

The extraordinary use of CNS stimulant drugs in Sweden poses a number of issues for the social analyst. Two in particular will be addressed in this paper. The first asks why the drug problem is different in Sweden than it is in other countries with similar kinds of social structure. Both Sweden and the United States, for instance, are characterized by affluence, heavy industrialization, urbanization, and demographic pyramids skewed toward the youthful tiers. In the United States, the criminalized addict population preeminently uses heroin, which produces depressant effects contrasting sharply with the stimulation afforded by the CNS drugs preferred in Sweden. The choosing of pharmacological products with such discrepant impacts could be nothing more than a quirk of circumstances, a function of chance historical developments. Or it could be, as this paper suggests, that the nature of the different drug sequelae are functional in providing the kinds of relief sought from cultural imperatives that differ in the United States and Sweden.

There is a second interesting question. The illicit use of amphetamines and their congeners in Sweden had a close parallel with developments in Japan. Amphetamines were widely employed in Japan during the war as part of an effort to increase working capacity, reduce food intake, and otherwise to aid the military effort. Following the war, drug companies dumped large stocks of stimulants on the Japanese market, pushing them with the advertising slogan that they would lead to "elimination of drowsiness and repletion of spirit." The advertising appealed to young persons who had had experience with amphetamines in wartime and who now suffered from feelings of frustration, loss of confidence, and the terrible fears that accompanied the holocaust of the atomic bombing of Japan.

In the 1950s, amphetamine usage had reached what commentators are prone to call epidemic proportions. The Japanese government instituted measures largely of a repressive and penal (in contrast to a treatment and preventative) nature. These proved strikingly successful in controlling, indeed, in virtually eliminating illicit recourse to amphetamines. The victory of the law enforcement approach was so stunning, in fact, that social scientists and medical practitioners were left at the starting gate; as Hemmi notes: "[The police] success was so dramatic that we [the narcotic treatment experts] have not fully discussed how to confront this kind of social problem."

In the United States, the Japanese experience is generally written off out-of-hand as a function of a very different social ethos, and a matter of no particular relevance to American policy. The Japanese people are said to be characterized by a robot-like obedience to authority, and to be ethnically homogeneous residents of a geographically small, manageable national enclave, all matters which are said to have made the control of amphetamine abuse a rather easy task. Sweden, however, is marked by many of the same kinds of conditions said to be responsible for the success of the Japanese campaign. Our second question, then, will be: Is there something distinctive about the Japanese approach as compared to the Swedish approach that might appear to account for the countries' different histories in regard to what were similarly high levels of illicit amphetamine use?

DRUG USE PATTERNS IN SWEDEN

A portrait of the extent of illicit drug use in Sweden puts the matter of chronic amphetamine injection into better focus. Drug use studies in Sweden, recently reviewed in a government publication, have focused on four population cohorts: (1) 15-year-old school pupils; (2) 18-year-old males registering for military service; (3) university students; and (4) persons arrested. These are some of the findings:

(1) Nationwide, the number of 15-year-old pupils who at any time had used drugs (the Swedes capture this concept in a single word, *knarkat*) decreased sharply in 1975, the latest year for which figures were available. Girls' involvement, which consistently is slightly higher than that of boys, declined from 17 percent in 1971, the first year of the study, to 8 percent in 1975. For boys, the drop was from 14 to 7 percent. Virtually all of the use involved marijuana (about 66 percent for the girls, and 63 percent for the boys). During the month previous to the 1975 survey, only 2 percent of the 15-year-olds said they had used drugs. That figure had been 5 percent in 1971.

How does this compare to the situation in the United States? It needs noting that generating truly reliable information about drug use patterns, a serious enough problem for national studies, is inordinately complicated in cross-cultural work. For one thing, among many others, inventories are not apt to ask for the same information in the same manner from the same kinds of populations. Word nuances suffer in translation, and cultural forms frustrate accurate comparisons. University students in Sweden, for instance, tend to be somewhat older than their American equivalents, and American high school populations less selective because Swedish youths are apt to conclude their formal schooling at an earlier age.

We will, with these strictures in mind, make some broad-gauge attempts throughout to compare the Swedish data to American information. A 1972 survey of the National Commission on Marihuana and Drug Abuse, for example, found that 10 percent of American 14–15-year-olds had tried marijuana, a figure not markedly different from that for Sweden.

(2) Males registering for military service in Sweden—all 18-year-olds must do so—showed an "any use" drug figure of 16 percent in 1971. This rose to about 18 percent in 1973, but decreased to 15.5 percent in 1975. More than half of the usage involved marijuana. Within this group, 1.3 percent had at some time injected a drug, a figure that remained quite constant during the five-year period.

A comprehensive nationwide survey in the United States by John O'Donnell and several colleagues embracing males registering for military duty found that about 60 percent of the group similar in age to that of the Swedish cohort had used marijuana at some time, and 27 percent had tried stimulants. These figures are much higher than those for Sweden. In the total American draft-registrant group studied, which included 2,510 men from age 20 to age 30, about 50 persons reported having injected stimulants, a rate of 2.0 percent, compared to the 1.3 percent for the Swedish 18-year-olds. Given the much longer exposure period of the Americans, and their strikingly greater use of other drugs, the near comparability for stimulant injection emphasizes the particular concentration in Sweden on this pattern of use.

(3) The highest usage among older students in Sweden predictably was found in the Stockholm University group. About 30 percent had used cannabis, and about 5 percent had used CNS stimulants in tablet form. Intravenous use of CNS or other drugs was virtually non-existent in the college group. For Americans, all surveys from this period report much higher drug use for university students. The National Commission found a 67 percent any-time use of marijuana on the nation's campuses, and reported that slightly more than 4 percent of the college students had used heroin at least once, presumably by injecting it. Groves has reported for 1970–71 that 18 percent of American college students had used amphetamines, a figure very close to that noted by a Gallup Poll. The general avoidance of drugs by Swedish university students, given their considerable reputation for political radicalism, a common drug use concomitant, provides evidence of a strong association in Sweden between abstinence from drugs and high social standing and academic involvement.

(4) The proportion of persons arrested who are found to be supporting drug habits has risen consistently in Sweden. Bejerot reported that one-fifth of the males arrested in 1965 were drug abusers, and that this figure had climbed to one-fourth by 1966 and one-third in 1967. A police study of persons coming to the Central Jail in Stockholm during May and June 1976 showed that 94 percent had some experience with drugs, and that 61 percent had used a drug at the time of the episode for which they had been arrested. Sixty-two percent used drugs more than four times a week, and 91 percent of this group did so by intravenous means. Eighty-eight percent of the sample employed CNS stimulants; 9 percent used cannabis, and 7 percent morphine and heroin. This last figure, bearing on a rather newly-arrived phenomenon, is further exercising Swedish authorities. There are now estimated to be about 2,000 heroin users in Sweden, and in 1976 there were 18 deaths reported from heroin overdoses.

DRUGS IN POSTWAR SWEDEN

That the Swedes attend so closely to the number of drug users in the criminal population is testimony to the same kind of anomalous, Alice-in-Wonderland situation that prevails in the United States. In neither country is adequate attention paid to the fact that the escalating criminality by drug users probably testifies less to growing individual evil and more to the ineptness of prevailing public policy. To the extent that trade and possession of drugs is criminalized prices will rise (a Swedish stimulant drug habit probably costs more than $60 a day now) and crime will become a defined necessity.

Edwin M. Brecher has argued with some persuasiveness that the Swedes created their own drug problem by the near-hysterical official manner with which they responded to the first inklings of undue citizen recourse to amphetamines Brecher suggests that a calm and reasoned, low visibility approach to drug issues is apt to be more effective than overreaction in limiting excessive recourse to the drugs. This thesis is illustrated in his discussion of an American crackdown on stimulants in the early 1960s. "Thus," Brecher writes, "the delights of mainlining amphetamines, previously known primarily to heroin addicts, became a matter of common knowledge and general interest." The difficulty with this theme, however near it may approach accuracy, is, as we shall see, its inappropriateness for interpreting the drug situation in Japan.

Amphetamines were first introduced into Sweden in 1938. A year later, 15 years before similar action was taken in the United States, the drugs were placed under prescription. It is likely that the profound social and political concern in Sweden with alcoholism underlay this move: the Swedes had what they regarded as one almost intractable problem, and they very much wanted to avoid another. It is estimated that about 3 percent of the Swedish population was using amphetamines in 1942, though there were only 200 cases believed to involve "serious" abuse. As in Japan, an advertising campaign employing a catchy slogan— "Two pills are better than a week's vacation"—probably contributed to the drugs' growing popularity.

In the immediate postwar period, amphetamines began to be used regularly by musicians, artists, and members of Bohemian groups in Sweden. The government's response this time was to place amphetamines on the National Narcotics Drug List in 1944, further restricting their medical use. This move had some temporary palliative effect. The surges of use thereafter brought only more restrictive measures, culminating in the virtual outlawing of the drugs, though there was an interval, 1965 to 1967, when permission was granted to physicians to supply some amphetamine users with drugs, an experience which, most sources agree, proved to be "disastrous."

Phenmatrazine, under the trade name Preludin, was introduced in Sweden in 1959 as an anorexigent and became, in addition to methylphenidate (Ritalin), a drug of choice for Swedish users. These soon were placed on the proscribed list. The panic of officials over drug developments was reflected in 1972 legislation that increased the maximum penalty for drug offenses to 10 years' imprisonment. Few crimes in the Swedish penal code carry such a harsh penalty; the maximum sentence for robbery with aggravated violence, for instance, is ten years.

The 200 Swedish problem cases of 1944 have escalated today to an estimated 10,000 to 12,000 intravenous users of illicit stimulant drugs. About half live in Stockholm, and most of the remainder in the Malmo-Lund area in the south of the country. It is noteworthy that usage is almost totally confined to the indigenous population and does not appear in any significant measure among the almost half million persons (Sweden's population is about 8 million) from other nations. This suggests that amphetamines and their congeners have a special meaning and utility for Swedes.

STIMULANTS AND THE SWEDISH ETHOS

There are a number of ways to regard the interaction between specific kinds of drugs and the social climates in which they appear. Perhaps the simplest is to define illicit drug use as symptomatic, and to ignore the particular effects of the substances employed. Two Swedish writers, for instance, noting the increase in heroin use, offer the following observation:

What is new in the abuse picture today is the injection of heroin. There is a connotation to the word "heroin" that is misleading. It is important, for example, not to overemphasize the difference between heroin misuse and amphetamine misuse. The significant difference is between misuse and no misuse, not between heroin and amphetamines.

There is, of course, some truth in this observation, but so would there be truth, and obfuscation, in the suggestion that the most significant fact is not the difference between homicide and suicide but their similarity as death-dealing acts.

Considerable research evidence indicates that rational discrimination will be exercised in choosing among drugs. A double-blind study by

Lasagna and his colleagues indicated striking preference among a group of medical students for amphetamines over opiates. The morphine was judged to make the user "tired and grouchy," to be "unpleasant," and productive of "distress and irritation." Subjects echoed the complaint of one of their number who said that he did not have "enough motivation to concentrate and read anything difficult." A typical reaction to amphetamine dosage, to the contrary, was that of a student who observed that "suddenly my body felt light and I became very happy, indeed, exhilarated. This new state filled me with excitement and joy. A delightful drug." It must be stressed that the discrepant reactions to the two drugs were from *medical students,* achievers who expectedly would be impressed with a drug that heightened their involvement with bourgeois standards, and would find repugnant a substance that made performance more difficult.

That "the drug of choice appears to be syntonic with the abuser's characteristic modes of adaptation" is also argued by Milkman and Frosch. "Whereas the heroin addict reduces anxiety via repression and withdrawal," they note, "the amphetamine abuser utilized a variety of compensatory maneuvers to maintain a position of active confrontation with the environment." Milkman and Frosch also found the low self-esteem of the heroin user to be in striking contrast to the narcissistic self-esteem and abstract communication of the amphetamine abuser. Finally, Kramer and his associates offer the opinion that "a difference in drug of choice occurs in drug users, some preferring chemical assistance toward activity approach, others desiring chemical assistance to pursue solitude."

What reasons, then, might be suggested for the particular popularity of amphetamines in Sweden? There is, of course, antipathy to things Swedish in conservative American circles that delights in any indicia of difficulty, and reflexively charges this to "rampant socialism," and similar defined Swedish horrors. The amphetamine situation, however, can hardly be regarded as convincing evidence of "failure" of the Swedish political system, though it may well be regarded as an unfortunate consequence of this and the Swedish personality. It is a truism that many, if not all, perfectly decent things can produce some untoward consequences.

The results of heavy intravenous amphetamine intake for the user have been thoroughly reviewed by Grinspoon and Hedblom. The sequelae include inordinate bouts of activity, in which persons suppose (and sometimes correctly so) that they can accomplish tasks beyond their non-drug capacity. An addict will generally show enhanced self-confidence, and manifest behavior that includes stereotypic, repetitive acts (such as endlessly taking apart and putting together things), restlessness, reduced fatigue, and a sense of rapid passage of time. The amphetamine user generally feels supremely in control of events, in contrast, for instance, to the LSD user who conceives that things are happening to him.

It has been argued by Seymour Fiddle that drug users tend to caricature aspects of their cultural milieu. Life in Stockholm, for instance, is marked by what Fiddle calls the "urban go-go," a hectic pace when compared to existence elsewhere in the country. This is a matter often remarked upon by the young Swedes from Västeras interviewed by Källberg when they refer to the capital city. Amphetamine users not only reproduce this theme of perceived frenetic metropolitan existence, but exaggerate it.

More generally, Gösta Carlsson, in a review of anecdotal and experimental literature dealing with "the Swedish personality," notes that the major theme that permeates such material is a view of emotional coldness and distance, together with stress on achievement and work rather than the warmth of interpersonal relationships. There is, Carlsson observes, a recurring idea covered by expressions like "reserve," "detachment," "psychological distance" and "lack of spontaneity." These matters are epitomized in a news story concerning recent assaults by Swedes against Assyrian immigrants. The immigrants, the story noted, "enjoy street life and lounging in cafes, which many Swedes regard with disdain." Amphetamines appear to be useful in providing drug-induced states attuned to the cultural emphases that Carlsson and others portray.

The matter of sex and amphetamines is instructive. The American literature, carefully reviewed by Grinspoon and Hedblom, offers highly contradictory evidence about the erotic potentiation of amphetamines. But there does not seem to be similar uncertainty among Swedish participants in the illicit market. Rylander notes of this group that:

The injections cause strong sexual stimulation in most addicts. According to my experience, Preludin and other central stimulants taken in this way are the most powerful aphrodisiacs known. "The shot goes straight from the head to the scrotum," as one of my rather experienced addicts said, and another stated that sex stimulation is up to 50 percent the cause of abuse. The addict's term [for an injection] is a "fucking pump." After a fucking pump I always need a couple of girls at the same time," two criminals confessed to me.

Swedish sexual mores are, of course, a matter of considerable international titillation. This external commentary probably has produced many problems for Swedish sexuality. To begin with, the Swedes, as noted, are socially inhibited, and probably (though this is only my speculation) rather sexually shy, so that for them intercourse may be more of a technical and mechanical act than it is in emotional kinds of societies. There is comparatively little personal discussion among Swedes on intimate matters, and many have poor information about sexuality beyond facts that they learn in school and from international opinion concerning what they are supposed to be experiencing. Surveys of sexual behavior indicate that Swedish girls and women are not individually that much different from their American sisters, both in terms of moral codes and sexual activity and attitudes. But both they and the Swedish men presume that others of them are marching to a different erotic tune, and this can create a malaise that amphetamines are notably able to relieve, again in a rather exaggerated and caricatured way.

The use of amphetamines by Swedes, and the general absence of their abuse among the immigrant population in Sweden, indicates the cultural homogeneity between users and the remainder of the population. Users probably share cultural values and personality traits generally found in Sweden, but for various reasons find the imperatives too demanding for routine, drug-free performance. It would be instructive to conduct a study among Swedish amphetamine users, the general Swedish urban population, and both heroin and amphetamine users in the United States as well as an American urban sample. I believe it would show considerable cross-cultural similarity among the Swedish urban group and amphetamine users both in the U.S. and Sweden, and distinctiveness between this cadre and the heroin addicts and the American urban group.

AMPHETAMINES IN JAPAN

The manner in which widespread amphetamine abuse was brought under control in Japan after the second World War is a dramatic case study in social constraint that, surprisingly, has received only cursory examination abroad. Brecher rather disbelieves it, noting that he would, at least, want much more information before he would concede that a law enforcement campaign really had managed to dry up an amphetamine epidemic. Reginald Smart suggests that the Japanese effort contained an amalgam of thrusts—punitive, rehabilitative, and educational—and that it is impossible therefore to generalize usefully from the experience. This observation, however, seems off-target, since the efforts of most nations include stress on education and rehabilitation. What was different about Japan, and what apparently made the campaign bear fruit, was the stern and immutable repressive police and criminal justice push against the use of the drugs. Other elements may have served as catalysts, including the remarkably effective system of policing in Japan.

Several similarities between Sweden and Japan were noted earlier, including their ethnically homogeneous populations. Bultena adds that "the thoroughness and speed of the transformation of [Sweden's] economy is perhaps paralleled only by Japan in modern times." Similarly, Richard Tomasson points out that, like the Japanese but unlike Americans, Swedes "believe in doing things according to rules and regulations." Then why did the Japanese effort to control amphetamine usage work while Swedish efforts seem to have had so little success?

Any definitive answer would require considerably more · field work in both nations, but two explanations offer suggestive starting points. First, it appears that the Japanese did not involve the amphetamine issue in a broader context of drug and alcohol usage and/or civil liberties questions. They attacked it as a separate, distinct matter, and concentrated exclusive attention upon this single issue, avoiding any tendency to embrace within the campaign a broader network of comparable matters. In Sweden, the tying of amphetamines into the long-enduring national debate regarding alcohol abuse made the analogous issue of amphetamine usage seem as no more than an added footnote in what for many persons had become a tiresome discussion.

The second matter, though part of the first, has distinctive implications. The Japanese, their literature on the subject indicates, had strong moral feelings about amphetamine abuse. They saw it as a wrong, not as an arguable, negotiable issue that might reasonably be the subject of national controversy concentrated on more fundamental issues, such as punishment versus rehabilitation. Part of this condition may have been a function of the speed with which the Japanese law enforcement program was launched and its quick success. The Swedes, on the other hand, were and still are only half-hearted in their effort to eliminate amphetamine abuse. Their campaign has been hindered (it is, of course, arguable whether this is for better or for worse) by the absence of a deep-seated belief that the defined "evil" was necessarily as bad as some insisted, and by a commitment in some circles to wider bounds of freedom for the individual.

These ideas remain speculative, as do those about the explanation for the specific focus on amphetamines as drugs of abuse in Sweden. It is suggested, though, that the issues stand among the most important, and the most understudied, in the realm of social inquiry about the illicit use of drugs.

Section 7

CORRECTIONAL POLICIES

As the Weissman paper in this section reveals, the direction of American correctional policy has experienced a recent upheaval. Previous articles of faith, such as the liberal rehabilitative ethic, are no longer afforded dogmatic approval. Traditional rehabilitative practices, including the flexible indeterminate sentence, are being rejected by lawmakers across the nation.

This policy shift represents anathema to designers of modern drug control efforts. As earlier articles have demonstrated, national policy has sought to establish a balance of drug demand and drug supply reduction activities. An essential ingredient to that calculus has been the availability of rehabilitative sentencing options and correctional programs for drug offenders. National drug control strategy has emphasized widespread utilization of rehabilitative alternatives.

The articles of this section address various dimensions of the application of that philosophy. The initial article reviews past strategies aimed at rehabilitative outcomes and describes the emergence of anti-rehabilitationism and its potential effects upon drug offender programs. Newman's brief article presents a forceful argument in opposition to correctional drug treatment within institutional settings. Finally, the second Weissman article explores drug offender diversion, the most popular drug rehabilitative program of the past decade.

James C. Weissman

CONSIDERATIONS IN SENTENCING THE DRUG OFFENDER

* * * * * * * * * *

GOALS OF 1960s CRIMINAL LAW

The fundamental tenet of the 1960s liberal-reform crime control movement was the rehabilitative ideal, i.e., the notion that criminality could be most effectively and humanely reduced by the application of medical-model treatment concepts. Today, that rehabilitative ideal is being reevaluated.

A review of the current criminological literature indicates that rehabilitation, as an organizing principle of sentencing and correctional policy, is falling into empirical and theoretical disfavor. With regard to the empirical criticism, the writings of the controversial Robert Martinson have persuasively questioned the efficacy of the treatment model. Martinson's acrimonious attacks notwithstanding, the New Yorker's research findings simply reinforce what criminologists and practitioners have known for years; rehabilitative practices are capable of producing only weak effects in terms of reducing offender recidivism.

Doctrinal examination of the rehabilitative ideal is also attracting weighty attention. Anti-rehabilitation disquisitions are appearing with frequency in the criminological and legal literature. The prominent names of Norval Morris, Andrew Von Hirsch, Richard McGee, Lawrence Pierce, M. Kay Harris, David Fogel, and Leslie Wilkins are being recognized as proponents of anti-rehabilitation correctional policies.

Before defaming these distinguished scholars, an explanation of anti-rehabilitationism is in order. Anti-rehabilitationism, as used herein, is not political conservatism, disregard of offender's human rights, or advocacy of a strict law enforcement approach to crime control. Rather, it is the systematic and reasoned investigation of the predominance of rehabilitation as the focal point of sentencing and correctional philosophy.

The tools of anti-rehabilitationism are historical analysis, assessment of empirical findings, and clarification of prevailing societal values. Already the anti-rehabilitationist writers are producing tangible results, offering alternative penal philosophies emphasizing utilitarian notions and goals other than rehabilitation. A more accurate, descriptive label for this movement would be correctional revisionism, which denotes the positive orientation of its adherents.

Although each of the correctional revisionists' products merit individual examination, space limitations require that only a representative output be considered. Chosen for analysis is *Doing Justice: The Choice of Punishments,* the report of the Committee for the Study of Incarceration, authored by Andrew Von Hirsch. *Doing Justice* is an eloquent statement of the revisionist philosophy conveying the substance of the penal reforms associated with correctional revisionism.

The Committee for the Study of Incarceration proposes radical modification of sentencing and correctional policies, unequivocally rejecting the rehabilitative ideal and advocating a penal philosophy based on the notion of just desert. Sentencing goals of rehabilitation, general deterrence, and predictive restraint are considered in agonizing detail, but are expressly dismissed as appropriate penal objectives.

The report argues that although the criminal law is necessarily a prospective and utilitarian social control vehicle, the rationale for allocation of a specific sentence may be retrospective and non-utilitarian. Thus, *Doing Justice* urges adoption of a penal philosophy establishing the principle of assessment and punishment of past criminal conduct. Blame-worthiness deserves sanctioning, reasons the committee, which then recommends that the seriousness of the instant offense and the number and seriousness of the offender's prior convictions determine the type and length of punishment imposed. Presumptive sentences are prescribed for each gradation of seriousness of the charged offense, and adjustments are effected according to the prior offense factors.

Seriousness of the offense is determined by "the harm done (or risked) by the act and on the degree of the actor's culpability." Harm is defined as "the harm characteristically done or risked by an offense of that kind," and culpability is defined as "the degree to which the offender may justly be held to blame for the consequences of his act."

Doing Justice provides a methodology for arriving at the normative severity levels of inflictable punishments. Both the internal relativity and the absolute magnitude of the scale are considered. The Committee's recommendations regarding severity of the punishments unmistakably reflect the decarceration bias of its members. Institutional assignment is reserved for violators of only the most serious offenses, and alternatives to incarceration are enthusiastically recommended.

In sum, *Doing Justice* offers society a new model for application of the criminal law. Its organizing principle, labeled by its author as commensurate desert, is a radical departure from prevailing American penal philosophy. The model sentencing philosophies which have previously dominated correctional policy are expressly disavowed. The sacred penal goals of rehabilitation, predictive restraint, and individual decision-making are abandoned.

In terms of real-world implementation, the future of commensurate desert and the correctional revisionism philosophy is understandably uncertain. No system accepts major change easily and the criminal justice system is notoriously resistant. Nevertheless, this writer accepts the inevitability of eventual acceptance of the revisionist penal philosophy. The task, therefore, is fashioning of drug offender sanctioning guidelines congruent with the tenets of correctional revisionism.

At first blush, this would seem to be an eminently resistable and inappropriate assignment. According to the conventional wisdom, drug offenders ought to be treated and therapized, not punished. And it has only been within the past decade that the politicians have acknowledged this fact.

But all signs indicate that the devolution of the therapeutic ideal is approaching. To those of us committed to a humane social control policy for drug offenders, the responsibility is formulation of a coherent sentencing and correctional paradigm which incorporates the principles of correctional revisionism.

DRUG ABUSE CONTROL

Consideration of sentencing and correctional guidelines for drug offenders should not be undertaken without some mention of the major perspectives which have shaped American drug abuse control policy. A glance at those events is essential to an understanding of current and proposed stratagems.

Examination of the historical dimensions of United States drug control policy has become a familiar topic to criminologists with analyses of the origins and current state of American drug abuse policy frequently appearing in criminological journals (e.g., the past two volumes of *Crime and Delinquency* reveal five articles pertaining to drug abuse, four of which contain analyses of drug control policy). For purposes of this paper, therefore, only a summary evaluation is presented, and the more ambitious reader is referred to detailed historical investigations, such as those of Rufus King and David Musto.

Most commentators would agree with the proposition that American drug control policy has passed through three distinguishable eras. The first era began in 1914, with the enactment of the Harrison Anti-Narcotic Law. The Harrison Act signified the permanent and significant incursion of the Federal government into the regulation of psychoactive drug consumption and distribution. The previous Federal policy of virtual nonregulation was dramatically recast into a policy of absolute repression or prohibition.

From 1914 to the 1950s, drug control remained relatively constant. The States adopted companion legislation to the Harrison Act demonstrating national acceptance of the prohibitory policy. Marijuana was added to both the Federal and State proscription lists, increasing the scope of psychoactive drug regulation. The only policy deviation of the era was Congressional authorization of the construction of two "narcotics farms" for rehabilitative and addiction research purposes.

The second era commenced with the "get tough" drug penalty legislation of the 1950s. Alarmed by evidence of increasing drug abuse during the post-World War II years, Congress extended the philosophy of existing legislative controls by drastically increasing prescribed penalties, particularly with respect to drug trafficking activities. At both Federal and State levels, lengthy mandatory minimum penalties became the exclusive sanction for drug offenders. Lawmakers explained these Draconian penalties as a conscious effort to effect a definitive and enduring suppression of the drug problem.

This middle policy era began to manifest signs of erosion during the 1960s. New criminal laws created to regulate "dangerous drugs" (i.e., hallucinogens, stimulants and depressants) were characterized by moderate penalty structures. In 1966, Congress passed the treatment-oriented Narcotic Addict Rehabilitation Act. The States experimented with addict civil commitment schemes, which were essentially quasi-rehabilitative social control models.

The current era was formally inaugurated by Richard Nixon who elected to confront the growing drug abuse problem with a coordinated and intensified Federal program. On both legislative and programmatic fronts, the Nixon administration sponsored exciting

developments in the "war on drug abuse." The Federal Controlled Substances Act replaced the former crazy-quilt of criminal drug law statutes,
and the Federal drug abuse bureaucracy was radically restructured.

At the Federal level, both demand-reduction activities (treatment,
rehabilitation, education, etc.) and supply-reduction activities (enforcement) received generous support. Budgets increased tenfold and more over
a several year period and the Federal government formulated an explicit
drug abuse prevention strategy. The Ford administration initiated efforts
to rekindle this intense and hopeful policy toward drug abuse, with
President Ford personally affirming his commitment by enthusiastically
endorsing the Domestic Council's *White Paper on Drug Abuse* and requesting increased drug program appropriations.

The states have not remained dormant during this period. Currently,
three discernible trends are developing among the state jurisdictions.
Most notable has been the decriminalization of marijuana possession.
In 1973, Oregon removed from its criminal code the conduct of possession of a small amount of marijuana for personal use. Nine other states
have already enacted variations of the Oregon law and more are certain
to follow.

Antithetical goals are being pursued by proponents of the creation
of a new round of "get tough" drug trafficking laws. Also in 1973, the
New York State Legislature, at the urging of then Governor Rockefeller,
adopted a stringent sentencing scheme for drug law violators. A handful
of other states have enacted similar legislation aimed more specifically
at drug trafficking conducts. Even Congress is considering a "get tough"
drug law, targeted towards high-level drug trafficking activities.

The final movement is less visible but promises to be a highly significant policy direction, consisting of interrelated efforts by Federal, State,
and local governments to establish "interface" between the operations
of the criminal justice and drug abuse rehabilitation systems. The
prototype interface or linkages strategy is the Federally-sponsored and
locally-administered Treatment Alternatives to Street Crime (TASC)
program. Ideologically neutral and oriented towards administrative
efficiency, interface programming is gaining solid political support.

* * * * * * * * * * *

Thus, the future of drug abuse control is clearly uncharted. Contradictory statutory and administrative developments are proliferating.
Jurisdictions are experimenting with new legislative programs based
on conflicting and poorly defined objectives. One important political
fact is clear nonetheless, drug abuse, as a public policy concern, has

attained a position of political prominence. The Federal drug abuse program is now considered a major domestic subject, and State and local leaders are devoting significant attention to drug abuse issues.

SANCTIONING GUIDELINES

Since development of an enlightened model for sanctioning of drug offenders is the primary objective of this paper, a broad definition of drug offender, the drug-dependent offender charged with any criminal violation and the defendant charged with any drug law crime is adopted. In this section, a sanctioning model is proposed from which sentencing and correctional guidelines may be inferred. This model offers a methodology enabling matching of individual offenders and appropriate dispositional alternatives.

The sanctioning paradigm operates under a triad of threshold assumptions implied or expressed earlier. First, the principle of commensurate desert, as defined by the Committee for Study of Incarceration and other correctional revisionists, is afforded doctrinal primacy. Decriminalization of the substantive drug offenses is accepted as a limited phenomenon, restricted to possession of marijuana for personal use. Finally, it is assumed that a degree of individualization remains a desirable commodity with regard to drug offender sanctioning, given the heterogeneity of the drug offender population.

The proposed sanctioning model employs a multivariate equational format. Selection of the appropriate sanction is based on an assessment of the identifiable harm associated with the proscribed conduct, the degree of the offender's drug use, and the severity of the alternative sanctioning options. The latter factor, the prescribable sanction, is the dependent variable and receives initial consideration.

Doing Justice defines punishment as "the infliction of consequences normally considered unpleasant" and recognizes a continuum of punishment reflecting severity of the sanction. Accordingly, a graduated sanctioning structure is proposed featuring progressively more restrictive dispositional alternatives.

The least drastic sanction is the *monetary fine* which affects only the offender's financial resources. It is recommended that a variant of the Scandinavian day fine be utilized, since the day fine concept introduces elements of individualization and equity into the fine-determination process.

Two classes of *pretrial diversion* follow on the severity continuum. The less onerous mode of pretrial diversion requires participation in either a drug education or community service program for a short period of time (e.g., six months). A more restrictive genus includes mandatory enrollment in a drug rehabilitation regimen for a like period of time. The remaining community-based alternative is *traditional probation* which more exactingly limits the offender's liberty. The probation term is longer (e.g., two years) and may include pertinent special conditions such as participation in a drug education or rehabilitation program.

Incarceration and *incarceration plus a monetary fine* are the most severe sanctioning options. The term of incarceration is intermediate (e.g., five years) and determinate in nature. Again, the monetary fine is to be individualized.

The first independent variable to be examined is identifiable harm. For each major offense category, perceivable harm is specified. Specification is generic to the offense class and is unaffected by the particular circumstances of a specific charged offense or named offender.

For purposes of this specification, four discrete categories of offenses may be established. The first category consists of drug consumption offenses (possession and use) and the ancillary to consumption offenses (possession of paraphernalia, loitering, disorderly conduct, etc.). Drug trafficking offenses (sale, distribution, manufacturing, etc.) comprise the next class, and the third class includes property acquisitive offenses committed to raise funds for the purchase of drugs. The final category is composed of all other crimes committed by drug offenders.

An excellent methodology for specification of the harms imputable to the first class of offenses has been developed by Robert Baker. Baker identifies two categories of harms ascribable to consensual crimes— self-directed harms and other-directed harms. The self-directed harms are obvious (e.g., the risk of drug overdose). The latter group includes harms inflicted on associates, drains on public resources, modeling harms, and culture shock harms.

Drug trafficking offenses involve a different and unquestionably more serious set of harms. The culpable offender realizes an illicit pecuniary gain and avoids tax collection aimed at the public good. The aggressive, extroverted role of the drug trafficker in depreciating the moral values embodied by the drug laws also activates the modeling and culture shock harms described by Baker. Proselytism is an intrinsic characteristic of drug trafficking.

Although each of the separate property acquisitive offenses, *viz.*, theft, larceny, embezzlement, false pretenses, forgery, bad checks, illegal credit card use, burglary, and robbery, involves substantially disparate degrees of harm, the general interest protected by this class of prohibitions is property rights. Commission of a property acquisitive offense is an invasion of the victim's property rights. Rank-ordering of the seriousness of this harm, in comparison to the aforementioned harms, requires a subjective evaluation.

The final offense class, all other crimes committed by drug offenders, is a potpourri of harms. Some of the harms are relatively minor, e.g., disruption of the public tranquility resulting from disorderly conduct, while others are extremely serious, e.g., the loss of life occasioned by willful homicide. Consequently, a general characterization of the harms pertaining to this encyclopedic category is not possible. Rather, each offense within this class requires its own harm specification analysis according to established criminal law principles. However, this specification is to be similar in methodology to the harm assessment of the offense categories; particular circumstances of a specific charged offense or named offender are irrelevant, and specification is generic to the offense.

The degree of the offender's drug use has been designated as the other independent variable. This is actually a substitute for the more traditional concept of offender culpability. *Doing Justice* states that "seriousness depends both on the harm done (or risked) and on the degree of the actor's culpability" and culpability is defined as "the degree to which the offender may justly be held to blame for the consequences of his act." As regards the drug offender, culpability has been uniformly defined in terms of the offender's drug-dependence. To a very limited extent, drug-dependent offenders have been excused from criminal responsibility on grounds of involuntariness, disease, and pharmacological duress.

Noteworthy progress has been made with regard to allowance for drug-dependency at dispositional decision-making, however remedial sentencing schemes permit the judicial decision-maker to consider not only the actor's conduct but also his drug-dependency status. The Narcotic Addict Rehabilitation Act is an example of this type of sentencing statute.

Legal commentators are proposing advanced sanctioning structures based on this general theme. The National Commissioners on Uniform State Laws have adopted the Uniform Drug Dependence Treatment and Rehabilitation Act which offers a range of treatment alternatives for drug-dependent offenders intersecting with the criminal justice system. New Jersey Attorney General William Hyland has proposed a classification system dividing the universe of drug offenders into six categories, with the type and length of sanction being adjusted according to the nature of the conduct and the presence or absence of drug-dependency as a mitigating factor.

These proposals consistently maintain a dichotomous conception of

FIGURE 1. Sanctioning Matrix

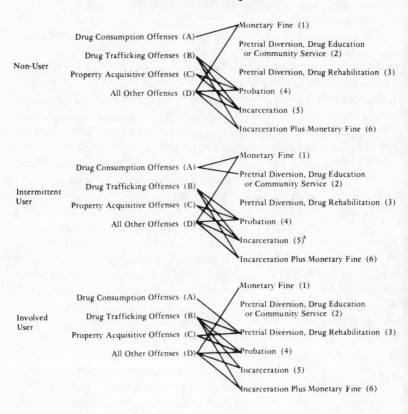

KEY

Non-User	Intermittent User	Involved User
A - 1	A - 1,2	A - 3
B - 4,5,6	B - 4,5,6	B - 3,4,5,6
C - 4,5	C - 4,5	C - 3,4
D - 1,4,5,6	D - 1,4,5,6	D - 1,4,5,6

drug-dependency. Either the drug offender is drug-dependent and *ipso facto* less culpable, or he is non-drug-dependent and undeserving of special consideration. A continuum of drug-dependency is proposed here, permitting a more sensitive adjustment of sanctioning alternatives.

A simplification of the National Commission on Marihuana and Drug Abuse drug use typology is offered. The construct features three patterns of drug use—non-use, intermittent-use and involved-use. Non-use refers to the offender who is not a user of psychoactive drugs. Intermittent-use consists of experimental, social-recreational, and circumstantial-situational use phenomena; the intermittent-user is a potential abuser. Involved-use includes intensified and dysfunctional use patterns. The involved-user manifests psychological and physiological signs of drug dependency.

The real task, of course, is manipulation of the paradigm's variables into a fixed equational format. Reference to the equation will suggest the appropriate sanction for the offender with a known drug involvement and charged with a certain class of offense. An outline of such an equation appears in Figure 1 of this paper. That design, however, only provides a sketch. The reader is urged to complete his own analysis of the model and develop suitable drug offender sanctioning guidelines.

Robert G. Newman

THE ARGUMENT AGAINST LONG-TERM ADDICTION TREATMENT IN PRISON

INTRODUCTION

Recidivism among released prison inmates—addicts as well as non-addicts—is generally conceded to be the rule rather than the exception. Factors outside the control of the correctional system share a major responsibility for this revolving door. Employers, licensing bodies and the general community commonly view the label "ex-offender" as a euphemism for "criminal," and "ex-addict" as synonymous with "junkie." As a result, problems of employment, education and training, and a pervasive sense of hopelessness and helplessness, are accentuated by a prison record, and incarceration not unexpectedly leads to more negative than positive consequences.

Lack of appreciation of the overwhelming influence of these *external* factors has led to numerous attempts to enhance the effectiveness of incarceration. Some of the innovations have been spurious, such as revising the terminology from prisons and penal institutions to "correctional facilities," and from guards to "correctional officers." Changing titles, however, accomplishes nothing: terminally-ill patients admitted to the St. Barnabas Hospital in New York City have no better prognosis than when that institution was named Home for the Incurables.

A more substantive and productive innovation is the increasing tendency to circumvent incarceration altogether, by providing probation for persons convicted of certain crimes. For those who are sentenced to jail terms, parole is widely used to limit the amount of time which must be spent in prison. Despite these humane and rational alternatives to institutionalization, the basic frustration persists: persons who are sent to prison for breaking the law are rarely better citizens when they are released, and the majority will return to be "corrected" again and again, with progressively less likelihood of success.

FOCUS ON THE INCARCERATED ADDICT

In the past few years, special attention has focused on the inmate who, at the time of arrest, was a drug user. Superficially, it is not unreasonable to attempt to differentiate this individual, who presumably *had* to commit a crime to maintain an expensive and illegal drug habit, from the offender whose criminal behavior was not associated with drug dependency. The widespread notion that addicts are "mentally sick," complemented by the almost limitless faith in the healing powers of the medical profession, lends credence to the hope that the implementation of appropriate treatment measures in the nation's jails will cure the inherent psychopathology which allegedly leads the individual into a life of addiction and associated crime.

The large proportion of inmates who have a history of drug abuse greatly adds to the temptation to view the addict as a special type of offender, distinguished by an underlying psychopathology which will respond to appropriate treatment. Addicts themselves, however, overwhelmingly reject this notion. One recent study, for example, found that while 95 percent of the staff members of a treatment program considered the clients to be suffering from "mental illness," only 7 percent of newly-admitted patients held that view. Generalizations regarding psychological deficiencies of drug addicts are also not supported by experience. Methadone maintenance treatment programs have found that the overwhelming majority of heroin addicts who are voluntarily admitted will be able to assume productive and self-fulfilling lives without psychotherapy of any kind; their primary needs for supportive services relate to problems of employment, housing, outstanding legal cases, and other pragmatic, *external* factors. Additionally, it would be curious indeed if there were some form of personality disturbance common to the large, ill-defined, extraordinarily varied addict population.

The question of an alleged psychopathological etiology of addiction, however, should not be relevant to the criminal justice process, since the rationale for incarceration has nothing to do with illness, but is the result of conviction of a criminal offense. The Supreme Court has explicitly ruled that drug addiction, *per se,* is not sufficient grounds for imprisonment. Inmates with a drug history are consequently incarcerated for precisely the same reason as all other inmates; they broke the law, were apprehended, found guilty by a court of law, and sentenced to jail. The purpose of imprisonment of addicts, as with non-addicts, is to punish the offender and serve as a deterrent to potential offenders. The prosecution does not and legally cannot base arguments to convict on alleged psychiatric illness which requires "treatment."

FUTILITY OF "TREATING" ADDICTS IN PRISON

The prison staff, likewise, must resist the temptation to provide special therapeutic programs for drug addicts on the premise that they are sick. The intent may be purely beneficent, and based on a sincere conviction that such programs will be in the interests of the inmate no less than of the society. Nevertheless, long-term addiction treatment in the prison setting will be socially unproductive, clinically dangerous, professionally unethical, and fiscally irresponsible.

From the perspective of society's interest, there is no reason to expect that psychotherapy, in whatever form, will be successful when applied to unwilling subjects whose only real desire is to get out of jail. Involuntary treatment has never been successful in the management of addicts, regardless of the nature of the care provided. This failure has characterized efforts employed against the unwilling addict subjected to involuntary commitment programs, where drug dependence alone is the basis for institutionalization, as well as the incarcerated criminal addict. The societal problem of addiction does not lend itself to simplistic solutions which can be imposed on imprisoned addicts.

The great danger in "treating" inmates who are in no position to refuse the services offered is that the "therapists" will be unable to restrain themselves given the unlimited scope of their authority in such a setting. Thus, most addiction treatment personnel who view addiction as symptomatic of character disturbance believe that other forms of deviance are simply expressions of the same underlying psychopathology. It is unlikely that homosexuality will not also become a focus of the therapists, or radical political views, or any other non-conformist behavior, values and attitudes. Once a psychiatric diagnosis is made, and the clinician has a captive audience, the misuse and abuse of the staff-client relationship is almost inevitable.

Unresolvable professional conflicts are created when the therapist is paid by, and owes primary allegiance to, a third party rather than the client. Rapport with an incarcerated "patient" who generally denies both guilt and illness is precluded. The clinician in such circumstances will function primarily as an agent of the institution, working against the perceived self-interest of the client. Success and failure under these conditions lose all meaning.

The enormous expenditure of money, personnel and physical facilities required by long-term addiction treatment programs in prisons cannot be justified. The results, from the viewpoint of the inmate as well as that of society, will inevitably be disappointing, and the resources can be used more productively for other purposes.

RATIONAL ALTERNATIVES

Arguments against the implementation of long-term addiction treatment programs in prisons by no means imply that institutional administrators should adopt a fatalistic callousness. To the contrary, abandoning futile and counter-productive efforts will make it more feasible to provide services which are indicated, and practical, within the penal institution.

Medical problems, including those directly associated with drug abuse, should be addressed. It is unconscionable for any prison which receives inmates who have a physical dependence on drugs not to provide adequate detoxification services. Detoxification is safe and effective when appropriately administered, as the experience in the New York City Houses of Correction has demonstrated during the past three years. Additionally, there should be diagnostic and therapeutic services available which focus on venereal disease, liver dysfunction, skin lesions, pulmonary disease, and other conditions which are known to be prevalent among the addict population.

The custodial care which is provided can and should be as humane as possible, consistent with the security needs of the institution.

Programs should be made available to provide education and training relevant to the inmate population.

Orientation and referral should be offered to resources in the community which provide services that might be needed following release. Such services should not only relate to addiction, but to employment, housing and other problems which the discharged prisoner will very likely encounter.

Prison officials have the unenviable task of trying to deal fairly and humanely with an understandably hostile group of people, who want little more than to be set free. There are very few so naive as to believe that imprisonment is a positive growth experience, and even fewer who fail to acknowledge the axiom that the smaller the inmate population, the more tolerable and secure the institutional life will be. It would therefore seem incumbent upon professionals working in this country's prisons to speak out in favor of decriminalizing the possession of marijuana, cocaine, heroin, or any of the paraphernalia by which these and other drugs are self-administered. The absurdity of marijuana laws is increasingly recognized; the other offenses appear paradoxical in view of the ruling by the highest court in the land that drug-dependence is not a crime. Whatever the legal rationale, those who work within prisons are perhaps in the best position to call attention to the futility of sending people to jail for these "crimes." By so doing, more can be achieved for the drug-user and for society than by the best intentioned treatment programs which might be applied to those who are behind bars.

James C. Weissman

DRUG OFFENDER DIVERSION
Philosophy and Practices

INTRODUCTION

Diversion of selected offenders from the criminal justice system has become a popular subject of contemporary social policy. Since the creation of a national treatment network in the early 1970s, policymakers at all levels of government have devised strategies aimed at channeling or diverting drug abusers away from incarceration and into community treatment resources. This policy direction has been variously referred to as diversion, systems interface, or linkage programming.

According to an analysis conducted by the National Commission on Marihuana and Drug Abuse, all but two states have enacted statutory provisions authorizing some form of drug abuse diversion, including eight distinct criminal justice options (e.g., prearrest vs. postconviction). A more recent examination by the present writer provides updated information. Utilizing a definition of diversion authority limited to statutes and court rules authorizing the dismissal of legal charges upon successful completion of treatment, 41 states were found to have formal diversion authority.

The federal government has supported the development of programmatic structures implementing the diversion concept at the community level. Since 1972, various federal agencies, now LEAA (Law Enforcement Assistance Administration) exclusively, have provided funding for the establishment of TASC (Treatment Alternatives to Street Crime) drug diversion projects. The July 1978 TASC Status Report reveals that 65 communities were in some stage of TASC sponsorship and more than 38,000 drug abusers had entered the TASC system.

149

Despite its ubiquitous presence, drug diversion is riddled with controversy. In fact, the status of the present relationship between the drug abuse treatment and criminal justice systems (epitomized by the diversion concept) is undergoing close scrutiny. The recent *Report of the President's Commission on Mental Health* recommended discontinuation of the diversion trend, proposing absolute divestment of criminal justice influence from the treatment process.

Numerous issues of civil liberties, program effectiveness, project design, and community values also affect drug diversion. Diversion has evolved as the product of conflicting social values regarding the treatment afforded the drug abuser by our social institutions. It serves as the compromise between authoritarian and libertarian views. Accordingly, it is natural that the program reflect ideological and empirical uncertainty as evidenced by these issues.

This paper will attempt to clarify the function of drug diversion and assess the associated critical questions. Emphasis will be directed at the origins of modern diversion programming, the policy base underlying the concept, prototype program models, available evaluative data, and anticipated future developments. It is hoped that this approach will furnish the reader with an informed and sensitive understanding of this important drug policy subject.

HISTORICAL PERSPECTIVES

The history of drug abuse prevention policy has been researched extensively. The treatises are too numerous to cite, although perhaps the most thorough bibliography and the most balanced perspective may be found in the final report of the National Commission on Marihuana and Drug Abuse. The Marihuana Commission report is particularly noteworthy for its incisive analysis of the influence of legal sanctions in shaping domestic drug prevention policy.

* * * * * * * * * * *

The purpose of this historical review is to illustrate several axioms concerning American drug abuse prevention policy. First, the basic thrust has been and remains a criminal law approach. Notwithstanding the outlay of considerable sums of money for health-directed programs, hopes for reduction of drug abuse continue to rely on direct and indirect applications of the criminal law. Liberal opinions and hopes aside (including my own), the evidence unequivocally supports this inference.

The emphasis on criminal justice controls has fluctuated over time and the current strategy seeks to improve the balance between demand-reduction and supply-reduction efforts. Both symbolic (e.g., marijuana decriminalization) and instrumental (e.g., stable treatment funding) gains are being recorded. Yet, it is an inescapable conclusion that in contrast to its sister alcohol prevention sector, drug abuse prevention incorporates a fundamental reliance on the status quo of drug use prohibitions.

This accommodation between competing drug prevention strategies (criminal vs. health) creates a significant level of tension. On both humanitarian and pragmatic grounds, Americans question the wisdom of application of harsh criminal measures to regulate drug use. The result is ambivalence toward existing criminal controls and attraction to less punitive remedial options falling short of formal decriminalization.

A demand is thus created for policy alternatives offering the symbolic features of the criminal law but the instrumental features of health care. Diversion serves as the principal policy option for reconciling these divergent demands and, as this historical analysis demonstrates, it has gained in impetus as the conflict has become more acute.

DIVERSION GOALS

As a general program emphasis, diversion is intended to accomplish both social action and rehabilitative aims. Although diversion may be defined in limited rather than expansive terms, diversion may also be conceptualized in a broad systems sense. Advocates of this latter view define diversion in terms of any recognizable effort, formal or informal, to lessen the degree of social control exercised over the offender.

Utilizing this broad definitional approach, diversion is a composite of various program interventions practiced by the criminal justice system. Some seek merely to minimize incarceration, while others aim at provision of community treatment services or avoidance of the stigmata of formal criminal processing. A commonality of these efforts is aptly described by Klapmuts:

The central feature of all these interrelated developments is their emphasis on minimizing the involvement of the offender with traditional processes and practices of criminal justice and correction and returning to the community at least some of the responsibility for its anti-social or deviant members.

In this writer's opinion, an even more fundamental commonality is the goal of reducing the proportion of institutionalized offenders through displacement with community-based alternatives.

The diversion movement is supported by both humanitarian and pragmatic values. Liberal proponents stress the matching of rehabilitative services with needy offenders. Furthermore, diversion is endorsed as capable of avoiding the stigmatizing experiencing of orthodox criminal justice processing considered a social culprit by advocates of sociological labeling theory. Finally humanitarians perceive diversion popularity as insuring continued reduction of institutional populations.

The pragmatism flows from various social calculuses that assess costs and benefits of social control devices. Diversion minimizes penetration into the formal processes of the criminal justice system, averting costs associated with traditional adjudicatory and correctional practices. In addition, society is expected to benefit from reduced recidivism rates presumably associated with diversion practices. The matching of offender and services, use of community-based resources, and delabeling are presumed to produce improved rehabilitation performance, translatable into reduced community crime rates.

Less manifest objectives are also sought by diversion advocates. Systematic diversion of certain classes of offenders, e.g., marijuana users, may achieve de facto decriminalization where formal legislative change is politically unfeasible. Another latent objective may be the substitution of observable and controllable diversion for the undetected, unregulated diversion practices traditionally exercised by criminal justice officials. The informal practices are believed to benefit the advantaged and discriminate against the poor.

Before addressing drug diversion specifically, it is necessary to examine more carefully the general issue of adequately defining diversion. This is of threshold importance. Scrutiny of the literature adduces the following meanings associated with the nomenclature diversion:

1. Statutory decriminalization;

2. Use of the "least restrictive alternative";

3. Administrative changes in police practices resulting in use of social services as an alternative to arrest;

4. Use of citations as an alternative to custodial arrest;

5. Use of community treatment resources as an adjunct to probation supervision;

6. Prosecutorial or judicial utilization of formally established pretrial intervention programs;

7. Deinstitutionalization of any type aimed at systematically avoiding use of incarceration;

8. Prevention activities designed to diminish community potential for deviancy through environmental intervention; and

9. Prevention activities designed to reduce latent criminal tendencies by promoting increased social integration of community members.

Typically, however, diversion is defined in relatively narrow terms. Most definitions stress preadjudication intervention, removal of the offender from rather than within the criminal justice system, and provision of individualized rehabilitative services. Ideally, variable definitions should be used, each descriptive of the program goals, nature of diversion activities, and locus of intervention of the particular diversion effort.

In terms of definition and program goals, drug diversion parallels the statements ascribed to the generic diversion concept. Drug diversion is considered generally to encompass all efforts aimed at lessening the degree of social control exercised over the drug abuser, although pure definitions restrict inclusion to programs offering formal preadjudication intervention and placement outside the criminal justice system.

With regard to the goals, the historical analysis presented earlier is instructive. Clearly, humanitarian and pragmatic values are associated with drug diversion efforts. Allegiance to diversion programming institutionalizes the social ambivalence toward methods of drug abuse prevention. A criminal law framework is maintained but application of harsh penal sanctions is minimized, treatment services are maximized, and the public receives benefits of reduced fiscal and social costs.

Even the latent diversion objectives are realized. To the extent that diversion achieves routinization, an informal (and imperfect) de facto decriminalization is accomplished. Furthermore, penal discrimination against drug abusers drawn from minority strata, traditionally considered to be a normative practice, is reduced as a consequence of the visibility and uniformity of the diversion process.

In sum, drug diversion functions as an archetype of the modern diversion paradigm. The social action and rehabilitative goals advanced by diversion advocates realize unquestioned acceptance in the drug abuse arena.

PROGRAM MODELS

For purposes of describing diversion program models, a narrow definition of diversion is adopted. Diversion models describe formalized
programs designed systematically to identify and refer drug offenders into
community-based treatment resources. Exclusively criminal justice-
administered rehabilitative programs and health care programs not directly
linked to the criminal justice system are excluded.

Although previous decades have furnished diversion models based on
institutional care regimens, programs meeting the above criteria are
principally a product of the 1970s. In fact, the genesis of modern diversion
programming may be traced to establishment of a national drug abuse
treatment system authorized by the Drug Abuse Office and Treatment
Act of 1972.

Earlier prototypes had existed in selected locales but it was the widespread availability of community treatment resources promoted by the
landmark federal legislation that catalyzed the growth of drug diversion.
Investigating the development of drug diversion models, the National
Advisory Commission on Criminal Justice Standards and Goals
described four pre-1972 community programs: Illinois Drug Abuse
Program, Cook County State Attorney's Office, New York City's Daytop
Village, and the District of Columbia's Narcotics Treatment Administration. These programs were selected as representative of the prevailing
diversion state-of-the-art.

Assessment of diversion models requires reference to an organizing
paradigm. Identified programs may be analyzed in terms of subscription
to recognized goals and incorporation of selected structural features.
In general, such analysis focuses on the following discriminant variables:

1. Program environment, e.g., community-based vs. institutional;
2. Primary sponsor affiliation, e.g., treatment agency, prosecutor,
corrections agency, etc.;
3. Referral stage, e.g., prearrest, pretrial, posttrial, etc.;
4. Basis of diversion authority, e.g., statute, court rule, administrative
order, etc.;
5. Target population, e.g., juveniles, first offenders, heroin users, etc.;
and
6. Program scope, e.g., community corrections, substance abuse,
vocational training.

The lack of a national data base prevents matching of programs and
numbers to this order of configuration. Despite the popularity of drug

diversion programming, reliable estimates of programs and client populations are unavailable. Neither LEAA correctional surveys nor the National Institute on Drug Abuse CODAP reporting system record these data.

Yet, a rich source of knowledge is supplied by the national TASC program, the largest and most successful drug diversion program. As noted earlier, 65 communities participate in the federally sponsored TASC program.

The TASC model was developed by the Presidential Special Action Office on Drug Abuse Prevention in the fall of 1971. TASC was conceptualized as a crime-reduction program, directed at interrupting the drug-driven cycle of addict street crime. SAODAP planners incorporated proven features of operating diversion programs such as New York City's Court Referral Project and the District of Columbia's Narcotics Treatment Administration court project.

The original TASC model was designed for a narrowly defined target group, heroin addicts charged with criminal offenses. Screening interviews in the local detention unit, coupled with mass urinalysis, were used to identify the universe of addicts within the preadjudication population. For those addicts determined to be eligible according to established criteria (e.g., nonviolent crime), pretrial diversion was offered. Diagnosis and referral to treatment followed and the offender's progress was monitored according to predetermined objective criteria. To insure the availability of adequate treatment capacity, the initial prototype subsidized treatment programs accepting TASC-referred clients.

The evolution of TASC has been linked to perceived changing social needs and empirical results reflecting the utility of existing practices. In addition, an important change developed as a result of reorganization of the federal drug abuse bureaucracy. With the creation of NIDA in 1974, funding for the nontreatment components of TASC was assigned to LEAA and responsibility for insuring adequate treatment capability was assigned to NIDA.

In terms of the evolving programmatic nature of TASC, several important modifications have taken place. Posttrial entry into TASC has been sanctioned, although the official emphasis remains pretrial diversion and pretrial release. Polydrug abusers are included, and alcoholics and juveniles may be accepted according to local option. Mass urine testing has been downgraded from mandatory to optional status.

These alterations demonstrate both the flexibility of the TASC model and the direction of its maturation. The flexibility is an important element. TASC does not attempt to dictate social policy goals to reticent local communities. Local communities applying for TASC funding are simply furnished the operational machinery to accomplish diversion goals of their own making. The diveristy of sponsoring TASC agencies is impressive—local treatment programs, probation departments, prosecutors, state drug agencies, judicial departments, and county drug coordinating bodies.

From its origins as a heroin addict identification program aimed at crime reduction, TASC has evolved into a social services and treatment brokerage system for criminal justice adjudicatory and offender-serving agencies. It has become a systems improvement rather than a crime impact program.

With regard to its internal operational activities, six fundamental diversion functions are practiced by TASC projects. These are screening/identification, court liaison, escort, assessment, referral, and monitoring.

These functions are intended to identify drug users entering the criminal justice system, assess their treatment needs on an individual basis, transmit these data to criminal justice system decision makers, and effect referral into treatment as authorized. Treatment progress is closely monitored or tracked by the diversion staff, which acts in part as a client advocate and in part as a representative of the judicial system.

A complete description of the diversion functions is available in other documents. Although TASC has refined and standardized these practices to a considerable extent, other diversion programs may exhibit somewhat different styles of operation. On balance, however, TASC is representative of the majority of formal drug diversion activities occurring in the United States. The TASC model has gained widespread acceptance as a prototype diversion methodology.

EVALUATION

Evaluation of diversion programming is not a simple undertaking. The social value of diversion cannot easily be translated into a standardized calculus yielding definitive answers. Assessment relies on the collection and analysis of sensitive qualitative measures and elusive quantitative data.

The discipline of program evaluation has only recently begun to gain recognition as a credible application of social science methodology. Evaluators are developing increasingly sophisticated research protocols fashioned to probe the effects of social action programs reliably. Drug treatment evaluation is measuring more than drug use and employment patterns and correctional evaluation is establishing indicators directed at other than recidivism outcomes.

Drug diversion is benefiting from this technological advancement. Although the conventional evaluation measures of drug use, retention in treatment, and socialization outcomes are employed, criteria of a different order are also being assessed.

For instance, much of the criticism of drug diversion centers on the potential for routine infringement of offender civil liberties. Perlman and Jaszi have meticulously documented these areas of vulnerability. Issues concern both procedural and substantive guarantees, touching on such matters as application of uniform eligibility criteria, protection of confidential disclosures, and uniformity in assessing diversion performance.

Although similar criticism directed at 1960s civil commitment diversion programs proved valid, little evidence has appeared attributing the same infirmity to modern diversion programs. Presumably, sensitivity to this possibility experienced by the architects of modern diversion programs has minimized abuse. The legal literature is remarkably devoid of reported instances of civil liberties violations associated with diversion programs.

A more critical evaluative concern relates to the charge that diversion has expanded the network of social control, rather than achieving its articulated goal of minimizing offender penetration into the criminal justice system. Proponents of this argument contend also that embracing of diversion as a policy alternative has blunted more constructive efforts to effect reform through decriminalization.

This is a complex and serious allegation deserving of close scrutiny. Unfortunately, insufficient data have been collected and advanced research designs have not been applied to the question. The rate of increase of drug arrests has declined in recent years, but the contribution of diversion alternatives is a matter of speculation. Similarly, the quantum of social control exercised under diversion circumstances as compared to non-diversion circumstances has not been determined.

To be sure, some of this line of criticism is undoubtedly substantiated. As Smith has illustrated, mass diversion of recreational marijuana users into unnecessary rehabilitative regimens has occurred in some jurisdictions. The extent to which diversion has expanded the social control reach is unknown, however. Accurate assessment requires an improved data base and application of refined research methodologies.

A closely related issue has also received considerable critical attention. Supposed adverse effects to the treatment system arising from the diversion process have been cited by a number of diversion opponents. Adherents of this view contend that diversion blurs the distinctions between the treatment and punishment institutions.

This opinion was endorsed by the *Report of the President's Commission on Mental Health*. Linkage with the criminal justice system was characterized as harmful to the autonomy of the treatment process. Quite obviously, this is not an isolated perspective which can easily be dismissed.

Evaluation of the national TASC program has yielded opposite conclusions, however. Investigators have discovered treatment system satisfaction with coordinated diversion programming. Perhaps the best that can be said is that this is an issue of great ideological importance and that qualitative assessments, the criterion data, are in conflict.

Of equal importance is the related question of community acceptance of drug diversion activities. Again, the TASC experience proves instructive. Of the first 16 TASC projects completing the full cycle of federal "seed" funding, 14 were institutionalized with state and local monies. This is strong evidence of compatibility with prevailing community social values.

The final dimension to consider is program effectiveness as measured by traditional outcome and cost criteria. Recently, Systems Sciences, Inc. completed the largest scale evaluation of this order directed solely at drug diversion programming. Commissioned by LEAA, Systems Sciences rigorously examined the national TASC program, complementing a preliminary evaluation conducted by Lazar Institute.

TASC received high marks from the Systems Sciences, Inc. evaluators. The TASC processes of screening/identification, assessment, referral, and monitoring were rated as effectively performed. Widescale acceptance by both the criminal justice and treatment systems was reported. With regard to outcome and cost measures, the following conclusions were noted:

TASC process outcome is beneficial when outcomes of TASC clients are compared with non-TASC clients. Treatment programs visited reported higher retention rates for TASC clients, which they attributed to close monitoring and TASC reinforcement of the treatment process. Process success rates (successful completions plus retention in treatment) amounted to 64 percent for all clients admitted, and three projects achieved 80 percent success rates. It is noteworthy that these three projects deal with many serious felons and one deals with hardcore alcoholics. TASC is cost effective. The median annual cost per TASC client was $637 and the median annual cost per successful client was $888. . . . Three measures of overall cost effectiveness were derived to assess TASC's contribution. These were:

—TASC costs vs. trial costs
—TASC plus treatment costs vs. trial plus incarceration costs
—Societal costs averted during the TASC process

In all three measures, using the most conservative estimates for comparative costs, TASC provided a lower cost alternative, cost benefits to both the CJS [criminal justice system] and the community.

FUTURE DIRECTIONS

The future of diversion as a permanent criminal justice innovation is uncertain. The beleaguered rehabilitative ideal is being challenged with philosophies emphasizing determinancy and retribution. Treatment as an instrument of penal policy is being questioned.

Yet, treatment concepts are not experiencing precipitous abandonment. Furthermore, drug diversion presents a special case. As long as drug use is regulated by means of criminal law framework, an ameliorative device is necessary. This is the function of drug diversion; it ameliorates the harshness of the criminal law, insures the channeling of criminal addicts into treatment resources, and sustains the symbolic values associated with our legacy of ambivalence regarding social control of drug use.

To be sure, there will be continuous modifications in drug diversion policy. Drug diversion reflects national and community policies toward crime control and drug use, and these policies change in degree. The *Report of the President's Commission on Mental Health* proposes a thorough review of the diversion subject, and such an examination can be expected in the near future. Developments in such diverse areas as intergovernmental cost-sharing formulae, tax-reform efforts, and reorganization of the federal bureaucracy may also affect drug diversion strategies.

Interjecting personal opinion, this writer suggests that the drug abuse treatment community assume an activist role in shaping future drug diversion policy. Rather than serving as a passive recipient of directives directly influencing the delivery of treatment services, drug abuse professionals may play a formative role in designing diversion policies.

In this writer's opinion, the present challenge is to reform diversion policies to effect a truly humane and enlightened approach toward the social treatment of drug use. Recreational and chronic drug use patterns must be distinguished. Drug use and its social and criminogenic sequelae must not fall prey to changing penological doctrines. Reform strategies such as the model Uniform Drug Dependence Treatment and Rehabilitation Act must be advanced. In short, drug abuse professionals are urged to emulate the pioneering social reform efforts of their alcohol abuse brethren.

Section 8

TREATMENT INTERVENTION

Because it is not a simple undifferentiated concept, drug abuse treatment is subject to scientific uncertainty and ideological influence. An appropriate analogy is cancer treatment. A variety of therapies are applied to identified cancer cases, ranging from experimental use of the controversial substance laetrile to orthodox medical techniques. Similarly, drug treatment methods include disputed therapies such as methadone maintenance and traditional interventions such as psychotherapy. For the most part, treaters and patients elect a particular approach based on scientific beliefs and shared values.

With respect to drug users, the frequently intervening variable of the criminal justice system introduces an ideological element of significant bearing upon treatment choice. The two selected articles recognize this factor and offer competing normative perspectives. The articles offer cogent arguments in favor of very different philosophical approaches to treatment of the drug offender. Central to both views is explicit acknowledgment of the influence of social values upon therapeutic practices.

With regard to empirical data, the Weissman article appearing in section 3 examines drug treatment outcome evaluations. The demand reduction component of that article scrutinizes the crime reduction effects of drug treatment intervention and offers detailed conclusions based on available research findings.

Robert G. Newman

WE'LL MAKE THEM AN OFFER
THEY CAN'T REFUSE

As the gap closes between demand for treatment and available services, it is inevitable that the controversy regarding compulsory treatment of addicts will become more intense. Unfortunately, as with many other controversies in the field of addiction, the polarization of opinion which exists stems at least as much from semantic confusion as from substantive disagreement. For this reason, a careful consideration of precisely what is and what is not meant by "voluntary treatment" is a prerequisite to any meaningful discussion of the principles which are involved in forcing people to accept therapy against their will.

Voluntarism is not precluded by the existence of outside pressures. Rather, voluntary "... implies the exercise of one's free choice or will *...whether or not external influences are at work.*" The difficulty, of course, is determining what constitutes "free choice." However unappealing the alternative presented, the addict nevertheless always retains the option of choosing the sanction associated with *not* entering a treatment program. One could thus argue that there are only voluntary patients. To avoid such abstract arguments, it is necessary to define voluntarism pragmatically by describing the relationship which exists between patient and practitioner.

Voluntary treatment describes a therapeutic relationship in which the primary responsibility of the clinician is to the patient. In an involuntary treatment setting the clinician's primary responsibility is to some third party. An obligation to report patient attendance, progress or termination to an outside individual or agency defines the relationship as involuntary, even if patients are induced to sign, in advance, open-ended authorizations for such reports.

Compulsory treatment of addiction has been justified on the basis of society's need to protect itself and/or on the grounds that it is in the interests of the unwilling addicts themselves. Regarding the former contention, there can certainly be no argument over the need for laws designed to protect individuals against infringement of their rights by others. Sanctions against those who violate such laws, however, must be equitable, reasonable, and imposed only after determination of guilt. These safeguards of our due process system are critical; the terminology used to describe the punishment which is meted out is essentially irrelevant.

It is inconsequential that penal institutions have been renamed "correctional facilities" and that guards have assumed the title "correction officers." These and similar euphemisms only take on a sinister quality when used to justify the abridgment of constitutional rights. Sanctions applied against addicts for the protection of society may be labeled "punishment," "treatment," or "rehabilitation," but they must be reserved for persons convicted of a criminal violation, must be applied to all people equally, and must be neither cruel nor unusual according to accepted standards.

It is significant that the constitutionality of involuntary commitment laws has not, in fact, been based on the rationale that society must protect itself at all costs. Rather, it has been stated that due process safeguards apply only to the prosecution of criminals, and have no bearing on the treatment of the sick. As suggested by a Presidential Commission on Law Enforcement and the Administration of Justice, the only condition imposed on compulsory treatment is that it be effective: "It is essential that the commitment laws be construed and executed to serve the purpose for which they were intended and by which alone they can be justified. This purpose is treatment in fact and not merely confinement with the pretense of treatment." This sentiment is also expressed in a recent New York judicial decision: "The extended period of deprivation of liberty which the statute (New York State's Narcotic Control Act) mandates can only be justified as necessary to fulfill the purpose of the program. . . . If compulsory commitment turns out in fact to be a veneer for an extended jail term and is not a fully developed, comprehensive and effective scheme, it will have lost its claim to be a project devoted solely to curative ends . . . and the constitutional guarantees applicable to criminal proceedings will apply in full measure."

Whether the key criterion of effectiveness is in fact met is highly questionable. Reports on the results of involuntary treatment have been consistent in the grim picture they present of extremely high recidivism rates.

The most widely accepted underlying premise in forcing addicts to undergo treatment for their own good is that they are mentally sick. Such a generalization, applied to a population as ill-defined and diverse as "drug addicts," must be suspect from the onset. Furthermore, empirical evidence of success of treatment which is not primarily psychotherapeutic in orientation (most notably, methadone maintenace) refutes the contention that addiction must be associated with some form of psychopathology.

In arguing against the desirability of involuntary treatment, it is tempting to dwell on the voluminous literature which demonstrates the widespread failure of this approach to addicts. To do so, however, would detract from the thesis that effectiveness, or "success," is a potentially far worse consequence for the unwilling subject. By definition, the involuntary patient enters the enforced therapeutic relationship rejecting that which the clinician sees as the desirable objective. Cure and rehabilitation therefore become synonymous with achieving that which the addict does not want, and this can be accomplished only by changing values and attitudes along with behavior. The all-powerful clinical director, acting for society, is the sole judge of what is healthy and appropriate: the clinician defines the disease and makes the diagnosis; the clinician decides on the therapeutic goals and implements the procedures he hopes will achieve these goals, though they are openly rejected by the patient; and, finally, the clinician measures the effectiveness of treatment. Should he decide that the therapy is not sufficiently successful, it is the patient who pays the price of continued, unwanted treatment.

By being labeled an illness, drug abuse is the activity which forms the spurious medico-legal rationale for permitting unwanted treatment to be forced on the addict. The objectives of the "rehabilitation" process, however, will almost invariably be far broader than simply eliminating the illicit use of drugs. All other forms of behavior which the clinician believes, on the basis of his own and society's prejudices, to be pathological will also be dealt with. Thus the addict who is a homosexual may well find his sexual preference a focus of the therapist, while the non-addict homosexual (despite the acknowledged burdens which society imposes) cannot be deprived of his liberty or forced into undergoing therapy in most states. The same is true of the involuntarily committed addict who belongs to a bizarre religious sect; or who is a member of a radical political group or who engages in any other activity which does not have the blessings of the general population and is thus classified as "deviant" and an additional component of the "symptom" complex.

Legal experts may argue over the constitutionality of involuntary treatment of addicts. Politicians and the lay public may consider the desirability and the dangers of such treatment. Economists may enter into heated debates over its absolute and relative cost-effectiveness. But the clinician who accepts patients rendered powerless by legislative fiat (as opposed to medical incapacity) to refuse his services, must be viewed in the role of persecutor. Rationalizations cannot obfuscate the issue; in dealing with an unwilling subject, a doctor is by definition striving to bring about a change in behavior which the patient does not wish, but which the government has mandated. He accepts payment from society in order to work against the perceived self-interest expressed by the patient; in such instances, the concepts of treatment and cure lose all meaning.

There are legal restraints against an internist who, in his professional wisdom, may be tempted to imprison a diabetic who fails to adhere to a prescribed diet. A surgeon, recognizing the inevitable consequences of ignoring a malignancy, is nevertheless restrained by professional as well as legal sanctions from operating on a cancer patient without informed consent. "Treating patients against their wishes, *even though the treatment may be medically correct,* should be considered an offense punishable by law. . . . Let us not forget that every form of social oppression has, at some time during its history, been justified on the ground of helpfulness toward the oppressed."

"Diversion" of addicts from the criminal justice system to a treatment setting is an increasingly common practice in many states. This approach, which purports to deal with addict-offenders as "patients" rather than as criminals, has been heralded as an enlightened, humane alternative to an expensive and ineffective prison stay.

In general, all of the problems of enforced "treatment" apply to this particular brand of compulsion: There is a serious question as to whether it conflicts with constitutional safeguard; there is no rationale for assuming that the label of drug addict is synonymous with illness, let alone illness that can or should be treated; there is no evidence to suggest that treatment provided addicts under coercion will be effective, and there is a basis for concluding that "success," even when attainable, may be more undesirable than "failure"; and, finally, the all-powerful role of the physician and other staff members creates a very dangerous potential for abuse.

Diversion from the criminal justice system also entails additional inconsistencies. For example, while the rationale is that the addict-offender is "sick," the period of compulsory treatment is determined less on supposedly medical grounds than on the nature of the *criminal* offense which brought the addict before the court. Generally, addicts convicted of misdemeanors are committed to "treatment" for shorter periods of time than those convicted of felonies, ". . . a differential which smacks of penal rather than therapeutic aims."

There are several mechanisms by which the criminal justice system forces addicts into treatment. In many situations the Court, upon *conviction* of an addict, may impose a sentence which specifically mandates a term in a treatment facility in lieu of prison. Such terms can extend either for an indefinite period of time, depending upon the "progress" perceived by the clinician, or for a minimum duration which frequently exceeds the longest sentence possible for the criminal act itself.

The other commonly used diversion technique offers a "choice" to the addict: either stay in prison, or "voluntarily" request release which will be conditioned upon entering and remaining in a specified treatment program. This practice is particularly invidious when it is applied (as is increasingly the case) to the pretrial addict-prisoner whose alleged offense is compounded by his inability to obtain bail money. Frequently, the prosecutor's agreement to the release of defendants is reserved for those persons whose charges are relatively minor (i.e., misdemeanors and low-degree, drug-related felonies). Those involved, therefore, are primarily poor people, arrested on charges of which they are presumably innocent under the law, and which even upon conviction would carry comparatively short sentences. They are "offered the opportunity" to enter a treatment program they may or may not want or need, and which will in any event provide society with the means of observing and controlling their activities for an extended period of time. Such coercion of legally innocent detainees is possible since overcrowded court calendars and other delays inherent in the judicial process make virtually any alternative more attractive than continued incarceration while awaiting trial. Incredibly, it is in precisely these cases that advocates embrace diversion as an especially humane and appropriate expedient.

A problem inherent in all of the diversion schemes is that the officials of the criminal justice system are put in a position of abrogating their appointed responsibilities, while simultaneously accepting roles for which they are not qualified. Judges, probation officers and parole officers have a primary obligation to protect society at large, and in exercising this obligation they must place consideration of the *community's* well-being ahead of all others. They cannot, and should not, have their roles re-defined as therapists, any more than physicians should attempt to make decisions regarding the need for incarceration of criminals.

Distinguishing between the functions and responsibilities of criminal justice personnel and clinicians does not imply a value judgment. The point is simply that the functions *are* different, and that both groups must retain their own priorities if they are to achieve their respective goals. Physicians, just like lawyers and priests, will be rendered totally impotent if they attempt to serve society *at the expense* of their clients. Similarly, judges, probation and parole officers will not be able to meet their obligations to those who elect or appoint them if they lose sight of their primary responsibility.

Neither role is easy. Those who work in the criminal justice system, for instance, are inevitably plagued by the knowledge that while prisons do not as a rule "correct" anybody, simply releasing convicted criminals without punishment is not feasible. The tempting middle road with addict-defendants is to force them, under threat of imprisonment, to enter a treatment facility with the assurance that the clinical staff will promptly report abscondence or continued involvement in "anti-social" activities. The attractiveness of such an approach is that it seems to offer something to everyone: The problem of ineffective and over-crowded jails is addressed; the judge is reasonably secure in the belief that the treatment facility staff will closely monitor the addict's behavior; the addict has been permitted to escape, at least temporarily, prison confinement for a more subtle (though perhaps longer) punishment; and finally, the treatment center frequently welcomes the added "business" and often believes that it will be more successful in dealing with what amounts to a captive population.

In fact, this type of program is a perversion of the role of all the parties concerned.

The *judge* engages in inequitable justice by providing different punishment to different people charged with the same offense, merely because one happens to be an addict and is deemed "treatable" and the other is not. Also, the judge imposes as the primary criterion of continued release attendance at a facility which may not offer society (let alone the addict) any benefits. The basic premise underlying such conditional release is that there is an inherent value in being in a treatment program; this assumption is as invalid as the belief that there is an inherent virtue in being a member of a particular religion, or political party, or any other group. Finally, the judge is frequently left with the task of deciding which type of treatment program should be required, a decision for which he is usually totally unqualified, and which will depend more on personal bias than on objective determination.

The addict-defendant is forced to accept "treatment" which he generally does not want for an "illness" which he more often than not believes is non-existent. The addict who has not yet been tried or convicted forfeits the opportunity to prove his innocence by accepting treatment in lieu of prosecution and the attendant pretrial incarceration.

The clinical staff, in agreeing to share the responsibilities of the criminal justice system, cannot meet its primary obligation to the patient. It thereby severely compromises its ability to serve *either* patients *or* the community. Clinical judgment is also compromised, since medical decisions (to terminate treatment, for instance) can and generally do lead to inevitable *criminal* sanctions against the client.

It would be wrong to assume that arguments against involuntary treatment in any denigrate the value and importance of *voluntary* services. Although a law mandating treatment of everyone over a specified weight would be unthinkable, people who are obese should have access to medical assistance for weight reduction.

If compulsory treatment as a form of punishment is to be eliminated, this should simultaneously preclude the addict-defendant from pleading illness as a justification for crime, or as a rationale for avoiding the usual penalties which the court imposes on non-addicts for similar offenses. Equal severity of the law is no less a principle than the corollary equal protection. The proposition that incarceration of convicted criminals serves no useful purpose may well be correct; whatever alternatives are suggested, however, should not distinguish between people on the basis of drug abuse.

Whatever the terminology and whatever the means by which coercion is applied, compulsory treatment of addicts is void of benefits and counter-productive of the goals which form the rationale for depriving people of their liberty. The interests of society cannot possibly be protected by ineffective attempts to force attitudinal and behavioral change on resentful and unwilling subjects; the rights of *all* Americans are severely threatened when the principle is established of ignoring safeguards of our criminal justice system. The assertion that compulsory treatment is in the interests of those who are forced into therapy is equally spurious; such efforts have been proven a costly, unsuccessful error in the past, and they are doomed to fail in the future.

The causes of drug addiction are as complex as society itself, and they must be faced directly. The analogy is frequently made between drug addiction and contagious disease. In that context, it should be noted that even where a readily defined illness exists (which is not the case with addiction), and even where that illness can be effectively cured by appropriate treatment (which also is not the case with addiction), elimination of the problem from a community generally requires far broader measures. Thus, tuberculosis was brought under control not by the introduction of chemotherapeutic agents, but by a substantial improvement in living conditions; in areas where that improvement has not occurred, the disease is widespread throughout the world, even though each individual patient can be readily diagnosed and cured. Similarly, we must recognize that addiction is a social problem which will never be eliminated by measures that are imposed on the addicts themselves, and until this is understood our effectiveness in dealing with drug abuse will remain severely limited.

James C. Weissman
George Nash

A GUIDE TO THE TREATMENT
OF DRUG ADDICT CRIMINALITY

INTRODUCTION

Social scientists and political decision-makers are paying increased attention to the examination of the relationship between narcotics usage and crime. In 1976 the National Institute on Drug Abuse released a comprehensive study of available drug use and crime research findings. Conducted by a panel of non-government scientists, that study, *Drug Use and Crime: Report of the Panel on Drug Use and Criminal Behavior* (hereinafter *Drug Use and Crime*), judiciously questions popular assumptions regarding the relationship between drug use and criminality. For example, after scrutinizing available research findings linking drug use and property crime, the study disputed the extent of causality commonly assumed between the two phenomena.

The present writers are veterans of drug use and crime research. We have investigated numerous aspects of the phenomenon, including the measurable effects of drug use upon criminal behavior patterns, the impact of drug treatment upon criminality, the relationship between female addiction and criminality, and the impact of diversion programming upon criminal behavior.

We have also been active in the administration of drug treatment and drug diversion programs. This combination of research and administrative experience provides us with decided views regarding the proper role of drug treatment in addressing client criminality. In this paper, we offer our recommendations on the subject.

To what extent have treatment programs really attempted to confront the issue of client criminality? To give you an idea of what might be tried, let us quote from a recent study:

"Patients were watched closely by two inspectors: John Hudson and Teddy Voight. Their primary concerns were that patients have a regular address, worked, did not sell their drug supplies or get in trouble with the police.

Persons who did not comply were not allowed to attend the clinic. Addresses of patients who were not already known by the clinic staff were checked by the inspectors regularly; so were jobs, but the inspectors were careful not to jeopardize the patient's relationship with his employer—this was stressed by clinic officials and apparently worked, judging from the variety of professionals who were patients.

"The inspectors' jobs were not, however, simply to control the patients. In fact a good deal of their work was to assist them. Both men were well known in town and assisted a number of patients to obtain jobs, housing and other necessities. . . .

"Unofficially, Hudson was Shreveport's narcotics agent. He knew all the addict-patients, and was quick to spot any unusual dealings among them. He held a tight rein on patients suspected of breaking the clinic rules. The other side of his nature was startling to Dr. Butler (the clinic director); Hudson could also be gentle and sensitive when the situation called for it.

"Another method of control used was fingerprinting. During the first year, the clinic attracted a large number of persons from outside Shreveport, and many were suspected of being criminal or having criminal records. Fingerprints were taken to control this group (this was discussed earlier). After the first batch of prints were made, 14 persons dropped out of the clinic and left town. When the reports were returned, all were known to the authorities, and some were wanted on warrants. Fingerprinting was continued routinely after that."

You may think that some of the ideas above sound a little strange and you may wonder why you have not heard more about them. The answer is easy. Although the study from which we are quoting was conducted by our colleague Dan Waldorf for the Drug Abuse Council, Inc. only a few years ago, the report describes not a contemporary treatment program but a public health clinic which distributed morphine to opiate addicts in Shreveport, Louisiana between 1918 and 1923. Clearly, this program did attempt to confront client criminality and the data indicate that its efforts were reasonably successful.

We quote from the Shreveport study to illustrate the novelty of the crime control approach in terms of contemporary ideology. With the exception of justice system operated rehabilitation programs, we have been unable to locate reports of community treatment programs practicing such direct means of addressing individual client criminality. To be sure, reduction of client criminality in the aggregate is universally espoused by drug treatment programs, but when applied to individual client treatment planning, that goal becomes diffused and attenuated.

We believe that treatment program administrators and staff have failed to appreciate the importance of crime reduction as a client treatment goal. It is indisputable that a consensus exists among funding sources and program officials recognizing the legitimacy of crime control as a treatment objective. Yet, operational treatment philosophy and practices typically exclude activities specifically aimed at reduction of individual client criminality.

In general, the prevailing rehabilitation ethic perceives criminality as a symptom of the client's pathology. The common treatment assumption contends that if a client demonstrates proper motivation, increases his level of self-understanding, and improves his psychological and social coping skills, he will consequently refrain from criminal behaviors. Thus, the conventional wisdom maintains that if a client's psychological and social problems are satisfactorily addressed, criminality will disappear of its own accord.

Of course, some treatment programs and treatment counselors deviate from this stereotypic characterization and do adopt specific crime reduction techniques. Further, few treatment programs fail to establish some type of elementary linkage with the criminal justice system, acknowledging the inevitable and significant interface relationship between the agencies. As a specific focus of the treatment process, however, reduction of criminality is largely displaced and occasionally disparaged. Some program administrators and staff, philosophically opposed to integrating criminologic concerns into the rehabilitative process, think of crime control as a dirty word and refuse to confront the issue directly. Others adopt a superficial approach, limited to polite cooperation with judicial and correctional officials. Only a small minority of drug treatment agencies and professionals develop complex crime reduction strategies evidencing sincere commitment to the task.

Policymakers funding drug treatment programs are becoming increasingly insistent that reduction in client criminality be tangibly demonstrated. Treatment programs are beginning to pay serious attention to the notion of addressing client criminality in an affirmative manner. To date, however, most community drug treatment programs have not dealt with the criminologic questions in a straight-forward and systematic fashion. The remainder of this paper focuses on that important policy issue and analyzes pertinent dimensions of the subject. Practical recommendations are offered for the benefit of funding sources, program administrators, and treatment workers.

* * * * * * * * * *

WHAT CAN TREATMENT PROGRAMS DO
TO REDUCE CLIENT CRIMINALITY?

At the outset, we propose that the legitimacy of the involuntary nature of drug abuse treatment be acknowledged. Although national NIDA data indicate that only 14 percent of drug treatment clients are involuntary admissions, this figure is clearly erroneous. Experienced treatment program administrators calculate that upwards of two-thirds of their clients enter treatment as a result of legal system coercion. Recent arrests, pending court hearings, and probation and parole orders account for most treatment admissions.

The actuality of this degree of involuntariness is an enigma to health care systems. On ethical grounds, many public health figures refuse to acknowledge the existence of this coercion. Adaptation of care-giving services to achieve compatibility with the legal system is unthinkable. Health care delivery is perceived as a totally voluntary system in which criminal justice input has no valid role.

A sizable group of less traditional health care providers, on the other hand, recognize the nature of the drug abuse treatment environment and attempt to integrate the coercive elements into treatment design. This adaptive position recognizes the existence of legal coercion and seeks to harness its benefits and minimize its potentially disruptive qualities.

We favor the latter approach. Since 1914, narcotics use has been an illegal activity in this country. Despite recent progress in decriminalizing possession of marijuana for personal use, we do not envision any realistic hope of decriminalizing behaviors pertaining to narcotic drugs in the foreseeable future. As in the past, the criminal justice system, i.e., police, courts and corrections, will play a significant role in identifying, detaining, adjudicating, incarcerating, and rehabilitating the addict.

Rather than denying the existence of this fact, we recommend that treatment programs utilize criminal justice system linkages and the omnipresence of legal coercion to augment the effectiveness of therapeutic interventions. Unless the client is free of criminality, he is not cured. If he continues to engage in criminal behavior, he will inevitably be rearrested and deprived of his freedom. Thus, a key task of treatment is addressing criminality in an explicit and affirmative manner.

What can treatment programs do to respond to this issue? The first step is attitudinal. Programs should be open and forthright regarding the goal of reducing client criminality. This is not to suggest that re-socialization and psychotherapeutic goals should be abandoned, but abatement of individual client criminality should be acknowledged as a primary treatment goal. This goal should be made clear to clients from the time of intake and should be continually discussed among staff and clients.

Although more is said later in this paper in regard to implementing this concept, it is important that the reader understand the primacy of inducing attitudinal change concerning this subject. Treatment program staff must truly believe in the utility of the reduction of client criminality as a function of treatment. The goal may be "sold" on two grounds. First, it is surely in the client's best interests to reduce his criminal behavior and to avoid deprivations of his freedom. Secondly, as a publicly funded activity, treatment is obliged to pursue valid societal goals reflecting community mores. Reduction of criminality is probably the foremost of community goals for drug abuse treatment and there is nothing unethical or improper in prosecuting that objective. Contrary to some traditional health care beliefs, treatment need not be amoral and should facilitate the practicing of ethical conduct by its clients.

At the time of induction into the program, treatment staff should obtain a criminal history in addition to the standard medical and psychosocial histories. If such information is routinely gathered, clients will usually be honest concerning their past criminal histories. The purpose of collecting these data is to gain an understanding of this element of the client's functioning in order to prepare a complete treatment plan.

A common oversight of treatment personnel is to view these criminological data as unidimensional. There are two distinct variables to be considered, the client's involvement in illegal activities and his relationships with the courts and correctional agencies. For example, a client may demonstrate a continuing and destructive involvement in group burglaries due to unsatisfactory peer relationships and he may also be experiencing a poor relationship with his probation officer due to the continuing criminal involvement. These are related but discrete phenomena. Each must be carefully diagnosed, evaluated, and planned for in the client's treatment plan.

Preparation of this component of the treatment plan requires a good deal of care. First, sufficient and accurate data must be obtained. Self-report data furnished by the client should be supplemented with and compared to official criminal history information. Appropriate consent to release of information forms should be used to protect client confidentiality. A thorough and complete correctional file provides a wealth of pertinent data, including arrest reports ("rap sheets"), presentence investigations, preparole reports, and institutional and community supervision records.

Scrutiny of the criminological data is a purposeful activity. The treatment worker has multiple goals in mind. First, the worker should identify patterns of criminality practiced by the client and possible explanatory or circumstantial variables. Was the armed robbery linked to a lengthy pattern of antisocial behavior, or was it a truly situational occurrence? Was the client involved in a criminal culture prior to the onset of addiction, or are all his criminal activities related to raising funds for the purchase of drugs? The worker must acquire an elementary understanding of the criminal code as well as a familiarity with the nuances of hustling and street life.

Secondly, the worker must assess the client's ability to function in the community as evidenced by prior probation and parole experiences. Analysis of prior probation and parole case records may be extremely revealing. For instance, the worker may ascertain that the client exhibits signs of an institutional syndrome which requires intensive clinical intervention.

Finally, the worker must evaluate the client's current relationship with his probation or parole officer. Design of an appropriate treatment response requires a good understanding of the goals, style, and expectations of the correctional agent. Is the correctional worker supportive of the client's rehabilitative efforts or is he surveillance-oriented and distrustful of the client? Ideally, these perceptions should be shared with the probation or parole officer and mutual roles and expectations should be negotiated between the officer, treatment worker, and client.

Action plans addressing each of these issues should be included in the client's treatment plan. Specific, measurable objectives should be established. The client's criminality and criminal justice relationships should be evaluated and treated in a manner similar to the client's other problem areas.

In addition to this strategy of incorporating this dimension of rehabilitation into treatment planning, we suggest several other prescriptions. In many communities, treatment programs are viewed as havens for the lawless. This is not only a poor posture in terms of effective community relations, but it inhibits staff efforts to reduce client criminality. Treatment programs must take affirmative steps to create an atmosphere of law-abidingness on and near the program premises. Staff must constantly monitor client activities and utilize informal and formal sanctions to enforce program prohibitions against illegal activities. Dealing of drugs and fencing of stolen property must not be tolerated on or near the program premises.

Treatment programs should maintain open communications with probation and parole personnel. The dialogue should not be limited to individual cases but should encompass comparison of casework techniques and practices. The technology of casework intervention should be freely discussed and shared between the agencies. Both treatment and correctional personnel will soon discover a striking similarity in their tasks despite fundamental differences in mission statements and philosophical orientation.

Improved dialogue and relations with the law enforcement community have also been suggested by an experienced treatment administrator. Swanson outlines a multi-stage strategy designed to improve treatment program–police relationships. His model includes: program policing of client activities on or near program premises; regular meetings with law enforcement officials to discuss treatment philosophy, goals, and achievements; involvement in training of police officers; cooperation with law enforcement with regard to encouraging clients to deal with outstanding arrest warrants; and arranging regular visitations of a police community-relations officer to the program. The majority of these notions are consistent with our recommendations and merit consideration.

Employment of a treatment program lawyer assigned exclusively to client affairs may also produce favorable results in terms of crime reduction. Current National Institute on Drug Abuse regulations require federally funded treatment programs to insure the availability of legal services to clients and programs have responded to this mandate with varied arrangements. Informal agreements with public legal service organizations, formal agreements with such agencies, and the securing of the services of a paid program attorney are the most common responses.

Lowinson et al. report significant benefits accruing to clients and program as a result of retention of a program attorney. Legal assistance is provided in both criminal and civil matters impeding the rehabilitation of the client. The personal attention afforded the client by the program attorney, in contrast to the depersonalized nature of the services traditionally rendered in the public legal services sector, can serve as a useful rehabilitative support mechanism. This may increase the likelihood of the client succeeding in treatment and abstaining from criminal conduct.

Another important topic pertinent to the reduction of client criminality is treatment aftercare. Re-entry into the community is fraught with peril. As Mecca and Pittel note in their incisive analysis of aftercare needs and methods, "Drug abuse treatment may eliminate the addict's need for drugs, but it cannot prepare him adequately for survival in a complex world whose values are unfamiliar and for which he has not been socialized." Mecca and Pittel outline a comprehensive model for after-care services delivery aimed at altering prevailing practices which terminate the rehabilitative process prior to adequate client socialization. Treatment programs lacking a satisfactory aftercare regimen may be passively contributing to the criminality of their former clients by failing to provide the support system necessary for adequate functioning in the community.

Do these practices really work to reduce client criminality? Since we know of no treatment program implementing all of these methods, the hypothesis is not yet subject to testing. Many of these practices are integral to the functioning of the national TASC (Treatment Alternatives to Street Crime) program, however, and preliminary evaluative data are available with respect to TASC.

TASC, operating in over forty communities, is specifically designed to augment traditional community treatment programming with regard to client criminality and criminal justice coordination. The results of the TASC program have done much to confirm our belief in the efficacy of addressing criminologic issues as a function of drug treatment. Although a comprehensive evaluation of TASC is still in process, preliminary data indicate that TASC has proven very effective in achieving its goals. Client during-treatment recidivism rates are low (5-20 percent) and linkages between treatment and criminal justice are productive.

We hope that readers of this article find our recommendations meriting serious consideration. Although the individual ideas are not original, the synthesis proposed herein combines philosophies and practices previously unconsolidated into a single approach. The emphasis on crime control is decidedly different from prevailing treatment ideology.

To be sure, the suggestions are controversial and subject to continuing debate. Further, operational definition of the concepts could benefit from more careful analysis. The notion of crime control as a valid function of community drug treatment is forcefully argued, however. We look to our colleagues to advance the discussion and to test the concepts.

Section 9

PREVENTION STRATEGIES

Prevention of drug abuse is as hard to object to as it is hard to define. Almost anything that seems good for young people has been defined at one time or another, during the last decade, as drug abuse prevention, as those concerned with youth have begun to recognize the epidemic increase in youthful drug use. The Brotman and Suffet paper thoughtfully dissects the basic elements of "prevention" and reviews the limitations of each, concluding that, despite our best intentions and highest hopes, "reality intrudes" with much disturbing information.

Taking a broader perspective, with much less data, DuPont speculates about the future of drug abuse prevention policies in the 1980s. The most likely new directions include more reliance on self-help approaches (modeled on Alcoholics Anonymous) and a family-oriented focus on drug use by those under the age of 16. This paper also suggests that drug abuse prevention is closely related to the broad area of healthy lifestyles, having much in common with such apparently unrelated public health issues as wearing seat belts and eating fewer calories as well as with (more obviously) smoking tobacco and overusing alcohol.

Both papers are appropriately cautious about the limits of any policy option, while supporting the importance of prevention as a goal.

Richard Brotman
Frederic Suffet

THE CONCEPT OF PREVENTION
AND ITS LIMITATIONS

Although the United States has frequently been characterized as a drug-oriented society, the use of certain drugs for purposes of pleasure or stress relief has, historically, been socially and legally proscribed. Drugs subject to proscription have included heroin and other opiates, cannabis preparations such as marijuana and hashish, LSD and other psychedelics, cocaine, and amphetamines and barbiturates when not used under medical supervision.

Broadly speaking, the proscription has two main sources. First, the use of such drugs is seen as potentially injurious to the physical and mental health of the user, particularly when use is immoderate. Second, their use, especially for reasons of pleasure, has been widely regarded as antithetical to the complex of moral values, including industriousness and maintaining control of one's rational faculties, often designated by the terms "work ethic" or "Protestant ethic." The former assertion hardly requires elaboration. Evidence for the latter may be found in many places, most recently in a survey of a national sample of adults sponsored by the National Commission on Marihuana and Drug Abuse. The survey revealed, for example, that 59 percent of the respondents thought marijuana use makes people lose their desire to work, and 64 percent said using marijuana is morally offensive.

Historically, the loci of responsibility for enforcing the proscription, that is, for the control of illicit drug use, developed initially in two main institutional realms—law and medicine. Stated briefly, the intended function of legal control has been to deter the use and distribution of banned drugs by threat of punitive sanctions. The intended function of medical control, as expressed through various approaches to treating drug users—

chemotherapy and therapeutic communities, for example—has been to terminate individual drug use careers. However, as the so-called drug explosion of the 1960s showed, both forms of control largely failed. The law apparently did not deter many persons from becoming involved in illegal drug activities, probably because the risk of arrest was demonstrably low. Few drug users came into contact with drug treatment programs, and of those who did, relatively few stopped using drugs permanently.

Consequently, there was, starting in the mid-1960s, a rising demand for another form of control which would complement law and medicine. This was a demand for prevention, for programs which would somehow keep people from entering into the world of illicit drug use. And, since in the 1960s drug use was seen mainly as a problem of the young, the demand focused primarily on the need to create or update school-based programs.

The upward curve of this demand, and the remarkable speed with which it became the basis of a significant aspect of national drug control policy, may be charted by federal appropriations over the past five years for drug education and information programs. In fiscal year 1969, $2.7 million was appropriated, followed by $10.3 million in 1970, $24.1 million in 1971, $43.7 million in 1972, and $40.5 million in 1973. These funds, disbursed through various federal agencies to establish programs at national, state and local levels, scarcely reflect the magnitude of the burgeoning drug prevention "industry," for an incalculable amount of money and effort for preventive programs has been generated by business, foundations, voluntary organizations, and other groups in the private sector. While it is probably true that most programs are based in the schools (a National Commission on Marihuana and Drug Abuse survey showed that as of 1971, twenty-four states required drug education at secondary school level, and in the other states many, if not most, local school districts had developed programs on their own initiative), it should be pointed out that many programs operate outside the schools in forums as diverse as the national television networks, local churches and civic groups, and so on.

It is clear, then, that the prevention of illicit drug use has become a major area of planned social action. It is also quite clear, as critics have begun to point out, that programs in this area, with few exceptions, have not been evaluated. As a result, there are few empirical clues as to what drug prevention actually accomplishes; no one really knows whether preventive programs, by and large, achieve their goals. Moreover, the assumption that the concept of prevention is applicable to illicit drug use has largely gone unquestioned. So strong has this assumption been, constituting as it does the fundamental premise of the entire preventive enterprise, that only within the past year or two has it been asked: Is the prevention of illicit drug use a realistic, achievable goal? Or is it just wishful thinking?

The purpose of this paper is to examine the concept of prevention as it relates to the use of illegal drugs and to make explicit some of its limitations. In doing this we outline a model or classifacatory scheme, in which we can locate the various approaches to prevention.

THE CONCEPT OF PREVENTION

The concept of prevention was first developed in the field of public health and epidemiology. In the classic epidemiologic formulation, the spread of contagious disease among people depends on the interaction of an agent (the disease germ) with a host (the human organism) as mediated through a particular environment (physical and social). Given this formulation, which is greatly oversimplified here, prevention may, according to standard public health categories, occur at three levels. *Primary* prevention is aimed at keeping the agent from infecting potential hosts by, for example, immunizing the uninfected parts of the population or quarantining those already infected. *Secondary* prevention, through early case finding and diagnosis, seeks to limit the disease process among infected individuals in whom the process is not far advanced. *Tertiary* prevention aims at limiting disabilities among, and if possible rehabilitating, persons in whom the disease process has reached an advanced stage.

As employed in the field of drugs, the concept of prevention has usually meant primary prevention and, to some extent, secondary prevention. In other words, the aim of preventive efforts has been to keep nonusers from becoming illicit drug users, and to help experimental or occasional users revert to nonuse, or at least to keep them from progressing to patterns of heavy use. Those who have reached the point of heavy involvement with drugs are typically seen as candidates for treatment; they are beyond the reach of preventive efforts. In this paper we shall adhere to the meaning of prevention commonly understood in the drug field; programs of treatment and rehabilitation for those already seriously involved with drugs will be considered herein to fall outside the area of prevention.

Since it is by now indisputably clear that most people are introduced to illicit drugs by intimate associates—usually friends, sometimes relatives—and not by the mythical pusher who loiters near schools, some persons in the field uphold a "contagion" or epidemiological model of drug use which views use as spread by direct contact. Under the auspices of this model, they propose classic public health measures, such as quarantining known users, or chemically immunizing nonusers. It should be noted that these measures are usually recommended with respect to heroin addiction.

In our view, however, the contagion model has a significant shortcoming. Namely, unlike the case of an infectious disease, people contract the disease of drug use willingly; they *choose* to use drugs. There is, in short, an element of volition in drug use which the epidemiological model fails to encompass adequately. Given this shortcoming, the model is of limited utility for discussing the wide range of efforts coming under the rubric of prevention. We therefore employ a different model, one which better fits the empirical facts. This is an economic model, first developed for somewhat different purposes by James V. Koch and Stanley E. Grupp, which treats factors of supply and demand as the organizing principles of analysis.

Under the terms of this model, prevention in its broadest sense may be said to include, first, all efforts aimed at reducing the supply of drugs, and second, all efforts aimed at reducing the demand for drugs. Attempts to reduce the supply of drugs, especially through monitoring and interdicting the illegal drug traffic, fall, generally speaking, into the domain of law enforcement. Such activity may validly be called preventive to the degree that it curtails the drug supply and, in turn, restricts opportunities for drug use. However, since in the drug field the term *prevention*, as commonly used, does not cover this kind of law enforcement activity, we shall eschew further consideration of the supply side of the equation and focus instead on the demand side, where virtually all preventive efforts, in the usual meaning of the term, may be located analytically.

In what follows we review the main approaches to prevention—that is, the strategies for reducing demand—and point out what appear to be the limitations of the various approaches. These are discussed under four headings: (1) coercion, or the threat of formal punitive sanctions; (2) persuasion, or education in the harmful consequences of drug use; (3) correction, or the eradication of the presumed causes of drug use; and (4) substitution, or the provision of alternatives to drug use.

Coercion. Throughout most of the twentieth century, the basic means American society has employed to reduce the demand for illicit drugs is the threat of punitive sanctions, as expressed through formal penalties codified in the law. This has been true at least since the passage of the

Harrison Act in 1914, and the general trend, in response to the stubborn persistence of illegal drug use has been to increase the severity of the penalties. The major exception to this trend has been the reduction, over the past few years, of penalties for marijuana possession.

The theory behind the drug laws is that the threat of punishment will act as a deterrent, that through the instrument of the law people can be coerced into acting in their own best interests. But despite its preventive intent, the law, viewed as a strategy to reduce the demand for drugs, has clearly not proved effective. One could discourse at length on why this is so; but since the detection and arrest of drug possessors, like the case of drug traffickers, is typically considered a law enforcement matter and not a form of prevention, let us consider another kind of coercion, one which is often closely linked to programs generally recognized as preventive in nature. This is the application of extra-legal administrative sanctions by certain organizations, schools in particular, to individuals discovered to be in possession of illegal drugs.

Schools, from elementary to college level, have become the key site for preventive programs, and for two reasons. First, young people are seen as the primary "population at risk" in regard to drug use; and second, school settings permit an in-depth presentation and discussion of drug information. The substantive aspects of such programs are treated below. Here we note that school-based programs, especially at secondary and college levels, often include, in addition to the strictly educational aspects of the program, a warning to students that administrative sanctions may be applied to any of them discovered to be drug users. Typically, these sanctions involve the possibility of suspension or expulsion from school, although in some cases school policy may include notifying the police. Whatever the arguments pro and con concerning the use of these sanctions, it is clear that such warnings are not always a hollow threat. In two noteworthy instances, midshipmen at the United States Naval Academy have been expelled for marijuana use. A national survey of schools conducted for the National Commission on Marihuana and Drug Abuse showed that 50 percent of the 363 secondary schools sampled had suspended at least one student for involvement in a drug-related incident, and 21 percent had expelled at least one.

Despite these facts, the use of administrative sanctions, considered purely as a means to reduce drug demand, has an important limitation. Most students, knowing school policy regarding illicit drugs, are not likely to use drugs in situations where there is a risk of detection by the school authorities. Given the high rate of campus drug use, it may be inferred that most drug-using students do not view detection as a significant possibility. It may also be, for obvious reasons, that many school administrators do not seriously attempt to identify drug users among their student populations. Thus it would seem that the most important function of the enactment of policies which include administrative sanctions is not to reduce the demand for drugs, but rather to placate parents, legal authorities and other interested parties outside the school, assuring them that the school administration is "doing something" about drugs.

No one, of course, pretends that administrative sanctions form the core of any prevention program; rather, they are ancillary to the main effort, which is to prevent drug use through nonpunitive means. From all indications, the most prevalent approach along these lines is education, or the attempt to persuade people by dint of information to abstain from drugs.

Persuasion. The effort to reduce drug demand through persuasion rests on a key rationalist assumption ". . . that given valid information about the consequences of alternative courses of action, most people will not elect the course most likely to result in self-harm." In a similar vein, Donald A. McCune, in his report on drug education to the National Commission on Marihuana and Drug Abuse, said:

The general consensus among the public at large as well as many in the drug bureaucracy has been that primary prevention can best be achieved through effective education. The traditional rationale has been very simplistic: if an individual knows about the drugs and their harmful effects and if he understands fully the variety of social controls and punishments associated with the use of drugs, he will abstain from using such substances in order to avoid the consequences.

In their review of school drug education curricula, Robert Boldt, Richard Reilly and Paul Haberman found that, "This concept, expressed in different ways, is the pervasive theme of all the drug curricula reviewed." Indeed, in their national survey of drug education practices of 342 elementary and 363 secondary schools, they discovered that, in the academic year 1972–73, the physical and psychological effects of drugs on the user was the single most emphasized topic in educational programs, with an identical proportion—85 percent—of the schools at both levels reporting this emphasis. They found, furthermore, that the most frequently utilized educational technique, presumably used to convey this information, was audiovisual presentation (reported by 67 percent of the elementary schools and 70 percent of the secondary schools).

The schools, of course, are only the most conspicuous example of this form of prevention. Persuasion has also been attempted at the national level through brief television messages, some developed with the support of the National Institute of Mental Health, which describe the dangers of various kinds of drug use.

The sheer proliferation of drug education programs of one kind or another suggests that the rationalist assumption which underlies them —that is, that knowledge of the possible consequences of drug use will promote nonuse—has in effect become an article of faith, one which until recently has gone unquestioned. It is becoming clear, however, that this approach to prevention has certain limitations.

First of all, attempts to persuade people not to use drugs, by force of information, fly in the face of a commonplace observation: even when they accept the information as valid, people often discount the risks and act against their own best interests. The use of cigarettes in this country is a classic case in point. This behavior might be termed the "not me" syndrome, which expresses the individual's belief that harm will not befall him, only someone else. For example, a study of 155 narcotics addicts undergoing treatment in the California Rehabilitation Center showed that 81 percent of them claimed that when they first began to use narcotics they did not believe they would become addicted.

Second, information may not be believed by its intended audience because its source is not seen as being credible. Several studies of students have indicated, for instance, that they often discredit drug information offered by law enforcement officers, clergymen, and school guidance counselors on the grounds that such persons are trying to promote "official" moral values.

Third, drug information offered by an education program may not be in accordance with information individuals obtain from friends or from firsthand observations of drug use. In the event of such discordance, the discrepancy may be resolved by crediting only the latter kinds of information, since these generally indicate to the individual that the risks attached to drug use are not nearly so high as official sources would have him believe. Howard S. Becker has pointed out that the drug sub-culture has its own informal ways of doing "research" on drug effects, and that the body of knowledge which results and is disseminated among users may be quite different from the information disseminated by official sources. In fact, officially produced information often may be faulty. For example, the National Coordinating Council on Drug Education re-cently evaluated 220 films on drug use and rated 84 percent of them unacceptable. Council president Robert M. Earle said that, "The majority of these films are inaccurate, unscientific and psychologically unsound."

The use of inaccurate information, especially that which exaggerates the dangers of drugs like marijuana, may produce, as a number of researchers have observed, an unfortunate "boomerang" effect. That is, if a program's audience disbelieves information on drugs which in their experience are not terribly dangerous, they may also discredit information on drugs whose dangers are more certain, and thus be induced to try them.

One might assume that the latter problem can be solved by having programs issue only accurate information. However, as the National Commission on Marihuana and Drug Abuse has noted, drug education programs face a special dilemma:

Prevention programs may proclaim goals which stress the prevention of high-risk drug use, or of drug dependence, or use of particular drugs, but in practice they must try to curtail *all* illicit drug use. Programs which expressly exmphasize the harm of certain use patterns imply that other patterns are relatively harmless and thus tacitly condone them. Since this is unacceptable, education-information programs usually take the opposite tack; they suggest that all use patterns are equally harmful, because all are likely to evolve into undesirable behavior.

The fourth limitation to the persuasion approach is that educational programs, even when they take care to deliver accurate information, may actually stimulate drug use rather than deter it. This possibility is suggested by the research of Richard B. Stuart, to our knowledge the only research designed to assess the effects of a drug education program on the drug use behavior of its audience. Space limitations prohibit details, but the search was done in experimental form, with 935 students in two suburban junior high schools being randomly assigned to experimental drug education or to control groups. The experimental group was given a ten-session fact-oriented drug curriculum, taught over a ten-week period. Pre- and post-measures were made of the use and sale of various drugs, as well as of drug-related knowledge and attitudes. For some students, follow-up data were obtained four months after the program (all data were collected in the 1971-72 academic year). The key findings, for this discussion, were that the experimental group, compared with the controls, showed a sizable increase in the use of alcohol, marijuana and LSD, and also became more involved in the selling of the latter two drugs.

Given these findings, a difficult problem arises: If programs which present distorted information induce a certain amount of illicit drug use through a "boomerang" effect, and if programs which strive for honesty also induce a certain amount of use (perhaps by a combination of increasing knowledge and reducing worry about possible harm, as Dr. Stuart's research suggests), is there a viable role for drug education programs? Are efforts based on persuasion a tenable means of reducing the demand for illicit drugs? The definitive answers to these questions are not known, but at the moment the evidence is not promising. It is not surprising, then, that in early 1973 both the National Commission on Marihuana and Drug Abuse and the federal Special Action Office for Drug Abuse Prevention called for a moratorium on production and dissemination of new drug education materials. It should be noted that neither agency recommended a complete halt to drug education efforts, but a moratorium would allow time for evaluation and critical appraisal of the goals, methods and results of programs currently in operation.

Correction. An approach to prevention which has recently gained currency is correction, or the attempt to reduce drug demand indirectly by dealing with the presumed causes of illicit drug use. A vast body of research on the etiological factors involved in drug taking indicates that the causes are multiplex, ranging from the individual level (personality attributes), to the interactional level (differential access to and involvement in drug-using groups), to the macrosocial level (for example, the evolutionary trend in our society toward acceptance of mildly hedonistic forms of recreation).

Obviously, some causal factors are beyond the reach of preventive efforts. For instance, a number of recent studies show that youthful drug users come disproportionately from families in which the parents use alcohol, tobacco, and prescription drugs. These youngsters, in effect, socially inherit a predisposing orientation to substance use which facilitates their decision to try illegal drugs when introduced to them by peers. The problem, of course, is that by the time a youngster is exposed to a prevention program, the substance use patterns of his or her parents have probably had their effect; there is no way to go back in time and try to change these patterns.

Because of such difficulties, preventive efforts which address causal factors tend to focus on the attributes of the individual, in particular his or her value system. The key approach along these lines, as practiced in many school-based programs, is what has been variously called "affective education," "humanistic education," or "value clarification." The thrust of this approach is to help youngsters, through a number of techniques such as role playing, to form their values consciously, so that in time they will become autonomous individuals, capable of making rational decisions based on those values. A typical statement of this approach is one made by Henry A. Kane and Doris Pearsall:

Students should be helped to develop a sense of inherent self-worth and uniqueness which will lead to the choice of positive and viable alternatives in life rather than self-destructive ones. . . . Assistance for each student in the clarification of individual values and value systems for himself and in relation to his individual choice of life style should pervade all areas of discussion. Students should be helped to develop a mutuality of respect for others who hold different values from their own, while at the same time developing a confidence and trust in one's own values and a willingness to live one's life in accordance therewith.

The assumption apparently underlying this approach is that once an individual's values are "clarified," he or she will refrain from drug use. But given the current absence of evaluation data, that remains, empirically, an open question.

Theoretically, the approach has an important limitation; that is, the overriding values it recommends—as distinct from whatever specific values students may form—may foster rather than inhibit drug use. The above quotation, taken on face value, advocates self-construction of individual values rather than unquestioning acceptance of received values; individual choice of life style rather than unthinking conformity to dominant life styles; and tolerance of differences of others. These are precisely the kinds of values which many studies have found illicit drug users to hold, and which distinguish them from nonusers to a large degree. These studies have shown that drug users, as compared with nonusers, tend to be more self-exploratory, more open to experimentation with different life styles, and more tolerant of unconventional behavior. If the affective education or value clarification approach truly promotes these values, then in the long run, whatever its other potential merits, this approach may do little to reduce the demand for drugs.

Substitution. A final approach to reducing drug demand is substitution, or the provision of alternatives to drug use, especially natural or nondrug "turn-ons." This approach is often recommended in prevention literature, but it is undoubtedly less widely practiced than are the approaches discussed above, at least in the sense of its forming the basis of actual programs.

The approach rests on the premise that there is something in the drug experience which users seek, and that this can be gained through nondrug means. For example, the National Commission on Marihuana and Drug Abuse has recommended that ". . . drug use prevention strategy, rather than concentrating resources and efforts in persuading or 'educating' people not to use drugs, emphasize alternative means of obtaining what users seek from drugs: means that are better for the user and better for society."

The question, of course, is: What do users seek through drugs? Some theorists see drug use as resulting from a lack of meaningful experiences, or a lack of relevant "connectedness" to others, a kind of socio-psychological isolation, as it were. They recommend that opportunities be made available for people to become involved in pursuits—community work, the arts, craft skills, and new recreational programs—which will provide personal fulfillment and a sense of meaningful involvement with others.

Others believe that drug users basically seek altered states of consciousness. Drug authority Andrew Weil holds that the desire occasionally to experience such states is an innate drive. Accordingly, somewhat more esoteric alternatives are recommended which will induce altered states of consciousness, including yoga and meditation.

The limitation to this approach is that, in principle, none of these alternatives is necessarily mutually exclusive with drug use. It may be perfectly possible to become intensely involved in community work, or in the arts, or to practice yoga—and still use drugs. Indeed, several studies of student drug users have shown that, compared with nonusers, they are more involved in political activities and in artistic pursuits.

More important, perhaps, is the real possibility that none of the alternatives provides what users seek from drugs. Marijuana users, for example, typically report that the drug is a sensory intensifier, that it greatly increases their enjoyment of music, food and sex. If this is one of the significant reinforcing aspects of the marijuana experience, it is difficult to see what can substitute for it.

CONCLUSION

Using a simple supply-demand model, we have asserted that most efforts at prevention, as the term is ordinarily understood, are strategies intended to reduce the demand for drugs. We have reviewed four major strategies or approaches: coercion, persuasion, correction, and substitution. And we have pointed out what appear to be the limitations of each.

The picture, frankly, is not hopeful. If the goal of prevention is to curtail *all* illicit drug use, then it is fair to say that, on the basis of currently available evidence, none of the approaches has proved effective.

Perhaps the time has come, as several observers have suggested, to admit that the prevention of all illegal drug use is not an achievable goal. Perhaps the time has come to adjust our goals and focus our preventive efforts primarily on high-risk patterns of use—on those patterns, that is, where drug involvement demonstrably and significantly increases the chances of self-harm. (This is not to suggest, incidentally, that prevention programs should not continue to reinforce those who have already decided to abstain from drugs. This is an important group, one which should not be neglected, and their decision should be given sustained support.)

Whether any of us likes it or not, reality intrudes. The reality is that some forms of drug use, particularly patterns of moderate recreational use, are firmly institutionalized in certain sectors of society. While the most troubling aspect of the drug problem—the high-risk patterns of use—becomes ever more visible and unquestionably warrants our deepest concern, we should not overlook the fact that there is an underlayer of episodic, moderate or low-risk drug use which is resistant to change. To try, then, to prevent all illicit drug use merely diffuses our energies, with the probable result that we will accomplish less than we otherwise could.

Robert L. DuPont

THE FUTURE
OF DRUG ABUSE PREVENTION

After my colleagues have dealt in this book with the solid stuff of the past and the present, it is left for me to dream of the future. I begin with a disclaimer: My track record as a predictor of the future is well known and undistinguished. To cite just one example: I confidently predicted a downturn in national heroin trends in 1973, only to see the heroin problem increase in 1974 and again in 1975 (but the trends from 1976 to 1978 were indeed down). I urge the reader not to take my predictions more seriously than I do: They are one person's attempt to read the present state of affairs and guess about the future.

I have divided my speculations into two areas, Programs and Policies, and then added two issues of importance: a concern about the impact of drug abuse on personal freedom and a reflection on what science can and—equally important—cannot do.

PROGRAMS FOR THE FUTURE

The drug abuse field has grown up in the last decade around the drug abuse treatment clinic—a location where typically as few as 20 or as many as several hundred drug abusers gather on a regular basis to quit using illicit drugs with the help of a trained, paid staff. The unique role of this clinical core is easily seen in the fiscal year 1979 budget of the National Institute on Drug Abuse. Over 60 percent of the total of $275 million to be spent during that year will fund treatment for over 200,000 people in over 1,300 individual clinics located in all parts of the country. These clinics provide a wide variety of services to a varied client population.

It is likely that categorical clinics will continue for the next decade to be the center of NIDA's funding. The categorical Government-funded programs are likely to focus increasingly on particular segments of the drug-using population: youth, the poor, women, and those people referred to treatment from the criminal justice system. These are the classically underserved in the health care system. But it also seems likely that more drug abusers will find services provided in more traditional care-giving institutions as the needs of these people and the treatments they can benefit from are increasingly accepted into the medical and social service mainstreams. A key test will be the coverage provided for drug abuse services under any proposal for national health insurance. While disappointments are certain in view of the long history of discrimination professionals and providers have established in dealing with drug abuse, it is inevitable, over the long run, that the achievement of stability and respectability which has characterized drug abuse treatment in the last decade will carry the drug abuser at least a little closer to the mainstream of health care during the next decade.

Similarly, it is hard not to predict the continued growth and development of the partnership between the States and the Federal Government which has been the single most important management-funding achievement in drug abuse treatment over the last decade. If this partnership is truly to flourish, it will be important to develop better techniques to meet the unique needs of the larger cities and the minority poor.

Is there nothing new on the treatment horizon? There are four general directions in which I expect to see new developments. The first, and perhaps the most important, will be the emergence of self-help as a key partner in providing services to drug abusers. The Alcoholics Anonymous model is too powerful, too effective, and too relevant not to spread to drug abuse. It is likely that most drug abuse programs of the future will make formal and informal alliances with self-help programs, and that increasing numbers of drug abusers in trouble will turn to self-help programs not only for "aftercare"—that is, posttreatment help—but also as the primary source of their care. Many AA chapters have already expanded their concern to include drug abusers. An organization was recently funded in New York called Potsmokers Anonymous. Narcotics Anonymous is already well established. Rather than seeing this trend in self-help as competition for the more traditional drug abuse treatment program, I see self-help as an essential partner in these efforts. This sense of partnership has certainly developed rapidly in the last decade in the alcoholism field.

The second new development will be the emergence of treatment programs (and self-help programs) for dependency on related "reenforcing substances" such as tobacco and alcohol but, I suspect, increasingly also for marijuana and prescription drugs. These treatment programs may even branch out to such related areas as weight control, exercise, and stress management.

The principles developed for the treatment of heroin addiction are generalizable to other dependencies, and I expect to see treatment programs and their clients make more use of these similarities in the future.

The third new area is related to the knot of issues raised by Betty Ford's courageous public admission of drug dependence and her use of treatment to deal with her problem. Nonopiate drug use, the misuse of prescription drugs, drug use by women, drug use by the non-poor, and finally drug use by the non-young are all part of this new development. Betty Ford punctured many of the stereotypes which had previously restricted the public view of drug abuse prevention and treatment to the problems of poor urban youth addicted to heroin. This new more comprehensive focus will encourage the facing of drug problems by drug-dependent individuals and their families who desperately need help. It will encourage the adoption of drug abuse programs by organizations and institutions which have traditionally dealt with the non-poor and the non-young. These range from mental health centers, to general hospitals, to private practitioners of medicine. The broad area will be a major growth area during the next decade. Although I expect most of this new growth to occur outside the drug abuse clinics, the process will also influence the client profile of these traditional clinics.

We can also expect a growing emphasis on the family as an integral part of both prevention and treatment efforts. It is unmistakable that drug use and quitting drug use are deeply imbedded in the network of human relationships of the drug user. For virtually everyone, that means the family in one of its many contemporary forms.

One more program change: There can be no doubt that the next decade will see the emergence of prevention as equal to treatment in terms of attention and support. It is unlikely that NIDA funding for prevention will ever equal that for treatment, but the overall social investment in drug abuse prevention will, I suspect, prove greater than that for treatment by the end of the next decade. We should have a better understanding of what works for whom, and we should finally find a way to conceptualize prevention programs on a community-wide basis. The recent emphasis on the basic modalities of prevention (information, education, alternatives, and early intervention) together with the emphasis on evaluation point the way to a brighter future for drug abuse prevention. The increased emphasis on prevention in health will also give a boost to drug abuse prevention.

In my overview of likely future program developments, I have not dealt with the major unknown: the possibility of entirely new techniques for both prevention and treatment. Surely we will at last have long-acting methadone and a nontoxic narcotic antagonist to add to our pharmacologic armamentarium before the end of the 1980s. The recent breakthroughs in understanding the body's own opiatelike substances offer hope that we may, before the next decade is over, have specific new tools. For example, we may be able to determine in advance who is susceptible to opiate and other drug dependence and who is not. We now know that some people can drink alcohol without being alcoholic and that many people use heroin once or twice and quit. (It is far less clear that any substantial number of people can use heroin regularly without addiction, although that previously unthinkable idea has received some support.) It may be that new research knowledge will permit precise determinations of vulnerability to drug dependence so that prevention and control measures can be better targeted. It is even possible that entirely new treatment techniques will be developed which will make our current techniques seem as old-fashioned as Sister Kenney's humane hot packs for polio victims now seem in the era of polio vaccine. However, a word of caution: The underlying problems we now label "drug abuse" have much to do with chemically reenforced behavior which is experienced by many as "pleasure." It seems highly unlikely that problems associated with people unwisely seeking pleasure will be eliminated in the next decade. We need not fear that our treatment and prevention programs with their humanistic techniques will become outdated. It is no more likely that even the most effective new treatment and prevention techniques will put today's preventors and treators out of business than polio vaccine put nurses out of business.

POLICIES FOR THE FUTURE

It is not yet assured, but it seems likely that the national commitment to dealing with drug abuse will remain steady and substantial. Thus, we can plan to build on the solid foundations of the last decade with much less worry that we may wake up one day to find that the whole effort has been "defunded."

Not only is it unlikely that the widespread public wish to "end the drug problem" will be realized, it is probable that at least for the next decade the overall levels of illicit drug use will continue to rise as they have over the last decade.

It is hard to imagine that the rates for the very young will continue to expand rapidly in the future, but the rates for those over 30 are likely to show substantial increases, particularly for marijuana and cocaine, today's hottest drugs.

A careful reading of the recent NIDA surveys shows clues to the future of our national drug policy. There is a growing and large consensus favoring a greater tolerance for adult occasional use of currently illicit drugs. There is, however, a large group who oppose public and regular use of any drug, including the legal drugs, alcohol and tobacco. There is also a growing awareness that a reasonable policy for drug use by adults (those over the unique intermediate age range of 16 to 21) is clearly different from a reasonable policy with respect to those under the age of 16. I anticipate a growing toughness about the use of all drugs (legal and illegal) in the under 16 age group—with schools, parents, and peers all joining in this effort. This change will result partly from the Nation's changing demography: The smaller number of youths and the larger number of young adults in the next decade will be in direct contrast to the youth explosion in the 1960s. This change will be associated with a reassertion of adult dominance and a general trend toward more conservative values. In addition, this increased toughness about "kiddy drug use" also reflects the growing awareness of the special dangers posed by regular use of any intoxicant in the fragile formative years of early adolescence.

Stepping back even farther, it seems that the potency of chemical reenforcers will have to be reckoned with as an increasingly serious health threat. The impact has not yet sunk in—the cost of letting each citizen set his own level of use of drugs such as alcohol and tobacco. The use of nonlegal sanctions against drug use of all kinds will surely increase. The social stigma increasingly being felt by the cigarette smoker will, I suspect, increasingly be felt by the user of other drugs, even— many will doubt my sanity here—the user of alcohol during the next decade. Simply because these sanctions are not legal does not mean they are not potent. I expect many of them will prove to be less than generous or reasonable, as is increasingly the case with the strident antismoking crusaders.

The use of formal nonlegal sanctions can also be expected to increase. For example, when one now gets life or disability insurance, one must have a physical examination which typically includes a urine test to screen for diabetes and other diseases. It is already easy to test urine for metabolites of cigarette smoke, and it is not outside the current technology to also test for recent marijuana, alcohol, and other drug use. Those with this objective evidence of use of health-related substances may find themselves—like the overweight and the hypertensive—paying substantially higher premiums for their insurance. Drug users may also find their use aggressively restricted in public places, as is now the case with cigarette smokers. These trends grow out of the large majority of the public who do not use drugs and who take a dim view of those who do use drugs on a regular basis. I suspect these negative attitudes toward frequent or high-dose drug use will increase rather than decrease over the next decade. The same antidrug trend can be seen in the attitudes toward the use of prescription sleeping pills, diet drugs, and tranquilizers. Use trends and public support for use of these medications are clearly downtrends which I expect to see accelerate in the future.

It is entirely possible that the link between drug use and "pollution," "herbicides," "pesticides," etc., will become much closer. Much of the public will probably see the use of these chemicals as increasingly unhealthy for the user and nonuser alike. Of course, this trend may not be strong enough to offset the potent biology of reenforcement any more than the current emphasis on "natural nutrition" has reversed the trend to "convenience foods" for the majority of the public. However, the health food boom may soon show up in "convenience" health foods. This antipollution reasoning will influence large segments of the population, and it may well be that the drug abuse treatment and prevention programs of the future will focus increasingly on those individuals who for one or another reason are unable to heed the culturally insistent warnings about the dangers of chemical highs.

Overhanging drug abuse prevention policy in the Nation and throughout the world is the dark cloud of organized and unorganized crime—the vast sums of money now generated by illegal drug trafficking. The full implications of this "business" and the consideration of the options for dealing with it will prove to be one of the most puzzling aspects of the policy debate in the next decade. Simplistic solutions like "legalization" will increasingly be discussed. Once the public horror of even talking about such issues diminishes, the harsh realities will push us toward the complex mix of prohibition and regulatory controls we now use. If one were to promote legalization, what drugs would be "legalized" and for whom, at what price, and under what circumstances? Our dismal experience with the open commercial exploitation of each citizen's setting his own level of alcohol and tobacco use hardly serves as an optimistic precedent for the legalization scheme. The explosive growth of the drug paraphernalia industry (from marijuana wrapper papers, to drug-oriented magazines, to coke spoons) will offer an important battleground for many of these policy issues.

DRUG ABUSE AS A SOURCE OF EROSION
OF PERSONAL FREEDOMS

Zealotry in drug abuse prevention poses real dangers. These dangers are now fairly obvious to many of us in terms of law enforcement, but they are less obvious in the treatment and prevention areas. For example, wiretapping, use of paid informers, unannounced breaking and entering by law enforcement agents, as well as many regulatory actions, pose fairly obvious risks. But how can drug abuse treatment pose a threat?

There is a paradox in all this which stands ready to take a bite out of our freedoms. For example, many reformers are now eager to divert marijuana and other drug users 'from the criminal justice system into treatment programs. Most of these marijuana users do not need or want treatment. Simply to move them from a prison to a hospital is to have achieved little social gain—especially if the hospital is equally depriving of individual liberties and more expensive! To sort your way through this one you must first think of what the goal of governmental action is.

With respect to the marijuana user, it seems to me reasonable for the Government to discourage the user and to provide him with information about the dangers of marijuana use, including the biological dangers, as well as the dangers of use of other drugs, the dangers of driving while intoxicated, and the impact of chronic intoxication on motivation and personal relationships. Such programs can also inform marijuana and other drug users about potentials for help with their habits should they desire such help. The State of Minnesota recently started such a program, funded primarily by the fines paid by the apprehended marijuana users. The Minnesota system requires attendance at a class on drug abuse, similar to the courses used in highway safety and alcoholism programs for people arrested for drunk driving. The marijuana user, in this approach, is not sent to prison, does not have an arrest record, does not use taxpayers' funds, and is provided with important and relevant information. He is also "punished" for his use of a prohibited substance by paying a reasonable fine, about $25. Some will, no doubt, argue that even this is an unwarranted intrusion on the marijuana user's liberties. The Minnesota program meets the test of moderation, and it helps sustain the reasonable point that society has decided that marijuana smoking is undesirable.

What about the heroin user? Despite the controversy over the point, the preponderance of evidence clearly shows that heroin use increases criminality. However, not all heroin users are criminals, and not all criminals are heroin users. It seems reasonable to have society set as a condition for release of heroin-addicted convicted criminals that they refrain from heroin use while they are on parole or probation—and enforce that condition by regular urine testing. But it does not seem reasonable to pick up heroin users who have not been found guilty of a crime and force them to take urine tests. And it does not seem reasonable to force the heroin-using parolee or probationer to enter treatment or, even worse, to enter a specific treatment program selected by the court or any other agent of the criminal justice system. The condition of refraining from heroin use on a regular basis is sufficient. If the parolee or probationer wants treatment to help him achieve that condition of his release, that is fine. If he can stop heroin use without treatment, so much the better.

These two brief examples hopefully suggest the range of areas in which drug abuse treatment poses threats to individual liberties and the need for balancing those threats with the needs of society. It is less important that you agree with where I draw the line than that you agree that the drawing of this line is of vital importance.

Few have thought through our generally laudable goals in the prevention field in terms of the potential threats to personal freedoms. The Government, the majority, want the minority of our population who choose to use illegal drugs to quit using them. Even more, the majority wants young people never to use illicit drugs. But where are the limits to efforts to prevent drug use? Who will be forced to do what? How will the problem people and the problem behaviors be identified? What limits will be placed on the techniques to be used? We want to promote healthy networks of concern in our communities. But how far are we prepared to go in mandating participation in these networks?

We are well served by making distinctions between youths and adults—being more forceful with the former and more permissive with the latter—and making distinctions between particular drugs and particular patterns of use, and most of all identifying dangerous behavior which warrants stiffer action. It is important to distinguish between "discouragement" and "elimination" in drug abuse prevention.

We must be prepared in the future to be much more open and realistic in our policy choices than we have been in the past. We must also be willing to live with the inevitable and often unpleasant complexities and contradictions that this openness will uncover.

These issues underlie many of our most familiar everyday problems. The boundaries are not easily defined. Drug abuse policy partakes of some of the most important and difficult areas of contemporary public policy.

SCIENCE GOOD AND SCIENCE BAD

We as a Nation have come out of a period which extended from the 1920s into the mid-1960s when our national drug abuse policy was set with little regard for the lack of scientific knowledge on which it was based. The policy was based on emotional and often ill-founded prejudices about who used drugs and what their effects were. (Parenthetically, most of the rest of the world is still back in this pre-1965 era in terms of their drug abuse policies.)

More recently, we have gone through a decade of profound reaction to this ill-informed early period. Many Americans, especially the most sophisticated, have concluded that we must turn drug abuse policy issues over to the scientists to avoid ever again repeating the errors of earlier decades. These well-intentioned people make two fundamental errors: They overestimate what science can tell them and they underestimate the vital importance of cultural forces in shaping behavior. With respect to the former point, science can tell us that tobacco increases the risk of lung cancer and heart attack. It can even estimate that tobacco use costs our society $18 billion a year. Science can tell us that the economic benefit from the cultivation of tobacco through the manufacture and sale of cigarettes is something like $12 billion. It can measure the highly ambivalent attitudes of our fellow citizens about our schizophrenic national tobacco policies. But when it comes to deciding what we as a Nation are to do about our most widespread addiction— and the most costly in terms of health damage and death—we are left almost where we started with our value conflicts—freedom of individual choice versus society's overall interests, the health costs of tobacco smoking versus the economic benefit of the industry and the taxes it produces.

Similarly, when one thinks about what should be *done* about illicit drug use, one always comes back to cultural institutions—the family, the school, and the church. And here too the potency of science palls in comparison to the shared values of those in our social systems. It *is* essential to expand our scientific knowledge about drug use and its consequences, but we must not overvalue this knowledge. We must not wait until "all the evidence is in" (it never is in science!) before making decisions and shaping policies. We have, in a word, overreacted during the last decade to our earlier overreaction in the other direction.

I certainly do not intend to demean the values of science for drug abuse prevention. Science has and can continue to provide more correct and rational bases for drug abuse policy, including more effective prevention, treatment, and law enforcement policies. It can also help develop new understanding of the nature of drug abuse itself and dramatic new techniques for prevention and treatment. In fact, we now need substantially more invested in science with greatly increased emphasis on bridging the gap between science and the practitioner and on targeting research more precisely on the most important questions.

My concern, however, is that we, in our shared confusion over drug abuse, not abdicate to science the responsibility which rests with each of us individually and collectively.

We will, in the next decade, have to search out a more balanced attitude which uses the great help science offers while retaining responsibility in ourselves and our institutions for resolving the enormous and recalcitrant value conflicts with which drug abuse prevention abounds.

Finally, the drug abuse prevention field has spent the last decade struggling for a stable, respectable identity. That struggle has been successfully completed. Now it is time to consider the opportunities for leadership in the wider health and social policy areas. The new global interest in prevention in health has forced us to recognize that the major gains to be made in the next few decades in improving the health and the quality of life in the United States and in other nations will come down to choices made by individuals—choices which, in their totality, we are increasingly calling "lifestyles." Improvements in health in the remaining decades of this century will have more to do with diets and exercise and drug use than with hospitals, doctors, and vaccines. The drug abuse prevention field has much to learn itself about this process of making life-style choices and the potentials for influencing these choices ranging from legal sanctions, to economic incentives, to health information, to direct intervention. As we solve our drug abuse problems, we will also contribute to the vital knowledge base which forms the foundation for the new field of behavioral health. The complex interactions of biology with economic and cultural factors which are familiar to those working in drug abuse prevention, are also at the root of other behavioral health issues. Cocaine and marijuana do make many people feel good—for a while. So do inactivity and sugar. Some of this good feeling from unhealthy behavior is biological. Genetics may play a role in determining which people are more likely to have which behavioral disorders. We also know, however, that social, economic, and cultural factors play major roles in lifestyle choices. Unraveling these interactions and developing techniques to promote healthy lifestyles are the major business of the future for the drug abuse field and for the health and social service fields as well.

SUGGESTIONS FOR FURTHER READING

SECTION ONE: EPIDEMIOLOGICAL PATTERNS

Chein, Isidor; Gerard, Donald L.; Lee, Robert S.; and Rosenfeld, Eva. *The Road to H.* New York: Basic Books, 1964.

Hunt, Leon G., and Chambers, Carl D. *The Heroin Epidemics: A Study of Heroin Use in the United States 1965-1975.* New York: Spectrum, 1976.

Richards, Louise G., and Blevens, Louise B., eds. *Epidemiology of Drug Abuse: Current Issues.* Washington, D.C.: Government Printing Office, 1976.

Rittenhouse, Joan D., ed. *The Epidemiology of Heroin and Other Narcotics.* Washington, D.C.: Government Printing Office, 1977.

Robins, Lee N. "Addict Careers." In DuPont, Robert L.; Goldstein, Avram; and O'Donnell, John, eds. *Handbook on Drug Abuse.* Washington, D.C.: Government Printing Office, 1979.

SECTION TWO: HISTORY OF LEGAL CONTROLS

Brecher, Edward M., and the editors of *Consumer Reports.* Licit and Illicit Drugs. Boston: Little, Brown and Co., 1972.

King, Rufus. *The Drug Hang-Up.* Springfield, Ill.: Charles C. Thomas, 1972.

Lindesmith, Alfred R. *The Addict and the Law.* Bloomington, Ind.: Indiana University Press, 1965.

Musto, David F. *The American Disease.* New Haven: Yale University Press, 1973.

National Commission on Marihuana and Drug Abuse, *Drug Use in America: Problem in Perspective.* Washington, D.C.: Government Printing Office, 1973.

SECTION THREE: DRUG-RELATED CRIME

Gandossy, Robert P.; Williams, Jay R.; Cohen, Jo; and Harwood, Henrick, J. *Drugs and Crime.* Washington, D.C.: Government Printing Office, 1980.

Greenberg, Stephanie W., and Adler, Freda. "Crime and Addiction: An Empirical Analysis of the Literature, 1920-1973." *Contemporary Drug Problems* 3 (1974): 221-70.

McGlothlin, William H. "Drugs and Crime." In DuPont, Robert L.; Goldstein, Avram; and O'Donnell, John, eds. *Handbook on Drug Abuse.* Washington, D.C.: Government Printing Office, 1979.

National Institute on Drug Abuse. *Drug Use and Crime: Report of the Panel on Drug Use and Criminal Behavior.* Springfield, Va.: National Technical Information Service, 1976.

Tinklenberg, Jared. "Drugs and Crime." In National Commission on Marihuana and Drug Abuse. *Drug Use in America: Problem in Perspective.* vol. 1. Washington, D.C.: Government Printing Office, 1973.

SECTION FOUR: ENFORCEMENT PRACTICES

DeFleur, Lois B. "Biasing Influences on Drug Arrest Records: Implications for Deviance Research." *American Sociological Review* 40 (1975): 88–103.

Epstein, Edward J. *Agency of Fear.* New York: G. P. Putnam's Sons, 1977.

Johnson, Weldon T., and Bogomolny, Robert. "Selective Justice: Drug Law Enforcement in Six American Cities." In National Commission on Marihuana and Drug Abuse. *Drug Use in America: Problem in Perspective.* vol. 3. Washington, D.C.: Government Printing Office, 1973.

Moore, Mark H. *Buy and Bust.* Lexington, Mass.: Lexington Books, 1977.

Williams, Jay R.; Redlinger, Lawrence J.; and Manning, Peter K. *Police Narcotics Control: Patterns and Strategies.* Washington, D.C.: Government Printing Office, 1980.

Wilson, James Q. *The Investigators.* New York: Basic Books, 1978.

SECTION FIVE: SOCIOLEGAL QUESTIONS

Baker, Robert. "Prolegomena to an Analysis of Victimless Crime." *Journal of Psychedelic Drugs* 6 (1974): 447–64.

The Drug Abuse Council. *The Facts about "Drug Abuse."* New York: The Free Press, 1980.

Duster, Troy. *The Legislation of Morality.* New York: The Free Press, 1970.

Rock, Paul E., ed. *Drugs and Politics.* New Brunswick, N.J.: Transaction Books, 1977.

Trebach, Arnold S., ed. *Drugs, Crime, and Politics.* New York: Praeger, 1978.

Zinberg, Norman E., and Robertson, John A. *Drugs and the Public.* New York: Simon and Schuster, 1972.

SECTION SIX: PENAL EFFECTS

Bonnie, Richard J. *Marijuana Use and Criminal Sanctions.* Charlottesville, Va.: Michie, 1980.

Hellman, Arthur D. *Laws against Marijuana.* Urbana, Ill.: University of Illinois Press, 1975.

Joint Committee on New York Drug Law Evaluation. *The Nation's Toughest Drug Law: Evaluating the New York Experience.* New York: The Association of The Bar of The City of New York and The Drug Abuse Council, Inc., 1977.

Kaplan, John. *Marijuana—The New Prohibition.* New York: World Publishing Co., 1970.

Packer, Herbert L. *The Limits of the Criminal Sanction.* Stanford: Stanford University Press, 1968.

SECTION SEVEN: CORRECTIONAL POLICIES

McGlothlin, William H. "Criminal Justice Clients." In DuPont, Robert L.; Goldstein, Avram; and O'Donnell, John, eds. *Handbook on Drug Abuse.* Washington, D.C.: Government Printing Office, 1979.

McGlothlin, William H.; Anglin, M. Douglas; and Wilson, Bruce D. *An Evaluation of the California Civil Addict Program.* Rockville, Md.: National Institute on Drug Abuse, 1977.

National Commission on Marihuana and Drug Abuse. *Drug Use in America: Problem in Perspective.* Appendix, vol. 4. Washington, D.C.: Government Printing Office, 1973.

Petersen, David M. "Some Reflections on Compulsory Treatment of Addiction." In Inciardi, James A., and Chambers, Carl D., eds. *Drugs and the Criminal Justice System.* Beverly Hills: Sage Publications, 1974.

Systems Sciences, Inc. *Treatment Alternatives to Street Crime (TASC) Projects Phase II Report.* Washington, D.C.: U.S. Dept. of Justice, 1978.

SECTION EIGHT: TREATMENT INTERVENTION

Bourne, Peter G. *Methadone: Benefits and Shortcomings.* Washington, D.C.: The Drug Abuse Council, 1975.

Lewis, David C., and Sessler, John. "Heroin Treatment: Development, Status, Outlook." In The Drug Abuse Council. *The Facts about "Drug Abuse."* New York: The Free Press, 1980.

Nash, George. "An Analysis of Twelve Studies of Impact of Drug Abuse Treatment upon Criminality." In National Institute on Drug Abuse. *Drug Use and Crime: Report of the Panel on Drug Use and Criminal Behavior.* Springfield, Va.: National Technical Information Service, 1976.

National Commission on Marihuana and Drug Abuse. *Drug Use in America: Problem in Perspective.* Appendix, vol. 4. Washington, D.C.: Government Printing Office, 1973.

Sells, Saul B. "Treatment Effectiveness." In DuPont, Robert L.; Goldstein, Avram; and O'Donnell, John. *Handbook on Drug Abuse.* Washington, D.C.: Government Printing Office, 1979.

SECTION NINE: PREVENTION STRATEGIES

Goldberg, Peter, and Meyers, Erik J. "The Influence of Public Attitudes and Understanding on Drug Education and Prevention." In The Drug Abuse Council. *The Facts about "Drug Abuse."* New York: The Free Press, 1980.

Grizzle, Gloria A. "Preventing Drug Abuse: A Comparison of Education, Treatment, and Law Enforcement Approaches." *Criminal Justice and Behavior* 2 (1975): 372-82.

Ramos, Manuel, and Gould, Leroy C. "Where Have All the Flower Children Gone? A Five Year Followup of a Natural Group of Drug Users." *Journal of Drug Issues* 8 (1978): 75-84.

Swisher, John D. "Prevention Issues." In DuPont, Robert L.; Goldstein, Avram; and O'Donnell, John. *Handbook on Drug Abuse.* Washington, D.C.: Government Printing Office, 1979.

Zinberg, Norman E.; Jacobson, Richard C.; and Harding, Wayne M. "Social Sanctions and Rituals as a Basis for Drug Abuse Prevention." *American Journal of Drug and Alcohol Abuse* 2 (1975): 165-82.